Between Psychotherapy and Philosophy
Essays from the Philadelphia Association

To the memory of Robin Cooper,
friend and colleague

Between Psychotherapy and Philosophy

Essays from the Philadelphia Association

Edited by

PAUL GORDON AND ROSALIND MAYO
The Philadelphia Association, London

W
WHURR PUBLISHERS
LONDON AND PHILADELPHIA

© 2004 Whurr Publishers Ltd
First published 2004
by Whurr Publishers Ltd
19b Compton Terrace
London N1 2UN England and
325 Chestnut Street, Philadelphia PA 19106 USA

Reprinted 2005

British Library Cataloguing in Publication Data

A catalogue record for this book
is available from the British Library.

ISBN 1 86156 401 5

Typeset by Adrian McLaughlin, a@microguides.net
Printed and bound in the UK by Athenæum Press Ltd, Gateshead, Tyne & Wear.

Contents

Contributors

Robin Cooper studied psychology at the University of Edinburgh. He was a member of the Philadelphia Association (PA) and of the Institute of Group Analysis and was involved for many years in the PA's community households. He died in 2002.

Joe Friedman studied psychology at the University of Michigan. He has lived and worked in Philadelphia Association households for nearly 20 years. He trained with the Philadelphia Association and has a private practice in London.

Miranda Glossop studied psychology and philosophy at the University of Oxford. She taught piano and repaired ceramics before training as a psychotherapist with the Philadelphia Association. She now works in private practice in London.

Paul Gordon studied law at the University of Glasgow and worked for many years as a researcher and campaigner in civil liberties and race relations. He trained as a psychotherapist with the Institute of Psychotherapy and Social Studies and later with the Philadelphia Association. His book, *Face to Face: Therapy as Ethics,* was published in 1999.

John M. Heaton studied medicine at Cambridge University and University College Hospital. He worked as an ophthalmologist for many years and wrote *The Eye: Phenomenology of Function and Disorder* (Tavistock, 1968). He has been practising psychotherapy since 1961 and joined the Philadelphia Association in 1965. He is the author of *Introducing Wittgenstein* (Icon Books, 1994) and *Wittgenstein and Psychotherapy* (Icon Books, 2000)

Barbara Latham grew up in New Zealand and found the PA in 1971. She practises psychotherapy in London and is involved with the PA training programme.

Peter Lomas has worked in different branches of child and adult psychiatry and trained at the British Institute of Psychoanalysis. He now practises psychotherapy in Cambridge and is a founder member of the Cambridge Society for Psychotherapy. He has written a number of books including, most recently, *Doing Good? Psychotherapy out of its Depth* (1999) and *The Limits of Interpretation* (revised edition, 2001)

Rosalind Mayo trained as a psychotherapist with the Philadelphia Association. She has a background in theology and spirituality and has a continuing interest in engaging with psychotherapy and the Judaic Christian religion.

David Smail is a retired clinical psychologist and formerly Special Professor of Clinical Psychology at Nottingham University. He is the author of several books looking at psychotherapy from a social perspective – most recently *The Nature of Unhappiness.* He maintains an informative Web site at www.djsmail.com

M Guy Thompson trained at the Philadelphia Association in the 1970s and obtained his PhD in clinical psychology from The Wright Institute, Berkeley, California, where he now lives and practises psychoanalysis. Dr Thompson is on the adjunct faculty of the California School of Professional Psychology, Berkeley. He is the author of *The Death of Desire: A Study in Psychopathology* (1985), *The Truth About Freud's Technique: The Encounter with the Real* (1994), and *The Enigma of Honesty: The Fundamental Rule of Psychoanalysis* (in press).

Acknowledgements

The following chapters were previously published and are reproduced by kind permission:

Robin Cooper (1996) What we take for granted. Free Associations 6(4): 530–50.

Joseph Friedman (1993) The *Odyssey*, community and therapy. Therapeutic Communities 14(1): 39–50.

M Guy Thompson (2001) Is the unconscious really all that unconscious? The role of being and experience in the psychoanalytic encounter. Contemporary Psychoanalysis 37(4): 576–612.

Page 113 *In my name* is used with permission of the publishers, Karnak House, and extracted from *I is a long memoried woman* by Grace Nichols, © 1983 Karnak House.

Page 121 *Pharaoh's Daughter* by Nuala Ní Dhomhnaill (1990), translated from the Irish by Paul Muldoon, is reproduced by kind permission of the author and The Gallery Press, Loughcrew, Oldcastle, County Meath, Ireland.

Introduction

For almost four decades now the Philadelphia Association has been ploughing its singular furrow within the field of psychotherapy. Despite having been around for so long we continue either to be misrepresented or misunderstood. At best, the PA (as we like to refer to ourselves) is still probably best known for its connection with the figure of RD Laing, one of our founders and guiding spirits, even though Laing died in 1989. At worst, there is a remarkable degree of ignorance and prejudice about us. *Wacky, mad, anti-psychoanalytic* are all terms we have heard from people who really ought to know better, yet of those who feel free to comment on our mental state how few really know anything of what we do – that, for instance, we have been running houses for the mentally distressed almost since our inception, something they would probably think *a good thing*? Of those who are so free with their opinions how many have read even one book by RD Laing, let alone anything by many others associated with us? Such matters may give rise to wry amusement on our part – those who advocate open-mindedness and approaching things without preconceived ideas prove themselves to be not quite so open-minded. But they can also be deeply revealing of the blinkered nature of the culture of psychotherapy

So who are we and what do we do? What makes us different? In our literature we choose to define ourselves by what we are not. We are not, we say, a school of psychoanalysis or psychotherapy. Nor do we promote any theoretical model or subscribe to any dogma. There are enough of these already. What we are, what we offer, is an approach, an orientation. We advocate a thoughtful approach to the practice of therapy, and a questioning of the cultural norms and assumptions that may be implicit in someone's suffering or in accepted ways of understanding it.

This thoughtfulness, we argue, can come about only through an engagement with philosophy. It is not that we are *interested* in philosophy, as is sometimes remarked. Many people are interested in philosophy, including a growing number within the world of psychotherapy. (Yes, this coming into fashion of what we have been saying for many years does raise a smile. It is not so long ago that the then director of the Tavistock Clinic told RD Laing that Kierkegaard's *The Sickness Unto Death* was an interesting example of early nineteenth century psychopathology.) Our particular involvement with the theory of psychoanalysis and the practice of psychotherapy is, at the same time, an involvement and engagement with philosophy, particularly the phenomenological tradition – from Husserl and Heidegger, through Bachelard, Sartre and Merleau-Ponty to Levinas, Derrida, Kristeva, Irigaray, Wittgenstein and others. In words that we might well take as a motto, Merleau-Ponty once remarked that psychoanalysis needs philosophy to be what it is. It is not possible, in other words, to think about subjectivity, experience, (un)consciousness, relationship, language and so on except philosophically.

The Philadelphia Association was set up in 1965 by the psychiatrists David Cooper, Aaron Esterson and RD Laing (who was also a psychoanalyst) and others, including the writer Clancy Sigal. Those involved were all interested in questions of mental health and mental illness and the PA's main founding objective was the relief of mental illness of all descriptions, and particularly schizophrenia. One of the PA's most important activities in its early life was the founding of its first therapeutic community at Kingsley Hall in east London, as a place where people in distress might find genuine asylum, a refuge from unwanted psychiatric (and other) intervention. Kingsley Hall was to be the first of over 20 households run by the PA. Around the same time the PA was very much involved in the Dialectics of Liberation conference at London's Roundhouse in 1967, an event attended by hundreds who came to hear such radical luminaries as Herbert Marcuse, Stokely Carmichael and Paul Sweezy. A training in psychotherapy was started by John Heaton around the same time. (A much more detailed account of the organization's origins and work in its first two decades can be found in the earlier collection of papers from the Association, *Thesholds Between Philosophy and Psychoanalysis,* published by Free Association Books in 1989 – in particular the first chapter 'Beginnings'.)

The political and cultural landscape in which we now find ourselves is, of course, vastly different to that of the mid-1960s. A time of political optimism and a belief in social and political change through common action has given way to a deep cynicism and individualism. Yet, for us, some of the basic issues that so moved our founders continue to be very much alive and in need of addressing. There continues to be a need for places of refuge, genuine asylum, from the omnipotence of mainstream psychiatry as well as other forms of well-intentioned intervention, households that exist outside of formal structures with their demands for goals and targets and performance measurements. There continues also to be a need for a scepticism towards established ways of thinking and understanding. Psychotherapy has mushroomed since the early days of the PA and while a greater awareness of our emotional lives and of the everyday forms of distress is undoubtedly welcome, no one could really claim that the growth of therapy and the proliferation of therapies has made the world a better place. (In many respects it has contributed to the individualism that now prevails, with its concern with the self to the exclusion of almost all else.) Intellectual confusion is widespread, as is sectarianism and a hostility to those who are different.

Our scepticism, however, is not just about theories of psychotherapy. It is also a scepticism towards established structures, particularly those that would seek to interfere in what we wish to do. Since the first collection of essays from the PA was published at the end of the 1980s, moves towards the formal regulation of psychotherapy have gathered momentum, threatening at times to drown a small organization like ours in paperwork and procedures. It is not that we are against regulation *per se*, but what is taking place now – and the process seems unstoppable – goes way beyond any minimum regulation that might, arguably, be necessary to protect the public. An agreed code of ethics and the means to enforce it, some minimum standards for training, compulsory malpractice insurance, for instance, would have been sufficient to meet any public concerns. But matters have gone far beyond this with a whole therapy bureaucracy now in place and thriving, not to mention the lawyers and consultants who are moving in to reap the various benefits. The truth is, and always has been, that there never was any real public drive for regulation of therapy. The impetus has a lot less to do with protection of the public and an awful lot more to do with assuring a professional status for therapeutic practitioners.

Despite all this (and despite a bitter split in the mid-1990s, which seems to be the lot of many therapy organizations) we have come through. This book is a testament to that. We are very much alive and keep burning a flame of inspiration from our founders and those who carried the torch since, a refusal to be ground down by bureaucracy or the trend towards sameness and uniformity, the eradication of difference. Our diversity may be frustrating for outsiders, our refusal to pin labels on ourselves an obstacle to neat categorization or definition, but for us it is a cause for celebration.

The essays that appear in this book reflect and celebrate the diversity of thinking in the PA today. The book opens with a paper by Robin Cooper. This is appropriate because, from the early 1970s until his tragic death in the summer of 2002, Robin had been a hugely important figure in the PA from the early 1970s and this book was his idea – just one product of his seemingly endless energy. His paper was first delivered at the PA's thirtieth anniversary conference and to some extent may be taken as a scene setting for the other contributions, all of which, in different ways, put into question what, as therapists, we too easily take for granted. As noted earlier, the PA's houses have been a central part of our work since our inception. Joseph Friedman, who has been involved in the running of PA houses for many years, offers a reading of the *Odyssey* highlighting the themes of home, hospitality and community that are at the heart of the lived lives of these communities-in-the-making. The notion of *rigour* is widespread in therapeutic discourse, especially in psychoanalytic circles where it is constantly held up as a standard separating them (who have it) from the rest of us (who do not). Miranda Glossop questions this received notion, arguing that it is too often a defensive move that ends up in a rigidity that is anti-creative and anti-therapeutic. One of the hallmarks of the PA has always been a scepticism towards accepted ideas and it is in this spirit that Paul Gordon, deliberately eschewing the idea of a sustained thesis, offers a series of sceptical thoughts, a lexicon, on a range of therapeutic issues. John Heaton questions concepts of normality and reason in his discussion of the nature of mental disturbance. He argues that neurosis and psychosis are disorders of reason. Their treatment, therefore, must attend to the logic of reasons rather than causes, involving questions of sense, meaning and truthfulness as opposed to truth and the discovery of mental mechanisms. Avoiding a linear argument that would distort more than it illuminates, Barbara Latham looks at the much-neglected but crucial issue of language in therapy from the standpoint of someone who is not just a therapist but a writer of stories.

For Peter Lomas, a contemporary of RD Laing in their early psychoanalytic days and who has for many years pursued his own independent-minded therapeutic path, psychotherapy has focused too much on what is wrong rather than on what is valuable; it has lost a sense of wonder at the world. If it is to be reinvigorated, psychotherapy must undergo an experience of re-enchantment. Psychotherapy, and particularly those forms of therapy owing allegiance to psychoanalysis, have for a long time been criticized, rejected even, for their claims about the female psyche, the nature of what has been called the *feminine*. Rosalind Mayo, drawing on theology and on religious iconography, shows some of the origins of this kind of thinking, connecting it to the founding father of psychoanalysis. David Smail draws on a lifetime working in clinical psychology and questions the notion of subjectivity implicit (if not explicit) in most therapeutic models – in particular, a certain voluntarism that holds that human beings are rationally, morally and aesthetically perfectible in principle through the efforts of their own will. Finally, M Guy Thompson subjects the idea of the unconscious to a rigorous scrutiny, drawing on several thinkers dear to the heart of the PA – Heidegger, Sartre and, of course, Laing.

As editors, we should like to express our gratitude to all the contributors for their generous co-operation. We should also like to thank other colleagues in the Association for their support and encouragement in this project.

Paul Gordon and Rosalind Mayo

CHAPTER 1
What we take for granted

ROBIN COOPER

I proposed the title 'what we take for granted' with two different inflections in mind. First of all, what do we, in the Philadelphia Association (PA), take for granted? What do we, for example in our conversations with one another, take for granted that other comparable organizations might not take for granted? Or what – for it comes to the same thing – might they take for granted that we do not? In framing this question as I do, I am of course presuming that – although we might not present a common front – there are shared assumptions that constitute some sort of common ground upon which we pitch our respective stalls. By the end of today you may feel that I am not entitled to take this for granted.

Secondly, what do we all take for granted? What we take for granted is – almost by definition – commonplace. The ordinary, the everyday, the familiar. It is at this point that an interrelationship between these two questions becomes apparent.

For, from the pre-Socratics – I am thinking for example of the Heraclitus fragment: 'even here the Gods are present' – philosophy has privileged the commonplace, the place that is in common, as the site of disclosure. Neither gods nor ethics are to be sought in some metaphysical topos, a separate region, but rather, as Heidegger puts it 'at this common place.' And for Heidegger, the common, the accustomed, the customary – the everyday – is the 'proper' (eigenlich) home of man.

In keeping with the phenomenological method inaugurated by Husserl, Heidegger regards ordinary experience as the domain within which human existence (Dasein) shows itself.

We must choose such a way of access and such a kind of interpretation, that this entity – Dasein – can show itself in itself and from itself. And this means that it is to be shown for the most part – in its average everydayness' . . . Thus by having regard for the basic state of Dasein's everydayness, we shall bring out the Being of this entity. (Heidegger, 1962, pp. 37–8)

And from its outset, the Philadelphia Association has privileged philosophy as being a tradition in which psychoanalysis is rooted, and has allied itself particularly with those philosophers who return philosophy to its proper place – as a guide to the art of, and through the perplexities of, being human.

Charles Rycroft proposes somewhere that psychoanalysis is less of an edifice than a quarry. This shift of definition is very instructive. I understand the distinction, more or less, as being between a field of knowledge and a tradition. The edifice – field of knowledge – calls to mind Kant's image of post-Enlightenment science as a 'self-sufficient whole . . . a separate and independent building and not a wing or section of another one.' By contrast with this self-sufficient and free-standing intellectual construction, the quarry – tradition – is something from which we all draw. It is kept alive by being continuously re-created, through retellings of the narratives that constitute the tradition. In Rycroft's instance, I assume that he means, amongst other things, that psychoanalysis enables a retelling, rereading of a literary tradition, and that without reference to the sources that constitute its tradition, psychoanalysis would dry up.

Psychoanalysis is just another story – powerfully generative, infinitely seductive and deeply mesmeric. It is a story that permits a different way of listening to stories. But it is not another story altogether.

For a long time the heading of 'phenomenology' served us as a reference point, and provided a name, from within the philosophical tradition by which we identified ourselves. Phenomenology is the disciplined study of the way things appear to me. It is a method of describing how the world shows itself, or comes into being for us. For the phenomenological movement the rediscovery or re-cognition of the ordinary was an explicit task, an awakening to the familiar so as to see it, in Plessner's phrase, 'with different eyes'.

Let us turn for a moment to *The Divided Self,* a work whose publication in 1960 delineates the concerns of the Philadelphia Association as well as anything. On the first page Laing writes:

> Existential phenomenology attempts to characterize the nature of a person's experience of his world and himself. It is not so much an attempt to describe particular objects of his experience as to set all particular experiences within the context of his whole being-in-the-world. (Laing, 1965, p. 17)

His whole being-in-the-world. 'Being-in-the-world' is, of course, a term introduced in 1927 by Heidegger. Heidegger had a massive influence upon Laing, who was reading his work closely during his years as a medical student. I can remember Ronnie asking – in that way that he sometimes would, implying that no one ever learns anything – whether perhaps this, at least, is a concept about whose importance and basic truth we can all, now, without equivocation, agree. That was maybe 15 years ago, and probably no one speaks about being-in-the-world any more.

The preliminary task of explicating the concept of being-in-the-world takes some 80 or so densely packed pages of Heidegger's (often rather turgid) prose. But just a quick dip, at random:

> What we 'first' hear is never noises or complexes of sounds, but the creaking wagon, the motor-cycle. We hear the columns on the march, the north wind, the woodpecker tapping, the fire crackling.
>
> It requires a very artificial and complicated frame of mind to 'hear' a 'Pure noise.' The fact that motor cycles and wagons are what we proximally hear is the phenomenal evidence that in every case Dasein, as Being-in-the-world, already dwells alongside what is ready-to-hand within the world; it certainly does not dwell proximally alongside 'sensation,' nor would it first have to give shape to the swirl of sensations to provide the springboard from which the subject leaps off and finally arrives at 'a world.'

(Heidegger, 1962, p. 207)

Heidegger is telling us that we hear the wind in the trees; we do not construct this 'auditory perception' out of 'raw sensations' that are more 'immediately' given to us. Hearing the wind in the trees is not merely the subjective and impressionistic account of how perception appears to the perceiving subject, which can then be swept aside by the analyses of cognitive psychology, taking their warrant from some system of immaculate perception called 'science'. There is no court of appeal beyond everydayness. But if we have wandered far away from a recognition of the primacy of everydayness – and Psychological Man has – what a long road we have to trudge to get back!

One of the significant contributions of Laing's first book – and this point remains as relevant today as it was then – is his demonstration that empirical/analytical thinking, and the psychologies and psychiatries to which they give rise, is often woefully inadequate to the task of describing the human forms of life with which it is confronted.

Heidegger's 'Being-in-the-world' is not an analytic or an empirical concept, for the world is not given to me through analytic thinking. The introduction of this concept does not provide us with any further facts about the world, or about human psychology. It is not about the mode of relatedness between two entities, the human being, and the world, about man and his relation to his environment. It is not primarily to do with entities, things or even processes. It is about being, and in particular about that being which is human being.

Many people find Merleau-Ponty's discussion of the lived world more evocative or approachable than that of Heidegger (perhaps because his language is closer to everyday language and less burdened with neologisms), and his argument better illustrated by reference to everyday experience.

> The world is not an object such that I have in my possession the law of its making; it is the natural setting of, and field for, all my thoughts and all my explicit perceptions. Truth does not inhabit only the 'inner man,' or, more accurately, there is no inner man. Man is in the world, and only in the world does he know himself. (Merleau-Ponty, 1962, p. xi)

With embodiment, it all comes as a package deal – everything under the sun – inextricably woven into a story of which I can speak, because I am of it.

'What is the source of our first suffering?' asks Bachelard. 'It lies in the fact that we hesitated to speak.... It was born in the moments when we accumulated silent things within us . . .' (Bachelard, in Gaudin, 1987, p. lix). Psychotherapy does not attempt to fill these silences, but to let them be heard in the words through which the world – in its depths, heights and surfaces, its light and darkness, its absences and presences, its awesome powers and its terrible fragilities – speaks. 'We do not hear because we have ears,' says Heidegger somewhere, 'we have ears because we can hear.'

Philosophy and psychotherapy have this in common: they are both concerned – in their different ways – with what it is to be. What it is – therefore – to have a world, and what it is for the world to come into being for us. Therapy is not to be trivialized as the removal of some obstacle to some task. Philosophy is not to be trivialized as mere 'talk about talk'.

Philosophy and therapy have this in common, too – one does them. They are practices, disciplines. To know phenomenology we must do phenomenology. As Heidegger tells us in the first page of *Basic Problems of Phenomenology*, we are not dealing with phenomenology but with what phenomenology deals with.

There are, of course, traditions in which the therapeutics of philosophy is quite explicit. For example, the Hellenistic philosophers, the Socratic/Platonic schools – or to bring us right up to the present day, the 'anti-philosophy' of Wittgenstein. Between the two, and with clear affinities with each, we might mention the figure of Montaigne. Montaigne, a heavily annotated copy of whose work was to be found in Freud's library, occupies an interesting position both as a precursor of psychoanalysis (as Masud Khan notes) and of existentialism.

Montaigne is of course relentlessly suspicious of human claims with regard to truth. 'We are born to quest after truth – to possess it is another matter.' It is clearly a small step from the dogmatism of believing we have the truth – we possess the truth writes Freud to Ferenczi – to fanaticism.

'I attribute a great deal of the world's woes to that propensity I recognize in my own mind, and that of other people,' states Laing, 'to become convinced that one is right' (Laing in Evans, 1976).

'Someone who knows too much finds it hard not to lie', says Wittgenstein. 'The truth can be spoken only by someone who is already at home in it; not by someone who still lives in falsehood and reaches out from falsehood towards truth on just one occasion' (Wittgenstein, 1980, p. 35). The importance of home truth, and of being at home in what we are talking about, permeates Montaigne. We find, throughout his essays, a priority being placed upon the practical sphere of personal engagement in the world, upon our common actions and deeds. What is important to him is no more or less than 'what is at our feet, what we hold in our hands, and what most clearly concerns the conduct of our lives' (Montaigne, 1958, p. 213). Knowledge is worth something only where it is embodied: 'What good does it do us to have our belly full of meat if it is not digested, if it is not transformed into us?' (Montaigne, 1965, p. 101). Or, perhaps more poetically: 'The bees plunder the flowers here and there, but afterwards they make of them honey, which is all theirs; it is no longer thyme or marjoram' (Montaigne, 1965, p. 111).

There can be few philosophers who have a keener sense than Montaigne of the capacity of the human mind to lead itself astray, and become cut off from its groundedness in the lived world. 'It is', he says, 'a dangerous blade'.

One of the PA brochures quoted a long extract from Montaigne's *On Experience,* which concluded

> For it needs some degree of knowledge to observe that we do not know...
> I, who pretend nothing else, find in myself such an infinite depth and variety that the sole fruit of my study is to make me feel how much I still have to learn. (Montaigne, 1958, p. 356)

We think of Montaigne, above all, as a sceptic – indeed his name has become almost synonymous with scepticism. The Glaswegian soul is naturally sceptical; and Laing is quite explicit about his affiliation to this philosophical tradition:

> I see myself in the sceptical tradition of Western thought. That's to say, to look at the nature of matter, the nature of man, the nature of the mind, the nature of phenomena without presuppositions to, to suspend judgement, as practised in the Greek schools ... I apply this scepticism to everything. (Laing in Evans, 1976)

I shall limit myself to mention three sources only, from within the PA, which show the direct relevance of a sceptical philosophical sensibility to our own concerns.

Firstly, Noreen O'Connor and Joanna Ryan's book: *Wild Desires and Mistaken Identities* (O'Connor and Ryan, 1993). In their phenomenological/ post-phenomenological study of sexuality they illustrate compellingly how the diversity of human experience is all too often homogenized within psychoanalytic theory – relying as it tends to on over-arching, universalizing, essentializing metaphysical concepts, saturated with what Robert Stoller refers to as 'highly abstract, theory laden, speculation-soaked, scientistic pseudo-explanatory jargon'.

Secondly, I would like to refer to a considerable body of work published by John Heaton in which a central theme is the nature of theory in psychoanalysis. (See, for example, Heaton in Cooper et al., 1989.) His work here reminds me of the example Wittgenstein uses to describe solving a philosophical problem – it is like getting to know a terrain, crossing it this way and that until one knows one's way about. At any rate John Heaton's criss-crossing of this particular terrain, informed by an invigorating reading of the philosophers – particularly Heidegger and Wittgenstein – constitutes an important demonstration of the relevance of the sceptical tradition to psychotherapy. 'The sceptics are enquirers', writes Heaton, 'but to enquire is not the same as to seek, for in inquiry there is no end to be gained and held. Inquiry does not seek answers' (Heaton, 2003).

Thirdly, another Glaswegian, Hugh Crawford. Hugh left no published writings, but played an important part in the evolution of the Philadelphia Association, and he had a considerable influence, I think, upon all who knew him. I quote here from unpublished notes to give some idea of his own weavings of phenomenology and psychoanalysis.

The Time of My Life

Turned backwards toward regret, I live in the wish for what I have not had; my intentionality is reversed and time passes me by.

I can live vicariously by watching others do it, but this is a cul-de-sac of fantasy; time still eludes me.

I can live where there is a lot happening, but they have no time for me.

I can live where nothing is expected because nothing is going on – but still there is no time.

I can sleep – slip into a cocoon of 'no time' – but each time I awake the party is over.

I can eat into deadness, into uncomplainingness, but the obscenity of it overtakes me.

I repeat endlessly.

So repression loses spatiality and becomes a separation from time a sin – albeit an illusion (as all the sins are).

To be condemned to live an illusion is indeed the Hell created by the Father of Lies, i.e. in repression nothing is absent, or it wouldn't have to be repressed.

The absence is the presence of what I have not had.

But since all I have to lose is what I have not had,

there is both nothing to lose and

a terrible impossibility of giving it up.

In these lines, time is everything. The lines allude to what Hugh called the temporal paradox of the phenomenological reduction. In the beginning is the lived act, or gesture, which is not so much in time, as the opening of time. The lived act is in the opposite temporal flow from any reflective awareness of it. It is toward a future in which it is realized. It is – to my reflectiveness awareness of it – already past. I can no more live by my reflective awareness than I can learn to ride a bicycle by studying the laws of dynamics. The lived act brings itself into being. As with speaking, we only know what to say by saying it (to someone).

But the lived act does not arise out of nothing; its 'cause' (which lies ahead of it) is its articulation with its context. And this context is the inter-subjective matrix, or potential space from which everything is born.

'Man is but a network of relationships' quotes Merleau-Ponty (1962) as the last line of *The Phenomenology of Perception,* 'and these alone matter to him.' Not: men have interpersonal relationships, and these are important to them. Man is a network of relationships. We are what we make of each other.

On this note, I would like to turn towards our communities. I do so because, whilst they are not our sole concern, they do play a quite essential part in what we are on about. Our houses – I have heard it said – keep us honest. At any rate, they provide a good point of departure with regard to our question: what do we take for granted.

The very first account of what goes on in a PA community house that I recall hearing was a story told by Laing in the course of the Dialectics of Liberation Congress, in 1967. It was a type of rather wild and improbable story that Ronnie would delight in telling and featured a rather flamboyant and extravagant character who had, I understood, recently been living in Kingsley Hall. This man was in the habit of going round the place with no clothes, except for a stuffed turkey, which he would wear upon his head. Driven, I understood, to a point of some exasperation by the persistent presence of this naked turkey-hatted nutter, another one of the Kingsley Hall residents suddenly picked up some rifle-like object, aimed, and shot him in the balls. Whereupon, said Ronnie, 90 per cent of his castration-complex – which had hitherto proved quite recalcitrant to prolonged psychoanalytic treatment – was cured, just like that!

Several things struck me about this story. I remember first of all the gusto with which Ronnie recounted it, which seemed to be inseparably linked with the state of anarchy which – one could not help but be given the impression – ruled in this house. It was rather implied that in these houses, or at any rate in this particular one, anything goes. To use a phrase which Ronnie was fond of – but which doesn't mean quite the same thing – it was all 'up for grabs'.

Secondly, this little drama seemed to me to have been an interaction utterly devoid of any treatment motive. There was nothing around this story to do with worthy good-intentionedness; it was more like youthful behavioural ribaldry. Yet, so went the story, it affected the parts the ordinary treatments failed to reach.

Now what is important about this story is what is taken for granted. The story is about something which happens within a context. The context is one within which what goes on matters. For example, a number of people had thought a very great deal about the guiding principles that might inform Kingsley Hall before it was even started. This project was contextualized within a broader context of interest, of which the conference at which I heard it described was one facet.

So it would be altogether misleading to think of the ethos of (even) this house as 'anything goes'. It is too facile, too saturated with the humanistic 'you do your thing and I do mine'. The ethos of the house was much more to do with letting be.

Letting someone be is a matter of some subtlety! 'Let' means to hinder (without let or hindrance) as well as to leave, to allow. Letting someone be is certainly an allowing, but it is not an indifference to the other. Letting someone be only makes sense in the context of some concern for him. But if it is not indifference, it is equally not that solicitude that leaps in with some idea of how the other should be. Letting be arises in the context of responsibility. It is contingent upon a capacity to respond rather than a propensity to react.

To take a rather extreme example there have been times – but not, it has to be said, for some time – when the 'holding' of a member of the community has extended to his or her being physically restrained from escaping from the house. The household has had to draw upon the resources of the broader PA network in order to maintain a degree of round-the-clock vigilance so as to protect the individual from the dangers associated with his being admitted to hospital and sedated. And sometimes all this in the face of the particular person concerned, helpless and vulnerable, screaming out 'Let me go! Let me go!'

What are the ethics of this? Well, in this situation letting be – i.e., if someone is mad let him be mad, if someone has a madness to go through let him go through it – cannot simply be a question of standing by indifferently. In this situation, on the contrary, letting be clearly seems to require some sort of sanctuary or asylum, whose ambience is conducive to this. In fact, this is a matter of very considerable sophistication. The provision of it is obviously predicated upon an assumption – clinical? ethical? aesthetic? – which may be borne out by experience – that this letting things run their course is all worthwhile.

The most important thing in an environment is the people in it ... so we have to experiment with how we can, in our context, be safe people for other people to meet. When we don't know people, people we've never met before, we have to show by our presence that we are not going to do anything to anyone in the name of anything (Laing in Evans, 1976).

We are not going to do anything to anyone in the name of anything. We have no plan in mind. We are not going to treat them. We are not going to cure them. 'We propose,' said Hugh Crawford, 'merely not to silence the unspeakable.'

During the past weeks, on the occasion of the fiftieth anniversary of their liberation, we have seen many images of the concentration camps on our television screens.

I do not know if this was mentioned on any of these programmes, but I learned from Peter Barham's excellent book *Closing the Asylum* (Barham, 1992) that techniques of extermination were developed by the psychiatrists of the Third Reich during the pre-war years. And so it was that when it was decided to convert the concentration camp at Auschwitz-Birkenau to an extermination camp, a group of prisoners was dispatched to the mental hospital at Sonnenschein to be gassed, in order to refine the technological know-how already being built up and adapt it for the extermination programme.

As many as 200,000 mental patients may have been exterminated in Germany prior to 1941, maybe 15,000 in Poland, where many of the techniques of the gas installations were perfected. Coming slightly closer to home, Barham refers to research which shows that in Vichy France, during the same period, psychiatrists co-operated in the starvation of some 40,000 mental patients.

The sociologist Zygmunt Bauman, whose *Modernity and the Holocaust* is cited by Barham, develops an argument that calls to mind Hugh Crawford's dark utterance: 'Hitler was ahead of his time'. Bauman argues that the programme of extermination carried out by the Third Reich was not so much a distortion or aberration of the modern civilizing process as one of its most accomplished products. (See Barham, 1992, p. 79.) Bauman's argument goes on to show how the rationalizing tendencies of the modem civilizing process have created 'the means whereby the requirements of rationality have been emancipated from the interference of ethical norms and moral inhibitions' (Barham, 1992, p. 78). What is crucial to this is the distantiation whereby 'the victimized group and the rest do not meet any more, *their life processes do not cross*' (Barham, 1992, p. 79, my italics).

In a manner reminiscent of Levinas's 'Face to Face', Bauman argues that responsibility arises out of proximity to the other person. If the conditions for the possibility of proximity are eroded, responsibility becomes silenced (Barham, 1992, p. 78).

Once the human bond has become broken it is the old story. They are not like us. What are we going to do with them? 'What should we citizens do with those who are not like us, whose ability to perform renders them unproductive; what are they here for, and how are we going to deal with them?' (Klaus Dorner, quoted in Barham, 1992, p. 81). Psychiatrists and others had come to see it as their social and professional duty to help restore the social body to good health. It is a social sanitization. The unsanitary become the insane and the issue becomes one of disposal.

They are not human. They cannot be human. We must feel touched and moved, then, by those heroic investigators, who, in the face of all the evidence, boldly continue to publish researches that demonstrate that, after all, they are human. In 1981, the *American Journal of Psychiatry* published a study in which it was demonstrated that 'people with schizophrenia are capable of experiencing human emotions such as depression.' Another piece of research concluded with the statement that 'it may well be that schizophrenic patients, like the general population, respond quite differently to different situations' (both examples quoted in Barham, 1992, p. 91).

I recommend to you Barham's analysis of what makes 'the project of schizophrenia' possible, and his historical analysis of the inauguration of the psychology of self-possession and concomitant moral distance between one possessed self and another. His point of departure is the Enlightenment de-narrativization of the subject, which he refers to as the 'clearing of the stage' to prepare the ground for what I have called earlier the psychological subject. This introduces what Barham calls a 'dissipation of the grammar of community' such that the possibility arises for individuals to find themselves put beyond the terms of a recognized human order.

The question of the ex-communication of the mental patient is, of course, enormously intricate, arising as it does at a complex interface or cross – articulation of interests and fears. Accordingly, it would be very naive to assume, as the project of 'care in the community' often encourages us to, that merely closing the hospitals and relocating the inmates itself changes anything.

The more inclusive terms that Barham employs, and within which he sets the hospital–community issue, are 'exclusive from' or 'inclusion within' the moral community.

An idiom of community predicated on notions of self-possession and self-expression is perhaps least qualified to amend that lack of nexus which schizophrenic and other vulnerable people often experience. To view the problem of community critically, by contrast, is to recognize that the crucial issue concerns not only the physical distance between hospital and community, or the formal distance between incarceration and freedom of the subject, but the moral distance between schizophrenic people and the society of which they are part (Barham, 1993, p. 181).

In reading Peter Barham's books, we are reminded again and again how strong is the wish on the part of those whose position in the community is marginal, who take up their place, as he put it, 'on the edge of the common' (and the common is shrinking!) to be treated merely as 'ordinary people'. And at the same time how difficult it is to become 'ordinary people.' I refer to a story written up by Melanie Phillips in the *Guardian* (November 9, 1990, referred to in Barham, pp. 110–112). In a number of respects it is reminiscent of the situation which arose between one of the PA households and the Royal Borough of Kensington and Chelsea.

About five years ago, Bath Health Authority bought two houses in a development to accommodate patients who had been moved out of a long-stay psychiatric hospital. Although these former patients caused no trouble of any sort, the developer – a subsidiary of a building society – on discovering the use to which the health authority intended to put these houses, took the matter to court, claiming that there had been a breach of the covenant which stipulated that the houses could be used for no purpose 'other than those incidental to the enjoyment of a private dwelling house'.

In the Court of Appeal, the Master of the Rolls, Lord Donaldson, maintained that the argument centred on the definition of a dwelling house. It was not enough that there had been no public nuisance. It was not enough, Lord Donaldson emphasized, that in many respects these health authority houses were quite indistinguishable from the other houses on the estate. He agreed that all of them were being used as dwelling houses, but no, this was still not enough. The crucial point for Lord Donaldson was that the persons concerned remained patients, he said, because they were ineligible for social security benefits and relied upon the health service for money to buy the necessities of life; and because they were supervised by a health service employee. The house was therefore being used 'for public and not for private purposes'. 'If a label can be attached to such a use,' Lord Donaldson went on to say, 'it seems to me that of hospital annexe or mental health hostel. This is not a use which would be regarded as a normal use of a private dwelling house.'

Melanie Phillips spoke to the building society in question about its attempts to preserve property value in the face of local prejudice. 'It's all about protecting the interests of other residents,' they said. 'But what were these interests that were so threatened if noone had complained and everyone who lived there was perfectly happy?' 'Well,' came the reply, 'just because this particular breach of the covenant hadn't caused any problems didn't mean that any possible breach of this or any other covenant might not cause a problem, so they couldn't turn a blind eye just because noone had complained. And anyway, any implications that this might have for community care policy was nothing to do with them.'

I find Michael Ignatieff's comment upon 'caring' very refreshing. Notions of the 'caring society' evoke, for Ignatieff, the image of the nanny state in which the care we get depends upon what the 'caring professions' think it fit for us to receive. He would, he goes on to say, 'much prefer to live in a society which struggles to be just, which respects and enhances people's rights and entitlements' (quoted in Barham, 1992, p. 113). A possible motto for the Philadelphia Association: 'at least we don't care'.

But there is, amongst the clamour of 'care in the community', a voice to be heard that does seem, on the face of it, to wish to address precisely this question of the moral separation. It is the contemporary inheritor of what was once called moral treatment, and which we now recognize as the therapeutic community. This voice, however, is not without its contradictions.

Bear with me whilst I try to illustrate this by reference to the writings of Tom Main. I chose him because he was a psychoanalyst of considerable influence in this field, having worked with Bion and Foulkes in the famous Northfield Hospital. He is widely considered to be one of the founding fathers of the contemporary therapeutic community movement.

I shall start with a suggestion that Tom Main makes with which I'm sure we'd all agree. We take it for granted. He proposes simply that the ways in which people treat one another, and are treated by one another, has a direct bearing upon their health and well-being. This surely is precisely what Main (1980, p. 53) is claiming when he suggests that 'a community may become therapeutic as a social organization no matter what individual treatments were or were not offered.'

The salient characteristics of a 'social system' that might be therapeutic for all are articulated in terms such as 'joint recognition of each individual's capacities and limitations', 'respect for the other', 'getting to know the other well as a person', and 'the attempt to create an atmosphere of respect for all' – all of which refer to 'the ways in which people relate to each other'. Now there is, of course, nothing particularly technical – medical or psychological – about any of these ideas, which are simply part of the vocabulary of everyday moral life. In effect Main is proposing here that what is determinative for 'mental health' is the ethical stand which people take up with respect to one another.

Main proposes to initiate what he calls a 'culture of inquiry', participation within which constitutes 'treatment for all'. That is, it is a treatment for the disorders common to the community as a whole, staff at all levels as well as patients. As examples of these disorders Main (1977, p. 17) cites:

- unconscious fantasies;
- blind mutual projection of evil;
- distorted perceptions;
- defensive use of roles;
- resistances;
- unthinking staff-based discipline;
- unbearable anxieties and rigid defences against them;
- projection of hostilities;
- loss of the hope of insight;
- creation and maintenance of various split-off sectors (into which are projected 'evil and disorder');
- projective defences against studying more painful interpersonal conflicts in depth;
- persecutory anxiety;
- disownment of responsibility;
- the fear of being attacked;
- acting out anxieties;
- suspiciousness;
- collusive splitting and projective defences against pain;
- social splits, especially insofar as patients may be used as containers of childishness and helplessness.

On reading this (abbreviated) list we surely agree with Main that 'the troubled larger system' itself needs treatment if it is to be therapeutic for all. The treatment that Main proposes is the creation of what he calls 'a total culture of inquiry, to examine, understand and resolve the tensions and defensive use of roles which are inevitable in any total system'. But now we ask: Is this treatment, the creation of this 'culture of inquiry' – a 'folkways of patient honest inquiry into difficulties' – sufficiently effective a therapy to heal not only the troubles and sicknesses characteristic of the community as a whole, staff as well as patients, but also mental illness proper? Main does not, incidentally, spell out in any detail the sort of characteristics whereby patients may be distinguished from staff, other than by maintaining that they are 'mentally ill', 'sick', 'ill,' display 'annoying inefficiencies', are 'liable to distort reality', and 'fail to understand others', although he adds, somewhat casually, that such failures 'are as common among staff as among patients' (Main, 1977, p. 10).

Main feels that the 'treatment for all' is not sufficiently effective a therapy to deal with these specific sicknesses, although it helps. He divides the mental patient into two parts, one of which may directly engage in the therapy of the treatment culture, the culture of inquiry, while the other part benefits indirectly, as a consequence of the staff being able to do their job more effectively. 'Psychiatric patients are sick as people, but not sick all through ... their skills and healthy parts need not be ignored in daily life in hospital as in the medical model which concentrates only on the sick parts' (Main, 1977, p. 13). He goes on to say that 'this attempt to create an atmosphere of respect for all, and the examination of all difficulties ... in a culture which is concerned with whole people ... would be a long way from the medical model' (Main, 1977, p. 11).

In all this we see an intention, which no sooner announces itself than seems to undergo collapse. We witness a failure of nerve. And whilst it would be churlish not to acknowledge the wide diversity of enterprises which come under the heading of therapeutic community, I think that this sort of failure of nerve is typical.

Main writes: 'Different pathologies need different social processes, especially designed for the special nature of the people they treat' (Main, 1980, p. 62). This is a very impersonal language. It does not say, for example, that it may be appropriate to conduct oneself differently towards different people, according to their states of mind and the circumstances in which they find themselves, as discerned by one's own sensibilities. Now, more is at stake in this than choice of words, for according to the words we use, different worlds come into being. I'm sure that our nerve fails us at all sorts of points. Let us, however, declare a position. We would like to be able to keep the door open to those individuals who find themselves drawn to a more personal world than one which exploits 'social forces' in 'especially designed' ways; to people who would like to take up home elsewhere than upon the barren wastelands of mental health.

'Their life processes do not cross,' says Barham, 'so that what happens has no meaning easy to translate into the vocabulary of human intercourse' (Barham, 1992, p. 79). The human bond has become broken. Our response to this essentially is very simple.

At the crossing of the ways, the meeting of the roads, the trivium – we start with a human dwelling. A place where 'life processes' do indeed cross.

A household where people may unpack, and live, and get on with it, with one another, as they wish. A place of co-habitation, where lives have implications for one another, where personal stories become woven together in the fabric, the 'nitty-gritty,' the textures of everyday matters. A place where what matters shows. A house which honours the venerable tradition of hospitality to the stranger. A place where paperwork, in the form of psychiatric records and clinical assessments, becomes irrelevant.

And who are the strangers who come our way? Those who have lost their way, in one way or another. Those who have become disarticulated from human belonging, in one way or another. Those who would like to come in out of the cold. Those who have something to go through, for which they feel they need more than their ongoing psychotherapy. Those who find themselves in one or other version of what used to be called Hell.

'I am human, therefore nothing human is alien to me' said the Roman poet Terence. What you are going through is human. The place to go through it is a human place, with people who have time for one another.

We assume that the business of living is able to include all its variations. The choice is not between order or chaos, but between a life curve which is flattened, or pulsating. Home is where you don't have to get it right. There is a great deal written about truth as a positive phenomenon, very little about error. One can always get one's lessons right, by careful preparation. The business of living in the world seems to be very different in that one learns, rather in the way that one does with a practical skill, by getting it wrong, by a process of embodiment of error. You take it on.

No one is in charge. But there are psychotherapists. They come and go, and come back again. This makes it all possible, for without the therapeutic presence – and the network to which the therapists belong – it is difficult to see how the thing could get started, or maintain itself with a sufficient degree of attentiveness.

But it makes a difference. And this is the one point where our houses suddenly cease to be quite like the ones next door.

And this leads to a final thought …

In the course of conversation the other day, a friend, Ian Simpson, told me that Colditz Castle, in one of its earlier incarnations, had been a mental hospital, and even had had some claim to fame as having been at one time a 'progressive' institution. Subsequently, of course, Colditz became a prisoner-of-war camp for British soldiers captured in the course of active duty during the Second World War. In comparison with the camps we have mentioned earlier, life in Colditz must have been like a gentlemen's club. So, at least, seems to have been my impression based upon a distant memory of having read Pat Reid's *The Great Escape*.

The dream of escape from Colditz was never far from the thoughts of most inmates, presumably for some more than others. There was an escape committee to assess the feasibility of particular schemes, and to ensure that would-be escapees were sufficiently prepared for their journey back to freedom. And those who made it out – some to get away, some to be brought back, and some to die – of course were invested heavily with the hopes, fears, and so on of those who remained.

And these thoughts, and the conversation in which they arose, raised a question. How well does leaving a PA community lend itself to the metaphor of escape? Escape plays on the idea of capability, of getting away with it, getting away with what you can, of a dash for freedom.

Of course the idea does not seem to rest easily alongside the things I would still want to insist upon, about the households as places of hospitality, as places conducive to finding oneself 'at home,' of spaces, to use Bachelard's fine phrase 'which invites us to come out of ourselves'.

And in any case, do we not speak of leaving as being a negotiation with the rest of the community? Indeed. And can we not say that one only leaves when one arrives, and then one can just leave? Freely? With, therefore, no need to 'escape.' Or are we now sliding – horror of horrors – into the metaphysics of full presence?

The point that I wish to raise is not simply to do with the difficulty of living in a PA community, although I think this needs to be fully acknowledged. 'Everyone can play his part in the farce,' says Montaigne, 'and act an honest role on the stage. But to be disciplined within, in one's own breast, where all is permissible and all is concealed – that is the point! To be orderly at home, in our common actions' (Montaigne, 1958, p. 239). Quite so.

Difficulty is one thing. But if psychoanalytic visitation descends into the living room, is there living room? If there is, what does it say about our therapy? Our households?

Love me and leave me, they say. For a great many people, to live – and I mean live – in a place such as a PA household, which unashamedly casts the spell of psychoanalytic mesmerization, may be necessary. But is it possible?

I would like to conclude by quoting a few lines from Philadelphia Stories, a booklet written to the PA on the occasion of its quarter century by Keith Musgrove. He lived in the Archway community for a few months between 1971 and 1972, and of his experience writes:

> I came here because I believed I had lost my voice, my self, my reason. I found none of these 'things' and now no longer expect or even want to. What I discovered instead was a place where I could at last be lost enough to say so, and a community of people to whom the gift of language means enough for them not to take the statement 'I am lost' to mean 'find me,' which it would anyhow have been beyond their possibilities to do.

I like, too, the epigraph that Keith chooses, from Samuel Beckett's *Malone Dies*: 'A bright light is not necessary, a taper is all that one needs to live in strangeness, if it faithfully burns.'

CHAPTER 2

The *Odyssey*, community and therapy

JOE FRIEDMAN

The *Odyssey*, the latter of Homer's great oral narratives, has two 'scenes' of action. The first is Odysseus' home, Ithaca, from which he has been absent for 10 long years. In this house, in which Odysseus still casts a long shadow, his son, Telemakhos (all spellings and quotations, unless otherwise noted, come from the Fitzgerald, 1961, translation of the *Odyssey*) has grown up, and his wife, Penelope, has grown older. His home is filled with uninvited 'guests', the loud and boorish suitors for Penelope's hand. They have declared they won't leave until Penelope takes one as her husband.

The second scene of action moves around, but largely takes place in what we would call flashback. It is the account of Odysseus' long and much-interrupted journey home – a journey in which he loses all his crew and all the spoil he has taken from the sacked city of Troy. The final part of the narrative is the story of Odysseus' return home, initially in disguise. The two separate scenes become one. The form of the book thus has that of a successful therapy. But the *Odyssey* has a great deal more to teach us about community and therapy.

Reading the *Odyssey* today, we are struck by how modern a world it depicts. Homer's first work, the *Iliad*, an account of the battle for Troy, shows a world in which a man is a man, and a woman's place is at home. In the *Odyssey* the old values no longer hold sway. People say one thing and mean another. Lives are destroyed by deception. Trust is shown as something rare and often undeserved. An awareness of the closeness of deception even characterizes Telemakhos' relations with his mother – when asked by Athena (in disguise) whether he is Odysseus' son he replies, 'My mother says indeed I am his. I for my part do not know. Nobody really knows his father' (Lattimore, 1965, p.32).

In many respects the *Odyssey* depicts a world which seems surprisingly Freudian, complete with what we would now call 'slips of the tongue' and an awareness of the importance of 'repressed' sexuality. An example of a slip of the tongue occurs near the end of the poem when Penelope speaks to her servant regarding her foreign 'guest'. 'Come here, stand by me, faithful Eurekleia and bathe – bathe your master I almost said, for they are of an age ...'. In this moment, Penelope seems to be unconsciously aware of the true identity of her guest. (The Nausikaa episode, below, shows Homer's awareness of repressed sexuality.)

The *Odyssey* is also centrally concerned with community – with questions such as 'what makes a community possible', 'what does coming home mean', and 'what is the nature of hospitality'. In all this, it can be a fruitful source for inquiry into questions that (should) centrally concern everyone involved in therapeutic communities (and for that matter, individual analysis).

In this chapter I shall take up a few of these issues, showing how they are understood in the *Odyssey*, and in the Philadelphia Association therapeutic communities. I shall also try to show how the *Odyssey* provides models for understanding the mappings and wish fulfilment that play so important a part in the notion of the transference.

Hospitality

In the *Odyssey*, Homer shows a deep concern with the nature of hospitality. Throughout the book, the way we are given to judge the various characters and houses is through their extension (or not) of hospitality. When Telemakhos pulls up at Menelaos' palace his servant rushes in to ask the king, should 'we unhitch their team, or send them on to someone free to receive them?' Menelaos replies in anger. 'You were no idiot before, Eteoneus, but here you are talking like a child of 10!' The Greek word *idios* refers to someone who lives in his own world – hospitality is thus defined as one of the essences of an interpersonal world.

Odysseus' story is set within two different contexts (both invoked in the prologue). One is Paris' abuse of Menelaos' hospitality, which brought about the Trojan war (Paris ran off with Menelaos' wife, Helen), the other of Aegisthus' abuse of Agamemmnon's hospitality (he sleeps with Agamemmnon's wife and kills Agamemmnon when he returns from Troy). The *Odyssey* itself begins with description of the suitor's abuse of (the absent) Odysseus' hospitality, and Telemakhos extending hospitality to Mentes (Athena in disguise).

Zeus, the most powerful of the Greek gods, rules the treatment of guests and suppliants. This denotes the important place hospitality had in the Greek world. Those who are civilized (of any station) recognize this. As Nausikaa, a princess, puts it, 'this man is a castaway, poor fellow, we must take care of him. Strangers and beggars come from Zeus.' As Odysseus' swineherd puts it, 'Tush, friend, rudeness to a stranger is not decency, poor thou he may be, poorer than you. All wanderers and beggars come from Zeus.'

Hospitality towards strangers involves an element of risk. The Greek word *xeinos,* both stranger and guest, guest-friend, embodies this tension. It seems extraordinary to us that the guest/stranger was not required to introduce him/herself. With the Phaiakians, more than a day has passed before Odysseus is asked to indicate who he is. Throughout the poem, hospitality has a general form: the new arrival waits at the entrance of the home until one of the company notices him and hastens to the doorway, taking him by the hand, and leading him in; he is offered a seat, and is invited to eat. However, Homer establishes that true hospitality is situational and bound by context.

In the *Odyssey,* Homer shows several extremes of hospitality; its low point occurs when in response to Odysseus' request for hospitality, the Kyklopes replies shortly 'you're a ninny', and then 'in one stride he clutched at my companions and caught two in his hands like squirming puppies to beat their brains out, spattering the floor.'

On the other hand is the hospitality of the Phaiakians, the first mortal men Odysseus has seen in seven years. He has been washed up on their shores after being kept prisoner for years on Kalypso's island, and a gruelling sea journey in which his raft was wrecked by Poseidon. Weary, hungry and naked he spends his first night sleeping between two bushes. I shall spend some time here going into detail about what ensues, because Homer, through the example of the Phaiakians, makes important points about the nature of true hospitality. Hospitality, he indicates, involves more than providing someone with a drink, good clothes and a full belly.

The night that Odysseus has been washed ashore, Athena sends Nausikaa, the king's daughter, a dream. Athena appears as a girl Nausikaa's age. 'How so remiss, and yet thy mother's daughter? Leaving thy clothes uncared for, Nausikaa, when soon thou must have store of marriage linen, and put thy minstrelly in wedding dress!' How psychoanalytic! Using a dream, and a disguised erotic one, to set the scene. Moved by the dream, Nausikaa goes to her father. She speaks of wanting to wash her brother's wedding clothes, but not her own. 'She had no word to say of her own wedding, though her keen father saw her blush.'

When Odysseus awakes, Nausikaa and her servants are washing clothes by the seashore. Her servants flee at the sight of the naked Odysseus, but Nausikaa stands firm. This establishes her as someone who might be secure enough to extend hospitality. Odysseus doesn't address Nausikaa as a suppliant which would give him rights. Rather, he speaks to her, initially flatteringly – 'Mistress, please are you divine or mortal?' and wins her over. Nausikaa gives him clothes and food but fails to take him home with her. This is the only way her hospitality falls short, as her father points out later. Interestingly, this is shown as her being ill-at-ease with her own sexuality. As she puts it, 'Some seadog might say, after we passed, "Who is this handsome stranger trailing Nausikaa? Where did she find him? Will he be her husband"? This is the way they will make light of me.'

Having arrived at the palace, Odysseus is granted hospitality and a passage home by the king, Alkínoös, before anyone knows who he is. At one point, while the minstrel is singing the story of Troy, Odysseus is moved to tears – 'only Alkínoös, at his elbow, saw them, and caught the low groan in the man's breathing. At once he spoke to all the seafolk round him.' He doesn't refer to Odysseus' tears directly but rather asks for the minstrel to stop singing and for the pentathlon to begin.

At the games, Odysseus is rudely challenged to compete, 'As I see it, friend, you never learned a sport and have no skill in any of the contexts of fighting men. You must have been the skipper of some tramp that crawled from one port to the next not by your looks, an athlete.' Odysseus responds with wit and spunk, 'That was uncalled for, friend, you talk like a fool. The gods deal out no gift, this one or any – birth, brains, or speech – to every man alike . . . You now, for instance, with your fine physique – a god's, indeed – you have an empty noddle.' Odysseus competes in the discus and makes the furthest throw. His prowess is acknowledged.

Thus, in Alkínoös' court, there is sensitivity, contentiousness, scorn, competition, vindication and recognition. There is the showing off of the things in which the house excels, and Odysseus' appreciation of this. And finally there is the space for Odysseus to tell his story, and an appreciative audience that wants to hear it all. Through all this, Odysseus is restored to himself. This, Homer indicates, is true hospitality.

Hospitality in the Philadelphia Association

In our increasingly technologized society (Friedman 1989, p.69-71), the home is impoverished by being stripped of all that makes a home homely. Children are sent off to 'learn', parents go out to 'work'; the sick are sent to hospital, the old to 'homes'. The home is thus reduced to a 'dwelling unit'. (On the block of council flats near one of our houses was the apt graffiti, 'Dwelling unit, sweet dwelling unit.')

Hugh Crawford, one of the early members of the Philadelphia Association, felt that in their small way our houses could be a place in which everything human is given a place, a home. This is the sort of home that Homer depicts in Skheria. This is what we aim to provide in a PA house, a home for the heart – which, of course, contains more than love. Not being fictional creatures like the Phaiakians, we mostly fall short of this. However, we are open to be seen to do so, and to having the nature of our hospitality explored.

At our Shirland Road household, we have one meeting a week which is open to people who are interested in moving into the house. These meetings are a potential resident's first contact with the house (apart from the initial phone call, 'can I come next Thursday? When is the meeting?' and so forth). They are ordinary meetings of the house, in which, depending on what is going on in the community, there may be time and space to open up a conversation with the visitor. A cup of tea and introductions around the table are in order. Sometimes the therapists are named as such, sometimes not. (If not, scenes reminiscent of 'Cuckoo's Nest' occur – the visitor is asked to guess which people sitting around the table are therapists. Sometimes, needless to say, they guess wrong, something which provides great amusement.). If something important is happening between people in the house, the visitor may well find it difficult to get a word in edgeways.

There is thus a parallel to Greek hospitality, in which the affairs of the house go on normally until there is space for visitors to introduce themselves. Some visitors who are reluctant to speak attend several such meetings before being moved to do so. Of course, if nothing much is going on in the community, or if people wish to avoid their own difficulties, the potential resident may become the centre of attention.

It is important for us that visitors see us at home, and get some idea of what being at home in this particular household involves. Their visits are not preceded by clinical interviews. At no time do we ask for medical records, etc. For those familiar with psychiatric or social work-based approaches, these mark us out as different. As often as not, the questioning of potential members of the community is led by residents, and rather than centring on clinical issues, revolves around shared interests and concerns.

People may compare notes on universities, hospitals, or other therapeutic communities. There is an honesty about the way in which what matters is whether they are liked, and whether they belong. So often, this central issue is hidden behind questions of diagnostic suitability.

At best, our visitors see a conversation in which nothing is excluded. Therapists can be criticized and made fun of. Usually forbidden language and subjects such as power and sexuality are all included in the conversation.

Homer's account of Nausikaa's meeting with Odysseus implies that part of what hospitality requires is a secureness in one's own position. Often, however, it is this security which cannot be assumed when residents meet potential new members of the community. Their own positions – of being house 'baby' or 'mother', most attractive man or woman – may be felt to be under threat. This often leads, as it did in Nausikaa's case, to failures in the extension of hospitality. When this happens, part of the therapists' function is to interpret what is going on.

Issues of hospitality, revolving as they do around the thresholds of 'inner' and 'outer' and the area between, show in a vital way how these are understood and embodied. When people do not grasp the nature of these thresholds, failures of hospitality result. An awareness of the complexity of hospitality is thus part of what our households hope to cultivate. When we first set up our house at Shirland Road, such awareness was almost entirely lacking. People would be set to move in without any recognition of what this involved, both for themselves and for those already living in the community – who didn't have much sense of it being their home, or indeed what a home was yet. Part of what is fascinating about our communities is the way in which people's awareness of the issues involved in hospitality develop. Some people see the question of moving in as one of following a certain protocol, having to touch specific bases. Others see it mainly as an opportunity to subject new people to what they felt they had been subjected to. One of the things that seems to be very difficult for people to get hold of is the way that hospitality involves obligations on both sides – because seeing this would involve a deconstruction of the notion of resident as innocent victim.

The heroic

As I noted earlier, the *Odyssey* presents a very different world from that of the *Iliad*. Odysseus' world is menacing with mysteriousness of underlying motives, inscrutable people, liars and cheats. Disloyalty and deception, not heroic rage and strife for honour, are causes of disaster. Odysseus struggles with mutinous sailors, offensive servants, disloyal subjects and with monsters and goddesses with whom heroic prowess is useless. (Griffin, 1980).

Indeed, the first time we see Odysseus, 2,400 lines into the poem, he is crying at the edge of the sea. He is a prisoner on the immortal Kalypso's island, impotent and despondent. All that life means for a hero – activity, struggle, achievement – has been taken away from him. There are no mountains for him to climb.

Most of what Homer has to say about the heroic is expressed in Odysseus' account of his journey, the story he tells over several days at Alkínoös' court. In his account, we (though seemingly not Odysseus) are faced with the question 'is heroic behaviour still possible, or even desirable, in this modem age?'

It is important to note that this is a story, told entirely in first person, one of many different stories Odysseus tells during the course of the poem. This has always been understood as crucial. As Aristotle put it, 'Only in tales told by Odysseus are there monsters and magic. The poet prefers not to vouch for their truth himself' (Griffin, 1980, p. 166).

His story begins in the framework of the familiar Aegean. Odysseus, the sacker of cities, leads his men in an assault on the Kikonês, who were allies of Troy and thus fair game. The old order – where everyone knew his place – is already failing, however.

His men turn mutinous, get drunk, and the Kikonês have time to regroup their forces and massacre them. Odysseus then gets caught in a storm off Cape Malea – the end of the world for the Homeric Greeks. After this, he has crossed a fundamental boundary, between the real and unreal worlds. He can only get back with help of godlike Phaiakians.

The first people Odysseus encounters after having crossed this fundamental divide are the Lotos Eaters. 'Those who ate this honeyed plant, the Lotos, never cared to report, nor to return; they longed to stay forever, browsing on that native bloom, forgetful of their homeland.' Though the Lotos Eaters are friendly enough, Homer makes the point that no community is possible for those who forget their 'homeland'. Unlike Dorothy in the *Wizard of Oz* ('I don't think we're in Kansas any more, Toto'), Odysseus never seems to recognize the divide he has crossed.

The next mythical figures Odysseus encounters are the Kyklopês – who help elaborate Homer's concern with community and what makes it possible. The Kyklopês 'have no institutions, no meetings for counsel; rather they make their habitation in caverns hollowed among the peaks of the high mountains, and each is the law for his own wives and children, and cares nothing about the others' (Lattimore, p. 140). This lack of community explains their lack of respect for the gods and hospitality.

Still ignorant of the fact that he has entered a different world, Odysseus speaks to Polyphemus of his heroic deeds:

> We are Achaians, coming from Troy, beaten off our true course by winds from every direction across the great gulf of the open sea, *making for home by the wrong way, on the wrong courses* ... We claim we are of the following of the son of Atreus, Agamemmon, whose fame now is the greatest thing under heaven, such a city was it that he sacked and destroyed so many people... but now in turn we come to you and are suppliants at your knees.... Therefore respect the gods, o best of men. We are your suppliants and Zeus, the guest god, who stands behind all strangers with honours due them, avenges any wrong towards strangers and suppliants. (Fitzgerald, 1961, pp. 164–5, my italics)

This is the sort of speech that Odysseus might have fruitfully normal sphere of existence, but he isn't in Kansas any more. Kyklopês tells him bluntly, 'You are a ninny, or else you come from the end of nowhere, telling me, mind the gods! We Kyklopês care not a whistle for your thundering Zeus, or all the gods in bliss, we have more force by far ...' (Fitzgerald, 1961, p. 165).

Without community, without a shared sense of values, such feats as the conquering of Troy have no meaning. In the face of Kyklopês, Odysseus seems merely pathetically proud. This episode also helps us to see more clearly that he is involved in a different, a 'magical', reality – for instance, his 'story' about Poseidon destroying his ship later becomes reality.

But Odysseus can't give up the world in which he is a hero. He has enormous resistance to this. Having managed to escape Polyphemos he has to vaunt. 'O Kyklopês! Would you feast on my companions? Puny am I in a Caveman's hands? How do you like the beating we gave you, you damned cannibal?' (Fitzgerald, 1961, p. 171).

His ship almost gets crushed by the rock Kyklopês throws and his men beg him to stop, 'Godsake, Captain! Why bait the beast again? Let him alone!' But Odysseus still hasn't seen the light, 'Kyklopês, if ever mortal men inquire how you were put to shame and blinded, tell him Odysseus, raider of cities, took your eye!' Now that Kyklopês has his name, he can curse him, which he does with dire consequences for Odysseus and his crew.

I could multiply examples of the way in which, during his account, Homer repeatedly puts into question the old heroic values but I will limit myself to one final example, which has particular relevance to any therapeutic enterprise.

In the popular myths of the Sirens, it was the sound of their voices that lured men to their doom. Homer changes this – his Sirens lure men on to the rocks by their message – which is a reaffirmation of the heroic values.

> . . . This way, oh turn your bows, Akhaia's glory, as all the world allows, moor and be merry . . . All feats on that great field, in the long warfare, dark days the gods willed, wounds you bore there, Argos' old soldiery on Troy beach teeming, charmed out of time we see . . . (Fitzgerald, 1961, pp. 227–8)

Homer explicitly shows here that doom lies in this message. There is of course a parallel here to the seductive power of transference love – house therapists, like individual ones – must not be seduced by the glory that is so often ascribed to them.

What does Homer's account of Odysseus' journey have to do with communities? I suggest there are two major parallels. Odysseus' journey has the same relation to the world of the *Odyssey* as our communities have to the larger world. Our communities are a sort of concentrated essence (of both fantasy and reality) of the community at large.

There is also a parallel between the world of the *Iliad*, where the heroic is still possible and the world of the *Odyssey*, and between the world of childhood and the world of the adult. People in our houses, like Odysseus, are bound to their 'heroic' deeds of yesteryear. They find it difficult to give up their 'heroic' childhoods, the childhoods in which they felt they had such compelling parts to play.

Some of the heroic roles one encounters in community (and individual) therapy are the 'one who attempts to (re)institute justice by punishing the parents for something for which they should feel guilty', 'the adopted one who makes the natural family feel more together', 'the one who saves the family by satisfying the father's sexual appetites'. These heroic roles have come to define our residents' images of themselves and, like Odysseus, our residents resist giving up these socially established places.

The clinging to the heroic possibilities of early childhood is also a holding on to a world where there are clearly recognizable heroes and villains, certainty regarding what is right and wrong. This childlike perception is difficult to give up, especially for the obscure and shifting uncertainties of the adult world.

One of the themes of the *Odyssey*, particularly in the journey to the underworld, is that there is no adequate reward for heroic behaviour. Akhilleus, the greatest of the Greek heroes, is quite explicit about this. This is also one of the themes of house (and individual) therapists. Though the 'preservation of the family' is felt to be a heroic achievement in early life, its cost later may call for it to be brought into question. This is part of the task of the therapeutic community where, through repetition and remembering, these originary families are always coming into play.

Many of the relationships that Odysseus encounters in his journey parallel those frequently seen in our communities. The monsters – Kyklopês, Skylla, Kharybis, and so forth – and the goddesses; Kirkê, Kalypso, Sirens – are often mapped on to other residents. Certain residents come to be seen as uncivilized savages, who either metaphorically or literally (depending on the degree of disturbance) eat other residents for lunch. Other residents are constantly in fear of being sucked down a whirlpool from which they will never emerge – often if they allow that they are part of a community rather than an isolated hero fighting collectivization. (It is common for these same residents to fear equally the therapists biting their heads off if they continue on this course.) Sometimes residents feel that they have been enslaved or seduced by the community, that they have lost their normal will – that the community (or the therapists) is a Kirkê or a Kalypso. Indeed, most of the permutations of the characters Odysseus meets on his journey are played and replayed between residents and therapists.

Transference and wish-fulfilment in the *Odyssey*

What is the position of the therapists in all this? Can the *Odyssey* help us understand this too? One way the therapists participate is through their involvement in the above mappings. They can be seen as Kyklopês – uncivilized oafs who barge in, eat up a few people, and leave, as Sirens – luring people to their doom, as Lotos Eaters – urging a sort of quietistic acceptance, as Kirkês – commanding a magical power to turn people into pigs or kings, as Teiresias – wise old ones who have been both men and women, and so forth. But in this, the therapists are in no way privileged – this is what comes from being part of the company, part of the magical mystery tour.

What is different about the therapists? The *Odyssey* gives us a wonderful image for the place of the therapist, in community and individual therapy. It is the image of Odysseus tied to the mast of his ship, listening to the Sirens. Because he is restrained, he is free to hear – and go mad through hearing – the Sirens' song. This is the therapist's ideal. Bound to their chairs, they are free to experience what has previously been experienced only by Odysseus. As the resident's unconscious heroic visions play through the group, the therapists become subject to them as to the Sirens' songs.

They can become aware of them, and can comment on their presence. In community therapy, where the Siren song can be very compelling, it is helpful to have more than one therapist present, so that if one is seduced by a particular tune, the others can pull him back from the rocks.

There is one episode during Odysseus' journey where he is, so to speak, pulled on to the rocks. Like all 'therapeutic failures', this and what Odysseus learns from it is instructive to us.

In his initial encounter with Kirkê, Odysseus is able, with Hermes' help, to avoid being turned into a swine by her, or be mastered by her in bed. But having, so to speak, established his place he then loses it. He forgets all about his journey home and spends a year with Kirkê, 'feasting long on roasts and wine'. One day his shipmates summoned him, 'Captain, shake off this trance and think of home – if home indeed awaits us . . . They made me feel a pang, and I agreed' (Fitzgerald, 1961, p.191) It is important, here, that what awakens Odysseus from his trance is the thought of home. He needs to be reminded of this by his fellow 'residents'. (This is reminiscent of Homer's earlier point regarding the Lotos Eaters – what enables them to wander around in a perpetual trance is that they have forgotten home.)

In relation to the immortal Kirkê, Odysseus loses himself in the fantasy of eternal wish-fulfilment. It is an awareness of home, which is here equated with the finite, that awakens him.

Later in his journey, in relation to a different desirable immortal goddess, Odysseus is able to hang on to this lesson. 'The enchantress in her beauty fed and caressed me, promised me I should be immortal, youthful all the days to come, but in my heart I never gave consent, though seven long years detained' (Fitzgerald, 1961, p. 158). When Kalypso is forced to release Odysseus through the intervention of Zeus, she asks in relation to Penelope, 'Can I be less desirable than she is? Less interesting? Less beautiful? Can mortals compare with goddesses in grace and form?' (Fitzgerald, 1961, p. 99). Odysseus' response, apart from showing his customary tact, also shows his new-found ability to resist the seduction of fantasy and wish-fulfilment. 'My lady goddess, here is no cause for anger. My quiet Penelope – how well I know – would seem a shade before your majesty, death and old age being unknown to you, while she must die. Yet it is true, each day I long for home, long for the sight of home' (Fitzgerald, 1961, p. 99).

In the magical space of the transference, when we are possessed by wish fulfilment, we forget the finite and temporal nature of human satisfaction and human relations. Therapeutic communities themselves can give rise to the fantasy of a life without lack. Potential residents often seem to think that all they have to do is get accepted into the community – after that everything will be taken care of. Any hints they get to the contrary don't seem to hit home.

'A caring community', 'a supportive environment'. Don't these phrases conjure up such a (wish) fulfilling situation? I'm never really sure what is supposed to be meant by these most promising of terms – but I know that they evoke the Hunky Dory Home, and that believing them means disappointment is guaranteed when people find not only is the fridge often empty but people hide as often as meet. Happy communal meals – almost always imagined as being cooked by someone else – are not always on the menu.

In our households, when this disappointing reality is encountered a common reaction is to go away for the weekend – a going away that can begin to extend into the week. 'No one was around' will be the airy response to enquiries about this. Surely the point of the community was to keep them from feeling anxious, lonely, empty, whatever. Often a result of the dashing of this expectation is that the therapists become increasingly idealized – at least they listen – and their fellow residents written off.

Hugh Crawford used to say the ideal upbringing was not to have all the love and support you needed, but all the trouble you could bear. Freud, of course, said therapy takes place in deprivation. But to many, the whole notion of a supportive or caring environment seems to promise the contrary. It is important to be able to bring into question what is truly 'supportive' or 'caring' in a therapeutic community. And therapists involved mustn't buy the idea that their job is to provide a corrective emotional experience through being perfect mothers/fathers.

Recognition

The scene in the *Odyssey* in which Penelope and Odysseus finally meet is one of most moving in the poem. In it, Homer displays a profound understanding of the nature and temporality of recognition, which is of course essential to the therapeutic process.

Penelope is summoned by her faithful nurse, 'Come with me, you may both embark this time for happiness together, after pain, after long years. Here is your prayer, your passion granted; your own lord lives, he is at home' (p. 443). Penelope, as befits Odysseus' wife, is cautious in her response, 'Do not lose yourself in this rejoicing . . . you know how splendid would be that return for us . . . But it is not possible' (Fitzgerald, 1961, p. 443). The nurse insists, 'Come down, I stake my life on it, he's here. Let me die in agony if I lie' (Fitzgerald, 1961, p. 443). But Penelope is still wary, 'It is hard not to be taken in by the immortals' (Fitzgerald, 1961, p. 443).

Penelope

> turned then to descend the stair, her heart in tumult … Crossing the door sill she sat down … across the room from the lord Odysseus. There leaning against a pillar, sat the man and never lifted up his eyes, but only waited for what his wife would say when she had seen him. And she, for a long time, sat deathly still in wonderment – for sometimes as she gazed she found him – yes, clearly – like her husband, but sometimes blood and rags were all she saw. (Fitzgerald, 1961, p. 444)

Here is a wonderful image of the therapeutic setting – Odysseus waits in silence, not even lifting his eyes. Penelope can't make out whether he is an image she wishes for, or someone else entirely.

Telemakhos, still in this moment a boy, is impatient. 'Mother, cruel mother, do you feel nothing, drawing yourself apart this way from Father … ? What other women could remain so cold?' (Fitzgerald, 1961, p. 444). Telemakhos is still tied to fantasy and wish-fulfilment. He longs for the scene in the movies (still yet to be made) where the hero and heroine run into each other's arms (preferably in slow motion across a field of tall grass). He, like the residents in our households, wants instant results, not understanding the temporality of recognition.

Penelope answers, "I am stunned, child. I cannot keep my eyes upon his face. If really he is Odysseus, truly home, beyond all doubt we too shall know each other better than you or anyone …' A smile came now to the lips of the patient hero, Odysseus, who turned to Telemakhos and said, 'Peace: let your mother test me at her leisure. Before long she will see and know me best' (Fitzgerald, 1961, p. 445). Odysseus, like a seasoned therapist, knows that recognition takes time, indeed that it doesn't happen in chronological time. (When during the initial interview I asked my therapist how long my therapy would take, he answered that therapy didn't happen in chronological time.)

After Odysseus has washed and is wearing new clothes, they face each other again, silently. This silence has great force, as if their fates are about to meet. Odysseus makes a provocative comment, 'Strange woman ... who else in the world would keep aloof as you do from her husband if he returned to you from years of trouble.' 'Strange man,' Penelope replies, keeping her cool, 'If man you are ... There is no pride on my part nor scorn for you – not even wonder, merely. I know so well how you – how he – appeared boarding the ship for Troy' (Fitzgerald, 1961, pp. 446–7).

Homer shows here that it is not so much a question of Penelope recognizing Odysseus but rather one of bringing her hopes and expectations and her new reality into tune with her own experience. She is faced with a recognition that will change her world.

She tells her nurse to make Odysseus' bed, and it is through his heated and passionate response, in which he describes the bedroom he built with his own hands, that she recognizes him. 'Now from his breast into his eyes the ache of longing mounted, and he wept at last, his dear wife, clear and faithful, in his arms, longed for as the sun-warmed earth is longed for by a swimmer spent in rough water where his ship went down ...' (Fitzgerald, 1961, p. 448). What a lovely image for recognition and homecoming. Coming home is like coming to solid ground.

Homer understands that home is always incarnate, bodily. Throughout his wanderings, Odysseus' thought has come back to the 'great, high-roofed, well-built house' (quoted by Vivante, 1985, p. 119). Penelope thinks of 'This beautiful house so filled with the substance of life; the thought of it will ever be with me, even in dreams' (quoted by Vivante, 1985, p. 119).

For both Odysseus and Penelope, the image of what Bachelard calls 'protected intimacy' is their house and, especially, their bedroom. As Bachelard puts it, 'our house is our corner of the world . . . The chief benefit of the house, I should say: the house shelters daydreaming ...' (Bachelard 1958, p. 6). Our dreams, and daydreams, always return to those houses in which we have dwelt.

Part of what makes community therapy different from individual therapy is that we do not just invoke homecoming metaphorically, but literally also. We invite people to inhabit a home, which will not always be theirs but is theirs for the making. We invite them into an encounter that is not just metaphorical, in which the place of metaphor and the concrete (which in the form of 'practicality' is so often a defence against recognition) can be put into question. An awareness of what being at home means, both in presence and absence, is crucial for community workers, whose involvement with a household must not be confused with work in 'an intensive treatment environment'. Texts on psychopathology and therapeutic process are not the only ones that need to be studied, but also those which evoke poetically what being at home, and coming home, means. Workers in such communities could do much worse than start with the *Odyssey*.

Chapter 3
The way of water

Miranda Glossop

The thoughts expressed here could be put in a nutshell like this: psychotherapy operates in practice more like an art than a science. Yet repeatedly its ideas and tenets are taught, learned or put into practice in a way more consistent with scientific thinking. I want to consider both why this happens and some of the confusions inherent in and consequent upon such thinking. Ours is a culture that favours certainty, fixed assumptions, essential truths, sameness. The language we use is too readily regarded as simply a means to an end, as a way of conveying these truths. In the name of (what we take to be) science, we concern ourselves with what language says but pay too little attention to what it does. Yet the effect of language is at the heart of what therapy is all about. We need to be able to defend the fluidity, aliveness and precision of what therapy is about and what it does (or tries to do) in a very different way.

> You are moving. You never stay still. You never stay. You never 'are'. How can I say 'you', when you are always other? How can I speak to you? You remain in flux, never congealing or solidifying. What will make that current flow into words? It is multiple, devoid of causes, meanings, simple qualities. Yet it cannot be decomposed. These movements cannot be described as the passage from a beginning to an end. These rivers flow into no single, definitive sea. These streams are without fixed banks, this body without fixed boundaries. This unceasing mobility. This life – which will perhaps be called our restlessness, whims, pretences or lies. All this remains very strange to anyone claiming to stand on solid ground. Speak, all the same. Between us, 'hardness' isn't necessary. We know the contours of our bodies well enough to love fluidity. Our density can do without trenchancy or rigidity. We are not drawn to dead bodies. (Irigaray, 1993, p. 215)

How aptly these words convey the spirit of the therapeutic endeavour (that deceptively simple task of having two people truly meet and speak to each other). But how can we and those with whom we hope to meet be all at sea together without completely losing our bearings, without the whole enterprise becoming sloppy (and actually, then, irresponsible and dangerous)? I want to argue here that whilst we do need fixed reference points (like the land, horizon, stars) to give us a sense of direction (our theories, techniques, our knowledge, presuppositions), it is our relationship to these references that is all-important; they are outside us and we do not possess them. We move continually in relation to them. I want to redress a balance and make the case for what one might call a more watery way.

Unfortunately a strict scientific attitude is often popularly somewhat starkly polarized against a stance that is pluralistic, anarchic and 'all over the place'. Often it is as though the best reason put forward *for* science is the (defensive one) that it keeps chaos at bay; that there must be the one true way. Perhaps it seems terrifying to accept that one might both know and not know at the same time. But does the correct perception of any matter and a complete misunderstanding of the matter need imply a contradiction? The danger is perceived to be that without science's ultimate causes there is too much fragmentation. In other words, that diversity is, in itself, seen as a weakness. But why should it be so? Andrew Samuels argues that it is precisely this not-having-arrived at the big story (both within and between the ever growing number of competing 'psychoanalytic schools') that is a sign of the aliveness and alertness to what might be going on that is itself a kind of integrity. 'Pluralism is an approach to conflict that tries to reconcile differences without imposing a false synthesis on them and without losing sight of the particular value and truth of each element in the conflict.' He goes on to describe how pluralism is a way to help open up a language of difference 'which is neither synthetic nor comparative' (Samuels, 1989, p. xi).

This futile quest for the one true way to be often besets the individual too. So often there seems to be a desire for a certain levelling out of fluctuation, a dislike of, or a guilt for, embodying difference, fluidity, the changeable, the seemingly contradictory. Yet, as Walt Whitman said, '*Do* I contradict myself? I contain multitudes!' So often, then, therapy seems to be, more than anything else, about enabling or allowing patients, as it were, *not* to be the same ... as their mother, father, therapist, as themselves on another day, at another time! Difference becomes pathologized insidiously, pervasively and on many levels by not being made explicit. Yet how can it be made explicit in a culture too much dominated by the explanatory, causal language of nature versus nurture? Therapy needs to open up another way to think that is less reductive or it simply becomes another trap, or like an archaeological dig with nothing, at bottom, to be found.

A structure will support or strengthen something else only if it is itself well founded. Husserl's rallying cry 'to the things themselves' was an attempt to go behind the unquestioned structures of science, dogma and the various absurdities and self-contradictions of logical positivism. In this sense his aim to promote philosophy, as 'rigorous science' was justified. A presuppositionless philosophy (or way of thinking) does not rely upon shaky empirical methods but sees things as they appear. How might this relate to the actual practice of therapy? One example would be to ask if one sees patients more or less clearly when one sees them for the first time without first having been given a detailed factual/historical account of them by someone else. What is it to know someone or to get to know them? My experience is that the more factual information one has about people in advance the less one is able to see them as they are, there and then. It is as though one finds oneself trying to make sense of them in terms of these facts about them rather than simply themselves.

Roland Barthes makes a similar point rather beautifully about the different ways one might understand. Although he is talking specifically about a text, one could substitute person, story or psychotherapeutic 'theory' here:

> Myth acts economically. It abolishes the complexity of human acts. It gives them the simplicity of essences. It does away with all dialectics – with any going back beyond what is immediately visible. It organises a world which is without contradictions because it is without depth, a world wide open and wallowing in the evident. It establishes a blissful clarity: things appear to mean something by themselves. (Barthes, 1972, p. 156)

By contrast, an explanatory structure can often cloud the issue, superimposed as it is on something else or someone else. Often, too, patients become caught in their own linguistic web of explanatory structures, meta-memories, meta-languages; everything then becomes about something (or someone) else.

So, then, there needs to be a shift from the explanatory to the descriptive. But which descriptions and stories are going to inform us? Why do some myths have such a strong hold? There are an infinite number to choose from, from the ancient Greek to the contemporary. Maybe there is another danger of being seduced by some myths at the expense of others. Oedipus is often taken as the defining myth for psychoanalysis. It speaks, and has spoken, in a multiplicity of ways since Freud, of the dynamics of three in a family. But who are these three? Always, coming from Oedipus, two parents and a child. Yet what about other kinds of dynamic: sibling rivalry, single-parent families ...? Is the relationship with the parents necessarily more critical and formative than that with a sibling, for instance? Is a single-parent family or same-sex parent family to be considered necessarily lacking or to be pathologized? In other words, do all situations have to be made sense of in terms of Oedipus first or shouldn't it rather be, as Husserl implied, the other way around: different myths, stories, theories may (or may not!) help to make sense of the things themselves as they appear. Myths, stories, descriptions do not contain truths. In some ways, however, Husserl contradicted himself. In his writing is the presupposition of a certainty or absolute truth or essence to be discovered. This was the one thing he believed in unquestioningly – hence his dislike of scepticism and his desire to make philosophy not just rigorous but also a science. Nevertheless, there is much to be learned from his methodologies – especially his meticulousness and the humility implicit in his attempt to think, as he put it, as a 'perpetual beginner'.

Much feminist psychoanalytic theory seems to propose a choice: between father and mother, system and silence, rigid structure and anarchy, presence/absence. Do we then want to cling on to our structures and theories because of what we think they confer in terms of potency or strength (or, conversely, because we don't want to be thought of as weak or castrated or not there)? Radical feminist writers have a much more interesting and persuasive argument: for them, the 'feminine' as a style or process is neither just a weaker option or even a necessary counterbalance but is clearly different in a way that needs to be made explicit. Women need to be able to represent this difference in their own terms rather than let it be subsumed under what might be called a 'male' heading. This is *their* strength and it is very much to do with a matter of style.

Irigaray, for instance, argues that female language is language that has an effect: a language that reintroduces values of pain, desire, joy and the body. (There are echoes here of Merleau-Ponty – and his notion of embodied being and embodied speaking.) A patient of mine expressed this like the difference between what she called 'mad speak via the idea' and the (kind of) communication that she wanted: 'speaking face-to-face or skin-to-skin'.

Irigaray's critique of Lacan is important because it is more than simply an attack on the obvious lopsided 'male-ness' of what he is talking *about*: (a phallocentric world where female is equated with lack and the symbolic and language is associated with the father – though one might well ask if there is any *a priori* reason within Lacan's conceptual framework for making the symbolic order, the third term, male?). It is, more crucially, a critique of the way that he uses language. In 'The mechanics of fluids' Irigaray criticizes the Lacanian emphasis on metaphor (quasi-solid or definite) over metonymy (which is more to do with fluids and the infinite). She complains that science has studied solids but neglected fluids. Metonymy is linked with the feminine and thus felt by Irigaray to have been neglected in Lacanian (and other phallocentric) writing. Irigaray says of the feminine voice: 'Woman never speaks the same way. What she emits is flowing, fluctuating. Blurring. And she is not listened to, unless proper meaning (meaning of the proper) is lost. Whence the resistances to that voice that overflows the "subject", which the "subject" then congeals, freezes in its categories until it paralyses the voice in its flow' (Irigaray, 1993, p. 112). Lacan himself gave a flavour of the difference of these two styles in defining metaphor, roughly speaking, as 'one word for another' – the vertical attribution of meaning metonymy as the horizontal relation word by word. Thus, in the metonymic dimension, the signifier can receive its complete signification only by deferred action. (Much of Derrida's writing, for example 'The trace', is concerned with a similar movement.) It is also useful to see how Lacan connects these two dimensions with different aspects of dream work that Freud speaks about: metaphor with condensation (repression) and metonymy with displacement (deferral, desire). Again the connotations of solidity versus fluidity are apparent. So, although Lacan has a lot to say about desire, there is perhaps sometimes too much of a ponderous attempt to look for meaning – for instance, in the reasoning behind his advocacy of the variable length session (a session that is brought to an end at a significant, meaningful moment rather than necessarily at the end of 50 minutes). Admittedly this might be one way to circumvent what Lacan calls 'intellectualization as procrastination, but can meaningfulness be pinned down, appropriated in this way? Who decides when the moment has arrived? The therapist! But maybe he, the therapist, could be wrong! Perhaps meaning is not such a neat function in time. Lacan was being the knowing analyst here. One's impression of the short session in practice (Schneiderman, 1983) is of the therapeutic encounter as a rather nerve-racking endgame – the patient sitting on the edge of his seat waiting for the meaningful moment or, even more paradoxically, trying to produce one! Perhaps in what one might describe as a more metonymous way, one might rather just let meaning (or indeed meaninglessness) speak for itself by creating 'an atmosphere of uncertainty', where meaning cannot be grasped. Phillips goes on to compare therapy with a kind of flirtation (with words) where one needs 'the art of making ambivalence into a game, the ironic art of making it a pleasure' (Phillips, 1994, p. xxiii).

Rigour has implications of discipline, 'to learn from disciples' says the dictionary. This has somewhat militaristic overtones and a suggestion that one could learn by rote. But how can psychotherapy best be learned, taught or transmitted – if at all? It certainly cannot be taught in quite the procedural, prescriptive way that a science can. One cannot, as it were, learn a formula for how to be a therapist (if A do B; if B do C). Neither can one learn the theory and then straightforwardly apply it. Of course one needs to know the historical tradition in which one claims to be taking up a part, what the arguments are, who said what, and so on. But this knowledge *per se* does not equip one to be a good therapist. An analogy

with music is apposite: if one learned all the rules of harmony and coun-
terpoint and then used them 'by the book' to harmonize a melody the
result does not sound like real music. It actually sounds rather odd –
'inaccurate' almost. This is because good music, like good therapy does
not always obey 'the rules' and contains an intrinsic logical pattern which
is non-transferable. (So far, no one has been able to make a computer
compose real music.) Likewise, could a computer take the place of the
therapist? Could it *ever* do so? It may seem ridiculous even to ask the
question. Yet much theorizing about therapy seems to work on the premiss that human interaction is nothing more than a very sophisticated
form of information transfer.

Roustang (who did not like to be quoted in large chunks because, he
argued, it turned him into a disciple) had quite a few irresistibly quotable
things to say on how psychoanalysis is passed on:

> There can be no transmission of analytic theory outside the actual practice
> of psychoanalysis. Every psychoanalytic session is unique as much on a
> practical as a theoretical level. The free speech of an analysand cannot come
> forth if the psychoanalyst, armed with a pre-established theory, waits for the
> analysand to fall into a trap. There can be psychoanalysis only if the trans-
> ference works both ways: if the analysand assumes that the analyst knows
> but also if the analyst knows that he does not know but that it is the
> analysand who knows. (Roustang, 1986, p. 70)

However, he makes two important qualifying remarks: firstly that it is the
experience with the patient that must be taken as the starting point and
not the end point. Or, in other words, that so-called 'theory' and 'practice' both have a place but cannot be artificially split off from one another.
Secondly, and more fundamentally, that the whole of psychoanalytic 'theory' is not rigid or fixed like scientific theory but is best regarded as
theory-in-the-making, an ongoing journey or movement towards.
Roustang uses the term 'scientificity' to distinguish a process of discovery
from assumptions of implicit truth (science). If one takes analysis for a
science, one acts as though the transference/countertransference does
not exist except in parenthesis. It becomes an optional extra!

Roustang goes on to say of Freud:

> Is not the history of Freud's theoretical productions marked by the fact that
> permanent testing is the best proof? If you attempt to consider the body of
> Freud's work as a whole as you could do for Spinoza, Kant or Hegel where
> each part illustrates the whole, you will understand nothing at all. This is
> even true for each idea taken separately. Studies of the vocabulary used by
> Freud throughout his work are exasperating . . . Variations in meaning and
> contradictions cannot be resolved or synthesised. (Roustang, 1986, p. 65)

Roustang goes on to describe how Freud created 'conceptual fictions' for the purposes not of classification but to get problems moving, and this is how he can perhaps be most fruitfully read – as an ongoing project, an unrealizable myth, where the inconsistencies and gaps are the most revealing.

Similarly, Lacan could erroneously be taken too literally as the theorizer of the word. One can only be stuck by his somewhat gnomic utterances (such as 'the unconscious is structured like a language') if one reads them as godly pronouncements of truth, as real rather than as metaphor. Whereas one could argue that Lacan's main concern was not in fact with linguistic theory but with how to be an analyst, how to listen, how to intervene – his interest was really more with speech (*parole*) rather than (as for Saussure and others) language (*langue*).

Another potential area of confusion relates to the matter of clinical reports. Again, the question comes down to whether one considers that, in this case, what the patient says, his utterances in the session, should be read or heard as pseudo-scientific statements – as representations of inner psychic states – or not.

Freud's dictum to attend to what the patient says with 'free floating attention' rather than with a conscious attempt to remember implies that he felt that it was essential to listen as much to what is not said as said, and to the effect/affect of what is being said on the hearer. Hence his coining of the term 'countertransference' in his later writings. (Although he alludes to this only rarely he does not underplay its importance: 'No psycho-analyst goes further than his own complexes and internal resistances permit.') This seems to me to be about the crucial distinction that needs to be made between hearing and listening.

As Spence (1964), amongst others, has noted, there are many problematics about the notion of what might be said to be accurate clinical reporting of what goes on in a session. In a clinical presentation, what are we trying to convey: what was actually said or what was actually meant? These two can easily become confused. For instance, a patient one is with starts to say something interesting, 'quotable', and one finds oneself consciously trying to remember what the patient is saying; one has stopped hearing because one has switched to listening-in. Hearing, as opposed to listening, implicates the hearer in the utterance of the speaker. In other words, the patient is no longer a subject but has become an object. Moreover, it is a moot point as to whether one has recalled what was said verbatim anyway (unless a session was actually to be tape-recorded) because might one not unwittingly have translated it slightly to fit what one was hearing was meant, rather than said? An example would be the 'translation' or the meaning of a double negative whose formal result might seem to be to arrive back at simple affirmation but whose discursive function is never that. Compare 'he is not unfriendly' to 'he is friendly'. What is the difference? In formal logical terms none but the former statement increases the concentration of interest, or self-regard, upon the 'I' in the act of uttering rather than focusing on the 'he' – the subject of the statement.

So there's a kind of catch-22 about verbatim reports. If one listens for actual words one may miss meaning. If one attends to meaning first and then 'remembers' the words, one may well have paraphrased what the patient actually said so that the words one quotes are literally inaccurate. Surely a false assumption implicit in our need for verbatim reports is that of language as primarily descriptive or connotative. Austin (1971) criticizes the reification of discourse implicit here. His argument is not dissimilar from what Lacan has to say about the relation of speech to language: the alienation of the subject in science. Austin says that the question is not so much whether utterances are true or false but what it is that an utterance does – he criticizes both the positivistic idea of language as consisting in poor approximations to scientific statements, and the notion that utterances are a representation of inner psychic states.

Or in Levinasian terms, saying is irreducible to the ontological definability of the said: 'Saying is what makes the self exposure of sincerity possible; it is a way of giving everything, of not keeping anything for oneself.' In so far as ontology equates truth with the intelligibility of total presence, it reduces the pure exposure of saying to the totalizing closure of the said.

There is a parallel, then, between the problem of the transmissibility of clinical material and of the transmissibility of psychoanalytic theory in general – and, as Roustang posited, it is the radical nature of transference that is at the heart of the difficulty. What makes a therapy session 'work' is precisely this two-way movement or entanglement, where the notion of subject versus object is quite alien.

As Lacan has pointed out, in its essence the efficacious transference which we are considering is quite simply the speech act. Each time a man speaks to another in an authentic and full manner there is, in the true sense, transference, symbolic transference. Something takes place that changes the nature of the two being present. It would be a mistake, one that psychoanalytic writers often make in the name of 'accuracy', to describe the transference or the transference-fantasy as a report on the patient's inner world made to a neutral observer. Both Lacan and Austin reveal this to be a constative conception of language limited to the language game created by modern science.

So although one should not abandon the possibility of being able to convey anything of what is going on with the patient to anyone else, it needs to be remembered that 'what is going on' can never be fully known, at least not by one of those involved in the therapeutic relationship. Furthermore, to the extent that it can be known, this 'knowledge', is not gleaned from an analysis of the content of the session as an abstract text in which the analyst plays an objective part. Finally, what is going on is best conveyed to others in a clinical report by giving a sense, a flavour of the therapeutic relationship, rather than by attempting to present either 'the patient' or merely one's own countertransferential position.

A 'good' (one might even say precise) clinical report, then, is one that seems to capture the spirit of what was occurring, rather than as many as possible of the words that were spoken. Of course, certain words, most especially slips or repeated phrases, are likely to stand out and thus be recallable verbatim, but because they are particularly, specifically revealing of (unconscious) meaning, not because one is actively listening out for 'Freudian slips'. Common sense all too often gets forgotten in the consulting room in the name of technique. After all, why do some slips seem 'Freudian' and others simply mistakes? Think how absurd it would be, how one could mis-hear the dyslexic patient, for instance, if one were listening-in in the 'scientific-analyst' way!

So it is beginning to look as though many of the fixed connotations of rigour are not what therapy is about, but rather that there needs to be movement. But where are we going? Do we need to be going anywhere? What kind of movement is involved? Do we march together or meander? A patient found the sense of embodiment and connectedness that she had been looking for when she had the opportunity to do a lot of walking on holiday: not going anywhere in particular, not rushing to catch a bus, not marching in time to someone else's tune (where there is the possibility of being OUT of step or out of time.) Whereas, as she said to me, 'How can you meander out of time?' We explored the qualities of walking that were therapeutic. This patient, for whom much of the impetus to come to therapy in the first place was that she felt herself to be too much 'in her head', found that the activity of walking was itself like another kind of thinking. (One is reminded here of remarks made by both Heidegger and Wittgenstein about thinking not being a hidden activity that goes on in the brain; not merely or even more closely shown by the thing that makes EEG graphs waver or eyelids flicker during what is known as REM sleep.) Walking is an activity both thin but deep: 'thin' in the sense of one's awareness of finitude, of being very small in the great scheme of things, of not being able to get ahead of oneself, of going slowly enough to notice and appreciate the little details of things. But 'deep', also, in the sense of losing oneself in the activity. For this patient this meant losing a very acute and at times paralysing consciousness of self. By contrast, one of the places in which she felt the most disturbed or unreal was on the

Underground. Here, of course, the only movement is passive. There is a surreal disconnection with the different places at which you might emerge. One has little real sense of how one might have found one's own way from one place to another. Perhaps good therapy has quite a lot in common with walking. Both are about autonomous movement. Both are also about going somewhere (without necessarily getting there), the seemingly irrelevant things, the little details, the casual 'asides' being shown to be what is significant, learning to enjoy the journey. Therapy is about learning too that, whatever the game is, it certainly isn't merely a mind game. It is embodied thought.

One of the commonest reasons why people become stuck enough to seek therapy in the first place is because they have become caught in technological scientific modes of thinking that cannot move or be moved. They have split the world into a straight-line world of bipolar oppositions (subject/object, inner/outer, good/bad, mind/body ... the list is endless). Then they find themselves struggling to make impossible and ultimately meaningless choices. This straight-line world is the imaginary world (in the Lacanian sense) – without joy, playfulness, detour or proximity: a very dry and lifeless place. As I hope I have illustrated a little, the very worst thing we could do would be to perpetuate this inflexibility of thinking by imposing more of it in or out of the consulting room. So how might the therapist help the patient out of the trap? By showing, over time, that 'getting better' is not to be achieved in the linear single-minded pursuit of an either/or. As Adam Phillips says, 'If we cultivate unbearable choices we create impossible lives' (Phillips, 1994, p. 130). It is not a point to be arrived at, but rather a state of being-in-time. It is the change from feeling fate to feeling destined, from stagnation to movement. Here the polarities of happiness/unhappiness, freedom/restriction coexist. Kierkegaard expresses this hauntingly:

> I am overwhelmed by gratitude for all that providence has done for me. How is it possible for things to go so well? Poetically speaking I can only say that there is nothing that has happened in my life of which I cannot say: that is the very best that suits my nature and disposition: I lack nothing. I was unhappy in my love: but I simply cannot imagine myself happy unless I were to become a different person altogether. But in my unhappiness I was happy. Humanly speaking, I am saved by one already dead, my father: but I simply cannot imagine myself having been saved by someone living. And so I became an author in exactly that way which suited the latent possibilities of my nature: and then I was persecuted – oh, had that been wanting my life would not have been mine. There is melancholy in everything in my life, but then again an indescribable happiness. (Kierkegaard, 1938, p. 771)

CHAPTER 4

Night thoughts of a sceptical therapist

PAUL GORDON

> Cause yet we continue. All of our lives. This is what we do, we continue. We really have to keep on being alert to this fact, because this is what it is, an actual fact. It makes yer head go. (Kelman, 1998, p. 72)

> If the construction of the future and the putting things to right for all time is not our business, it is all the more clear what our present task is. I mean the uncompromising criticism of everything that exists, uncompromising in the sense that it does not fear its own results and just as little fears conflicts with the powers that be. (Marx in Kovel, 1981, p. 30)

Many years ago, when psychotherapy was being subjected to one of its periodic attacks in the media, I spent some time trying to write a piece called 'In defence of therapy'. The article came to nothing but it was some time before I realized what was wrong. The problem was and is that one cannot defend something called 'therapy', any more, indeed, than one can really criticize it. The beast of therapy is hydra-headed and one has to be specific, whether in criticism or defence. Ultimately I can defend and stand up for only what I do, what I think, not for what others may do, unless of course I have chosen in some way to associate with them. Even then differences in thought, style and approach are quickly and easily apparent. This chapter, which borrows its title from Russell McCormmach's dark and elegiac novel, *Night Thoughts of a Classical Physicist* (Penguin, 1983), sets out not a sustained thesis about therapy or even a linear argument. It is rather a sequence, almost an alphabet, of observations written under the sign of scepticism.

An aesthetics of therapy?

A therapy that wishes to renew itself might well look to some writings on art for paths to follow. In his book *The Intimate Philosophy of Art*, John

Armstrong argues that what helps us to get more out of works of art – pictures, buildings and so on – what aids a genuine appreciation is not information or knowledge, the traditional art historical approach whereby one learns about artists, periods, styles, methods and so on. Rather it is our own resources, in particular our capacity for contemplation, reverie and sensitivity. If we allow these to inform our engagement with a painting, say, our appreciation will be deep and authentic:

> It is in the quality of our engagement that the human worth of art is apparent – art matters in virtue of the kind of experience it invites the spectator into. There is no access to art except in private – in looking, thinking, feeling as we stand before an individual work. Cultivation requires that we draw upon our own resources of sensitivity, reveries and contemplation, our capacity to invest our ideals and interests in the process of looking. Without these we can only know about art as detached observers who look on without being able to participate . . .' (Armstrong, 2001, p. 195)

Bad behaviour

The therapeutic relationship is not, as some claim, an inevitably abusive one. If it were, no one could be involved in it in good faith. But it is surely beyond doubt that it is a relationship that can become abusive, and very easily so. All this has been well documented. What more is there to say about such things? When therapist and patient engage in a sexual relationship, whatever is going on it is no longer therapy. It is no longer a talking about things but an enactment of them.

What concern me more in a sense, because they are more widespread, are other forms of questionable behaviour. There are simply too many stories of such things – of therapists who hold on to patients long after the therapy seems fruitful, of therapists who seem unable or unwilling to engage in any real dialogue, particularly where it involves them being questioned or challenged. (Herein lie the dangers of dogma, of therapists who think they are the ones who really know what is going on. See for instance Gordon, 2003.) Here I want to address a couple of other issues.

Among the stories are those of therapists who seem distracted or bored or who go to sleep. Now here we are on difficult ground. Of course, as therapists we are affected by the people we are in the room with and these effects can be strange indeed, especially to people outside the world of therapy. To speak of someone falling asleep sounds terrible, a gross dereliction of duty if you like. And yet all therapists must be familiar with the urge, or something similar. It is, after all, what theories of countertransference are all about, that one person can affect another, quite wordlessly, quite profoundly. These feeling states can be crucial communications from the patient, I do not doubt it for an instant. Indeed, the longer I work the more I trust these silent, sometimes bodily communications. And yet, when we hear such stories and maybe, too, if we are really honest in thinking about our own work, how often do we sense that 'countertransference' is just part of what is going on, that it might even be just a therapeutic excuse for, well, bad behaviour, not being in a fit state of mind for the work? Countertransference, Lacan (1988, p. 228) remarked, in the 'coded language we wallow in' is what we call 'being an idiot'. Therapists frequently work far too much, putting in hours that they would rightly question if a patient said they were doing the same. A certain omnipotence, a self-importance, hides behind the offered excuse of financial uncertainty. But maybe therapy isn't something you can do in this way – the intensity of the encounter is just too much hour after hour after hour.

As for the question of money, here one enters taboo territory, something therapists are extremely reluctant to discuss. There is, it seems to me, nothing wrong with charging fees for therapy if people have the money to pay and this is how I have chosen to make a living. What is questionable, however, is the notion that paying for therapy is somehow good for the patient, an integral part of the treatment. Now if this were true it would surely follow that any form of treatment that did not involve direct payment, for instance in outpatient psychotherapy departments or GP practice counsellors, must be flawed, but this does not seem to be argued. Otherwise arguments about the supposed benefits to the patient of paying are simply self-serving mystifications designed to obscure the fact that paying for therapy is good only for the therapist. Not only that, but psychotherapy must be the only profession where patients can find themselves being charged high fees because of what they earn. A plumber does not charge the well-off client more than someone else, nor do doctors in private work or osteopaths. Yet it is quite common to hear of therapists doing this. The claim that this allows them to see others for low fees must in some cases at least be treated with just a little scepticism. The truth is that therapy is a business as much as anything else these days and the logic of the free market, where one gets as high a price as one can, prevails as much here as anywhere.

Coming to terms

A great many of people's difficulties in life arise from an inability to accept who they are. We berate ourselves for not being something we feel we are not – attractive, successful, intellectual, younger, slimmer, gregarious –

whatever. The list is probably endless. And people who have significant emotional or psychological difficulties berate themselves for these too, something therapy can play into with its confused talk of people 'taking responsibility' for their problems. The idea of a 'coming to terms' highlights a process of acceptance, an acceptance of who one is, of one's experience, both of what one has done and what one has suffered. The process is, of course, by no means easy. The idea that we are not, after all, masters of our fate is one most people find hard to accept. Coming to terms is not a surrender, nor a resignation, nor a quietism – 'there is nothing to be done' – but a modest aim that can make a difference.

Dogma

> For you apparently it makes a difference who the speaker is, and what country he comes from; you don't merely ask whether what he says is true or false. (Socrates to Phaedrus)

In the world of therapeutic theorizing, one encounters not competing theoretical positions – not the blooming of a hundred flowers, not the contending of a hundred schools of philosophy – but dogma, theory that has set into quasi-religious stone. And, as many of our critics point out, the religious parallels are all too obvious – the sanctified figures, the holy texts, the lines of therapeutic succession, the sects and the sectarianism. This is something, it should be remembered, that can be traced back to Freud, the great debunker of religion who was not without his own mystical views. There was all that nonsense about numerology and periodicity for instance, which he shared with his great friend Fliess, and all that nonsense too of the secret circle of followers, given rings by the great man himself as a sign of their electedness.

Today dogma continues to have its authorities to whom reference is made in almost sanctified terms, not just historical figures who may have some claim to our attention because of their intellectual contributions, but people who are seen as important because of their current professional status. It is 'the hem of the garment' syndrome, where to be in the same room as certain people, to have a conversation with them, let alone to have been analysed or supervised by them, is to have been touched by their supposed greatness. For a profession which sees itself as a great debunker of myth, a great demystifier of illusion, psychotherapy seems just as prone as any other field to idealising leaders, especially those with any hint of charisma, with an uncritical and unquestioning position towards those in clinical authority. (In this regard psychotherapy, as Roger Bacon has remarked, is a curious discipline in that the reputations of its leading figures cannot by definition rest on their actual work as therapists, which is private, but on their theoretical contributions which may bear no relation to how good they were/are in the clinical encounter. (Bacon, 2000, pp. 8–9)

Ethics

The other does not exist: this is rational faith, the incurable belief in human reason. Identity = reality, as if, in the end, everything must necessarily and absolutely be one and the same. But the other refuses to disappear, it subsists, it persists; it is the hard bone on which reason breaks its teeth. (Antonio Machado quoted in Paz, 1990, p. 5)

The 'other' (usually capitalized) has undoubtedly become a fashionable word of contemporary discourse, a word without which no contribution is complete. Indeed, sadly, it may be falling into that category of words that are being emptied of content, which will be impossible to use with any real conviction. Yet what it speaks of continues to matter. It may sound paradoxical but there is a sense in which most psychotherapy has lacked any real sense of the other. Theories of therapy are based on concepts of an atomized individual, isolated from any context. Moreover, these theories place the individual at the centre of things, as a sun around which other entities must revolve. Even those theories that seem to grant more place to the other, primarily the mother, still depict the individual as centre stage, with others standing in adjunct, albeit important roles. The other is not only other but secondary. The great achievement of the philosophy of Emmanuel Levinas is to put this into question. For Levinas, ethics is my responsibility for the Other, and this responsibility precedes any knowledge I may have of that Other and it is this ethical responsibility to and for the other that makes me a human being; it constitutes me as a subject (see Gordon, 1999, Ch. 2).

Levinas's work is a sustained and radical questioning of the preoccupation in Western thought with knowledge in which even other human subjects are treated as phenomena – objects – to be known and to be understood. In this process their essential and fundamental otherness is lost. Levinas's conception of ethics also goes against the grain of thought that sees in the other only a version of my self, which appropriates the other through some assumed knowledge or claimed understanding. Against this Levinas argues that 'there is no exceptional place for the subject'. For Levinas the important question is not 'To be or not to be?' but, rather, how being justifies itself.

Fictions (clinical)

> The clinical eye . . . cannot explain a poem, but a poem is quite capable of
> revealing to the clinical eye what it does not know. (Rivas, 2002, pp. 136–7)

Like most other therapists, I imagine, I grew up – cut my therapeutic teeth
as it were – on the clinical writings of people like Harold Searles,
Christopher Bollas, Patrick Casement and Robert Lindner. In a different
way I have enjoyed, as have so many others, the allegedly 'true psychoanalytic tales' of Irvin Yalom's *Love's Executioner*. And yet the more one thinks
about these matters the more problematic they become. Take the question
of confidentiality. Do people who write about their patients really seek
their consent beforehand? And if they do, does this not inevitably skew the
therapeutic process? Is it not exploitative of the patient? How free really is
a patient to say no? How would any of us, therapists that is, feel if the roles
were reversed? Would we like to be written about either as patients of therapy or indeed written about by our patients? I doubt it very much. (The
literature is of course massively skewed in terms of who writes about
whom. There are, relatively speaking, few voices from the other side of the
room.) Clinical accounts frequently have a kind of detail that, if it is true,
must surely point to particular individuals, at least to those who know
them. If they are fictions, then what place do such artifices have in what is
supposedly true? But such case studies are fictional in a deeper and more
mundane sense. They are always stories made by the therapist. As anyone
who has ever had to write any kind of clinical paper knows, one is
inevitably selecting, condensing, shortening, and always under the sign of
recalling and remembering. The only true alternative would be a full tran-
scription of every session rather like the cartographers in Borges' story
whose map becomes the same size as the territory they are mapping. And
even that would pick up only what is said, which is only a part of what goes
on when two people are together. Not only that, but the therapist is invariably imposing an order, a pattern, on what is inevitably disorderly. There
is a process of selection. Most material is inevitably left out and what little
is remains inevitably supports the therapist's ideas. (I once had what is
probably not a very common experience of hearing a colleague give a
paper part of which was about a woman I had seen, so I was in a strong
position as to the facts of the 'case'. Something that had indeed happened
in this woman's life was spoken of but emphasized in the presentation in
a way that quite distorted who she was.) And of course the pattern or order
that seems clear to one therapist is not at all clear to others.

Furthermore, as many people have written, therapists write about their
work with one eye over their shoulder, anxious about what their

colleagues, real and imagined, will think. People are not only afraid they might look stupid in something they have said or done, or failed to say or do – they fear their membership of a group or theoretical affiliation being called into question; the terror of hearing the words, 'Oh that is not psychoanalytic'. (This is part of the reason for the popularity of Yalom's writings – that sense of freedom that says 'I don't really care how this will be judged; I stand by what I do.') Similarly writers will frequently make reference to an unnecessary number of other texts, not just to impress but as a statement of affiliation with a particular position and as a kind of intellectual self-defence. The words, 'As XX says' give us an alibi.

Gap

'Between the experience of living a normal life at this moment on the planet and the public narratives being offered to give a sense to that life, the empty space, the gap, is enormous. The desolation lies there, not in the facts.' (Berger, 2001, p. 176) A psychotherapy that wishes to be meaningful must dare to step into that space.

History

'History throws its empty bottles out the window' (from Chris Marker's film, *Sans Soleil*).

Individual

Psychotherapy, as we understand it today, came into being in what has justly been called the century of the self. It has both been shaped by its historical situation and contributed enormously to it. How we see ourselves today as individuals is a lot to do with the project of psychotherapy. The problem is that the theories on which psychotherapy are based invariably extract the individual from the social context. In fact, they rarely are able to see that the very concept of 'the individual' is one that is socially, economically and culturally determined and one that is possible only in a particular context. There is a paradox here. As David Smail has pointed out in many of his writings, therapists (of whatever kind) will readily accept the not-too-contentious notion that each of us is the product of our environment, that the individual man and woman is not self-generated or self-created, that all of us, if we are human, are to some extent influenced, moulded, shaped – whatever – by social (including familial), economic and political forces. Yet, once people step inside the clinical encounter all this disappears and patients and clients are treated as though they exist in a vacuum. (At best one may hear some acknowledgement by the therapist of the 'external world' – 'But that's a reality issue', as though there were nothing further to be said and as though that is not our concern.) Now it may be said, and is said, that what happens outside is not our business, that there is nothing we can do about these matters. But even if this is true, there may indeed be little we can do, as therapists, about the material circumstances of people's lives. But something we can do is refuse to collude in the idea that people's problems are somehow all 'in them', in some supposed 'internal world'. This metaphor has become so concretized as to have become mystification, no longer a possibly helpful way of thinking, if indeed it ever was, but an obstacle in the way of truthfulness, of seeing the world, and the patient's place in it, for what it really is. (In the hands of some therapists, everything becomes a question of the internal world. Even torture and trauma, it is all in people. If psychoanalysis had been around at the time of slavery would it have told slaves that their problems stemmed from their internal worlds? Probably.) We are in the world and of the world. From the moment of our conception we are social beings, requiring other people to make us – literally – to nurture us, to give birth to us, to look after us, to give us the recognition as another human being without which we would be nothing. None of this is inside me, even metaphorically. It exists as social and material fact.

Judgementalism

To say that therapy has become a substitute for religion in a secular society has become something of a cliché. But, as with all clichés, there is something true in the allegation. Anyone who looks for the trappings of religion – sects, texts and rituals – can find them all too easily. But what is more problematic in this regard is the judgementalism of psychotherapy, its moralism and its normativeness. Note that I use the word moralism and not morality. I have no objections to morality, although the word ethics is preferable, suggesting something more wide-ranging than rules. In a society when the force and authority of religion have rightly been superseded it is only right that we should give some thought to moral issues – how should we live, how should we act? But moralism is something different, with unavoidable connotations of prescriptiveness, of telling people what to do, how to live, how to behave, how to be. This is implicit, if not explicit, in many forms of therapy.

In the case of psychoanalysis, this is something that, like so many things, goes back to Freud. He may have been relatively liberal, for instance, in thinking people should not be made to suffer for their sexual leanings but Freud clearly thought them perversions, in the literal sense they were turnings away from something that was designated normal, that is heterosexual intercourse The record of psychoanalysis since then has not been a good one. Women, generations of psychoanalysis has claimed, suffered from penis envy. Homosexuality, of course, was a form of pathology. Indeed, there is an argument that Freud's whole notion of the individual moral sense, located in the superego, is based on what he regarded as purely masculine attributes, born of the oedipal struggle between a boy and his father waged under the threat of castration. In this model, the pre-oedipal, the relationship between mother and child, is obliterated (see Sagan, 1988).

It will be objected that this has changed, that psychoanalysis, for example, has made a decisive turn to the pre-oedipal, that homosexuality is no longer regarded as an illness, and so on. And, of course, this is true – in some quarters at least. Nevertheless, one looks in vain for some self-criticism, some acknowledgement of errors in the past, some sense of the suffering in the pathologizing of individual men and women to which psychoanalysis contributed. (At the same time the public statements of psychotherapy, that homosexuality is not pathologized for instance, are contradicted by individual stories too numerous to ignore.)

Today the moralizing continues, albeit with different emphases and inflections. What is one to make, for instance, of the neo-Kleinian position that holds that the fount of all genuine creativity lies in parental procreative sexual intercourse? At a more ordinary and everyday level listen, in so-called clinical discussions, to the implicit judgments that are made all the time – people are envious, narcissistic, defensive, engaged in projection and projective identification, and while it will be readily acknowledged that these are universal attributes, somehow it is always others, the objects of the discussion in question, who are engaged in these manoeuvres. Hear, too, how much traditional (and deeply conservative) ideas of male/female functions and roles permeate the discourse. Fathers, it is said, are needed to help children separate from their mothers, to set boundaries which, one presumes, women cannot do. Listen to how easily therapists in their everyday discourse about patients cross the line from understanding to judgement, from 'mad/bad'. As therapists, we are among the first to dismiss any notion that people who are emotionally distressed and disturbed are somehow bad. We say, quite rightly, they are the products of their histories, of their experience, and it is this that makes them who they are and do what they do. And yet how easily under pressure of the intransigence and intractability of suffering this slips into its opposite, judgement and even condemnation, as though people choose to be unhappy, to cut themselves, to starve, as though their suffering were a sign of moral failure.

Too often this moralism infects the practitioners in a way that is insufferable. One encounters not an atmosphere of humility in the face of human suffering and human complexity but positions of presumed knowledge, insufferable preciousness and suffocating sanctimony. Therapists behave as though they are an elect, superior to other more ordinary mortals who have not come to share in their truth, who have not been enlightened. The common view of therapists as arrogant, earnest, smug, self-satisfied, lacking in ordinary qualities – a genuine warmth, a lightness of touch, a humour and spontaneity – is more than a little true. The 'plain speaking' claimed by many is in truth a lack of manners, a failure of tact.

The self-satisfaction is of course misplaced. Therapists live lives that are no better than anyone else's. We are just as petty, envious, narcissistic, self-aggrandising, mean-minded as anyone else. The claims to greater insight and self-awareness can not only be a little hard to take but also alibis for bad behaviour, where 'insight' becomes an excuse, as in the frequently heard 'I know I'm deeply envious . . .' or 'I'm a terrible narcissist but . . .'

At the level of groups the history of therapy is the history of doctrinal disputes, organizational schisms and bitter fighting with an awful lot of demonizing, processes that continue to this day, as all involved know only too well and often to their cost.

Kindness

'Kindness is what matters, all along, at any age – kindness, the ruling principle of nowhere!' (Morris, 2001, p. 186).

Language

A political economy of the sentiments has developed in mimicry of all the sacralized marketings elsewhere. When interrogating our profoundest relationships, we ask, 'What's in it for me, is it a good emotional investment, what do I get out of it, what is the pay-off, where is the bottom lime?' 'I gave you everything', cry the debtors of psychic economics, 'and I was conned, swindled, taken in, cheated'. A language of pecuniary fraud is deployed to describe our broken bonds and ruined attachments. Will it pay dividends, will I get a good return for love or friendship, how high is my stock right now. I staked everything, and I came away empty-handed. A bankruptcy of the soul and heart that is filed in no court. (Seabrook, 2002, p. 21)

Music

Music may be the one cultural form that evades the psychotherapeutic grasp to understand and to subjugate. Psychoanalysis for example, George Steiner (1989, p. 46) remarks, is almost helpless in the face of music. This may be, as the saying has it, the exception that proves the rule. Freud, famously, did not like music. 'I am almost incapable of obtaining any pleasure' from it he said in the first page of his essay on Michelangelo's statue of David (Freud, 1914, p. 211). Is this not astonishing? Even Lenin, now one of the most vilified figures of the modern world, found Beethoven's *Appassionata* sonata unbearable, that such beauty could exist in such a terrible world. But he could hear it for what it was. In music as in no other art, Oliver Sacks suggests, we find expressed a whole range of emotions, some of them not even nameable, and their resolution. Maybe it is this unnameability that is so problematic for therapists, 'Why it circles and returns/ instead of giving a straight answer/ as the Gospel demands' as Adam Zagajewski puts it in his poem, 'Late Beethoven'. (RD Laing once remarked that music told him, a lonely child, that other people had the same thoughts and feelings as he did, that he was not alone in this. It was 'a connection to the heart of humanity'.) For some time I wanted to write a story about a character, the music healer, who would advise people on music they might listen to accompany them in difficult (indeed not always difficult) periods in their lives. 'Maybe,' he might say, 'you should listen to Miles Davis' *Kind of Blue* every evening for a while, or Shostakovich's Preludes and Fugues for piano or try Arvo Part's *Fratres* ...' (Incidentally, as the musician and writer David Toop remarks sharply, the music produced by men in popular genres surely gives the lie to the nostrum that men cannot express what they feel.)

Narcissism

A therapeutic buzz word, without a doubt, as the mountain of literature attests, not to speak of the confusion and doctrinal disputes. But is there not another kind of narcissism, a narcissism of the consulting room, not to say a solipsism, in which nothing exists outside of the room and where the patient's utterances are to be taken as referring either to himself or to the therapist? To speak of a colleague who is a bully and oppressive, for instance, is to be speaking not about a colleague who is a bully and oppressive, but about the 'bully in oneself' or the bully and oppressive therapist. In such situations is it any wonder that people feel unheard, that they are being driven mad?

Ordinary

What is ordinary is pathologized – loss, grief, ageing, illness, jealousy, obsession, anxiety, redundancy. Psychotherapy becomes part of the process of what Tana Dineen calls 'manufacturing victims'.(Dineen, 1999) Having started out as an attempt to normalize the pathological, or at least place it on a continuum with the normal, therapy has ended up making the normal a problem. What is called for, as Peter Lomas has consistently argued for a long time, is a return to the ordinary, to the everyday ways of being and thinking that are too easily dismissed by the professional. Indeed, the further the therapist moves from the ordinary and everyday, in the speculation and investigation of fantasies for instance, which are in any case unprovable, the further he may disable the patient from being ordinary and living an ordinary life (Lomas, 1999).

Politics

Attempts to apply psychotherapy to political and social issues wrongly conflate two domains – the domain of psychotherapy and the domain of politics – that are separate. My work as a psychotherapist does not give me any special insights into matters that are, ultimately, political. Is there anything useful or meaningful that a psychotherapist can say, as a psychotherapist, about the environment or the economy, for instance? I doubt it very much. Therapists may well think a great deal about these and other issues but the resulting ideas do not emanate from what they have decided to do in their working lives. More than this, once therapists start to think psychotherapeutically or psychoanalytically about these things, a grave mistake is being made, a category error, mixing up terms from one discourse with those from another.

This is why so often attempts to speak about social and economic issues from the viewpoint of psychotherapy sound so unconvincing or even confused. Even if what is said is true, it is often just banal – for example, when people speak of group psychology, for instance about the nature of leadership or people's need for strong leaders. It is why much of Reich's work, for instance, is simply embarrassing. (That said, not all of it is by any means and one must in any case acknowledge Reich's commitment for which he paid the unique price of expulsion from both the official Communist and psychoanalytic movements.)

This is what is wrong with attempts in recent years by psychotherapists to have some political influence, to inject what they would see as an emotional dimension into areas of policy such as economics, education and the environment. Here, too, there is a confusion between what belongs in the personal lives of individuals and what belongs in the world of politics. Not only that, but there is also a dangerous reduction of material issues to psychological ones, as clearly shown in a proposal by one such group to investigate the 'emotional meaning of money'. What on earth does this mean? It is not that money does not have an emotional significance but this is hardly its most important attribute. A moment's reflection tells us that ours is a society that values money above all else and that money allows one a considerable degree of control over one's life. A shortage of money signifies a lack of value in what one is or does and the absence of any meaningful control over one's life. The emotional significance follows from these lacks. And only people who are comfortably off could possibly pose this question.

This kind of thinking, aimed at making politicians more aware of the emotional or psychological implications of their policies, is quite wrong-headed. While it is true that passions are aroused in politics, this does not mean that politics is or should be about emotions. Politics is about, or should be about, power and the distribution of resources. If politicians want to improve the psychological lives of the majority of men, women and children then they have to address this question.

Questions

'Oh my body, make of me always a man who questions' (Fanon, 1968, p. 165).

Recognition

Despite all the criticism and qualifications, therapy matters, or can do. It is certainly not the most important thing in the world and there are many types of work that are more beneficial to the world. But, in small ways, and maybe not so small ways at some times, it is important and can help people to lead lives that are less disturbed and more creative, more alive.

In therapy we do what? We listen to another and in doing so we recognize her as another human being. We put into practice the idea of the Roman poet that 'Nothing human is alien to me'. This is not something other to me but this is also me, at least in possibility. This may be the first time that someone has ever taken this stance in relation to this person.

We listen to the people who come to see us and we listen in a way that other people do not listen to them, and maybe never have listened to them. We engage with them. We reflect with them and we offer a space in which such thought and reflection might, against the odds, take place. We are interested, and if we are not we are interested in thinking about why not. We help to clarify and demystify. We offer, as David Smail puts it, a form of solidarity. We show people that they are not alone. 'Do not leave me in my solitude', as the philosopher Emmanuel Levinas puts it, is the cry of the other to me (Mortley, 1991, p. 15). We offer our thoughts drawn from our own experience in life as much as our work. We help people come to terms with who they are, to accept who they are with all their faults and limitations and, in so doing, maybe help to open up new possibilities of who they might become. Recognition is not about some phony niceness, although there is nothing whatsoever wrong with tact and manners, something too many of us have forgotten in our professional (de)formation. 'I would meet you upon this honestly', as Eliot puts it, an honest meeting, an attempt at one, where everything can be talked about. And if I experience someone as arrogant or mean or self-obsessed I have a responsibility to articulate this in a manner that is appropriate to the occasion and I must be prepared to hear difficult things about myself also.

Scepticism

Scepticism is not to be confused with cynicism – to know the price of everything but the value of nothing, as Oscar Wilde put it. Nor is it to be confused with a posturing, usually associated with a certain kind of post-modernism, which appears to hold that we can know nothing or that all positions and perspectives are of equal value. Scepticism holds, rather, that we are entitled, indeed enjoined, to question. 'What is the basis of your belief or assertion? How do you know that?' If we are unable to ask these questions we might as well give up whatever it is we are doing. 'Language' says the philosopher Emmanuel Levinas, 'is already scepticism'. The very fact of language enables us to put things in question, not to take things for granted. This is part of the responsibility of being a human, speaking being.

Whether it is an epistemological position valid for all seasons is debatable. That it is a valuable, even necessary position for the psychotherapist seems less so. Scepticism is not some easy option, an excuse for mental laziness. Far from it. A sceptic has to work a lot harder, think a lot more for herself. Like the agnostic in the field of religion there are no easy dogmas to follow, to fall back on. ('It's in the Bible/Koran/Torah'; 'It's God's will', 'Jesus/Moses/Mohammed decreed . . .') Life is a lot harder when you have to think for yourself.

Therapization (of everyday life)

The growth of therapy has also contributed to what one might call, if rather inelegantly, the therapization of everyday life, the ways in which the language and culture of therapy have infiltrated spheres of life outside of the clinical encounter as well as the ways in which people have come to see themselves. In some ways this is no bad thing. It is right, for instance, if institutions such as prisons and the criminal justice system become less punitive and more understanding of what it is in people's lives that lead them to do the things they have done. It is right that we increasingly recognize that the experience of learning is a profoundly emotional one as well as an intellectual one. But there are other ways in which therapy affects the culture that are much less welcome – indeed, which ought to make us rather worried.

At an everyday level there is the way in which therapy is proffered as a solution for almost everything – bereavement, redundancy, illness, separation and divorce. It is shocking how quickly therapy or counselling will be offered or suggested to someone who has suffered in some way. Moreover, the suggestion, 'maybe you should think about seeing someone?' can, all too often, be a way of saying, 'actually I don't have time for what you are going through'. In this sense the culture of therapy can justly be accused of contributing to the weakening of more ordinary bonds, especially those of family and friendship. In the same vein, there is the terrible language of therapy that has invaded the culture. People don't talk to or with one another, they 'share'; people don't cut or burn themselves, they 'self-harm'; people don't refuse to do things, they are 'resistant' to them; people do not disagree about things but are 'in denial'; people are not oppressed or exploited but have low self-esteem.

There are more far-reaching ways in which therapy has invaded the public culture that are far from welcome. There is the way, for instance, in which the provision of therapy is seen as the answer to deprivation which is material. The denial of material resources to schools, for example, which prevents them doing the job they are supposed to be doing, not to mention the vilification and denigration of teachers that has become a regular feature of public discourse, is not going to be set right by the provision of psychological help. This is not, it must be emphasized, an argument against therapy. It should go without saying that schools should have access to whatever help they need, psychological or otherwise.

Universalization

One of the most regrettable tendencies in psychotherapy is the tendency to universalize, to make general statements from specific situations.

Practising therapists fall into this trap all the time when they use a highly specific clinical example as proof of a general theory. More fundamentally, Freud generalized hugely from his own experience or, rather, his thoughts about his own experience. He assumed, for instance, from his own love for his mother and jealousy of his father, a universal syndrome, the Oedipus complex. What was true for Freud had to be true for everyone at all times, a pretty narcissistic view of things (Heaton, 1993, p. 116). Not only that, but Freud drew from his own experience of an authoritarian father–son relationship the conclusion of an inevitably authoritarian politics. This helps us to understand, although not forget, Freud's dedication in 1933 of a copy of *Why War?* (his exchange of letters with Einstein) to the Italian dictator Mussolini with the inscription 'with the respectful greetings of an old man who recognizes in the ruler the cultural hero' (Brunner, 2001, p. 170).

Virtue

In his attentive and thoughtful reading of the writings of Primo Levi, Robert Gordon argues that what makes Levi meaningful to millions of readers who have never experienced a fraction of the horror that Levi endured, what can make him seem almost like a friend, are his 'ordinary virtues'. These are the virtues of listening, of common sense (not really that common of course), of friendship, of wit, of discretion. From every page exudes 'a practical, engaged sense of living, working and writing' along with an unceasing commitment to various forms of practical intelligence (Gordon, 2002, p. 89). It is this practical wisdom which through intelligent engagement with the world can clarify or humanize experience.

Wonder

There is a predictability of intellectual life, a deadness even in the therapeutic culture. Nothing surprises. Nothing cannot be explained or understood. The book, the film, the play and, of course, the person – none can escape the grasp of psychotherapeutic theorizing. But let us be honest. How often does one really want to read that book or article or attend that lecture or seminar, particularly after formal qualification? Very rarely in my experience. The reason is simple. Before one has even opened the book or gone to the lecture one knows what one is going to hear. It is all so predictable, so lacking in any kind of freshness, let alone excitement. (Of course there are exceptions; there always are. But all too often the exceptions are less illuminating in themselves than as signifiers serving to point up what is wrong with all that is not exceptional.)

Wonder, Peter de Bolla writes, is not the same as awe, or rapture or surprise, each of which can involve a paralysis of other senses. By contrast, wonder requires us to acknowledge what we do not and indeed may never know, to acknowledge the limits of our knowledge: 'It is ... a way of knowing that does not lead to certainties or truths about the world or the way things are. It is a state of mind, of being with the world and oneself that, like being in love, colors all that we know we know' (de Bolla, 2001, p. 143).

> Because everything connects in the end, or only seems to, or seems to only because it does. (DeLillo, 1998, p. 465)

Acknowledgment

I am, as always, grateful to Melissa Benn for her encouragement and constructive criticism in the writing of this chapter.

CHAPTER 5

What is normality? Reason and its loss

JOHN M. HEATON

Viola: Thy reason, man?

Festa: Truth,sir, I can yield you none without words, and words are grown so false, I am loath to prove reason with them.

Twelfth Night III. i. 19–21.

In this chapter I shall consider the ordinary notion of reason and show its relevance in understanding people who are 'mentally disturbed' or in states of mental conflict and pain. It often used to be said that a mad person has lost his reason and that a neurotic person tends to be unreasonable, at least over certain matters. Thus if someone claims to be Judas Iscariot, or to be pursued by demons, or to 'see' and 'hear' things we do not perceive, then most of us are at a loss to understand them. And if someone fears to go outside their house in ordinary circumstances, or feels compelled to wash their hands for half an hour after going to the toilet then both we and usually they feel there is something unreasonable about this behaviour.

We are at a loss to understand them. But many experts in psychiatry, clinical psychology, psychoanalysis, and psychotherapy produce theories that claim to explain these 'deviations' from reason and produce techniques of treatment based on them.

To ordinary people the loss of, or deviation from, reason is the mark of mental illness; basically they cannot understand or make sense of certain actions that they themselves feel compelled to do or that others do. These confusions about reason in ordinary people are admirably brought out by Laing and Esterson in *Sanity, Madness and the Family* (1964). But psychological experts change these confusions to the question of what is a normal personality or, even worse, to what is a normal person. But can one be impersonal in judging personality? What is the authority that grounds the judgement?

The field of psychotherapy is full of ungrounded judgements of people. There is the belief that we are all neurotics, more or less, other than those who have been successfully analysed by an analyst belonging to the International Psycho-analytic Association. This implies that the experience of the doctrine that underlies the therapy is an essential ingredient of normality – an Olympian belief indeed! Nearly all the definitions of a normal personality, such as resolution of the Oedipus complex, overcoming of the depressive position, raising of repressions, and so forth, contain a grain of truth but are implicated in psychological doctrines of one sort or another. They all encourage the cult of personality; the analysed person – or best of all the approved analyst – is special and has a personality superior to the rest of us.

Psychotherapy, when it is understood as attempting to normalize a person, is the way psychological man tries to heal himself. As Philip Rieff wrote: '"Therapy" has become a general word describing our present distraction from the unavoidable soul-making journey' (Rieff, 1979, p. 390). It is subject to one of the most archaic of phantasies: that we can command ourselves, which is tantamount to being uncommanded. Hence the endless proliferation of different therapies and versions of psychoanalysis and our ability to have our transgressions disguised as 'optional lifestyles'.

All talk of what is normal or not brings in the question of value. It is assumed that it is better not to be neurotic, to have worked through the depressive position than not, and so on. Freud claimed that psychoanalysis is a science and its 'endeavour is to arrive at a correspondence with reality' (Freud, 1933, p. 170). He thought religion and philosophy were inferior to science, while art and its illusions are 'almost always harmless and beneficient' (Freud, 1933, p. 160). He gave no cogent argument or evidence for these remarks. Few scientists, religious people, philosophers, or artists would agree with him. For example, his view that science just seeks correspondence with reality leaves out the importance of logic and mathematics in science. Logic does not deduce truths about reality but elaborates the internal connections between propositions and the conditions under which scientific language makes sense; and many mathematical structures vital to physics do not describe any empirical reality. Freud's thought on what is normal and of value is strongly biased by his stubborn insistence that his understanding of the natural sciences is the only correct one.

Now it has been pointed out by Janik (2001, p. 218) that Wittgenstein and later Laing questioned what 'normal' could possibly mean with respect to human personality.

Laing's views on the concept of normality are summarized in Burston (2000, pp. 98–131). His critique of normality unfolded in several stages. First he thought of normality in terms of primary ontological security;

later what was abnormal was unconscious complicity in 'social phantasy systems', then he thought of normality as being linked to some sort of transcendental experience, and abnormality as being the denial of it. He tried to link this with Buddhism and other traditions but he remained an empiricist wedded to experience. The Classical tradition in both East and West would not agree that transcendence could possibly be an experience that can be pursued or obtained in any way, it is not a source of gratification. As Burston (p. 118) points out, Laing took an élitist attitude to human existence; it is difficult to see by what authority he claimed that the particular creative geniuses that he idealized should be the model for everybody; surely human life is far more varied and there is a place for butchers and bakers as well as for Van Gogh and Artaud without either claiming the other is abnormal. Nevertheless, Laing made an important contribution by moving away from judging personality according to psychological doctrines and by questioning the source and authority of norms.

Wittgenstein was not an empiricist and much of his work is concerned with breaking the spell of the ideal; he was fond of the line in *King Lear* (I.iv.86): 'I'll teach you differences'. Imposing standards of normality on human life easily falls into the trap of idealization and obliteration of difference. Attending to ordinary notions of reason, and understanding the claims it makes on us, can perhaps help us see the sources of normality and respect the variety of human life.

Reason

Reason is not a skill belonging to any particular group of people. It is forged in the spontaneous responses between caretaker and child. We do not learn to reason, but by being in a family, taking part in rituals, playing games at nursery school and so on we 'catch on' to reason. It is intimately connected with the possession of language, the ability to affirm oneself freely as a subject, to say 'I'. It requires the availability of logical devices signifying negation, conjunction, implication, and disjunction. These are not specifically taught but their use is learned at a young age. Certain areas of knowledge play a special role in reasoning such as logic and mathematics. Thus mathematical statements are used to describe certain empirical facts and so empirical facts cannot revise mathematics, hence its apparent certainty. It may be reasonable to predict that it will rain tomorrow but of course one might be wrong; but that $2 + 3 = 5$ seems to be more than reasonable but veritably inexorable because it is a matter of logic, of the way our propositions represent things.

Reason is a perfectly ordinary word used to justify, condemn, guide, or give an account of our acts, desires, beliefs and thoughts. It is as varied as human activities, for they depend on human attitudes and responses that antecede the development of reason. It follows that it is not monolithic and is not confined to argument. Thus a perfectly good reason for me to buy chocolate is because I like it. Reasoning comes before reason. There is a tendency to try to define the essence of reason. But this can be done only by reasoning, so there is no such thing as reason apart from reasoning. The phrase 'we must be guided by reason' is problematic, for it depends on the particular notion of reason that the speaker holds. If I say I do not believe in reason and simply follow my desires I am still appealing to reason – the reason I do X is because I want to or feel like it; that is my justification. Of course, others may not agree that this is sufficient, but nevertheless it is my reason. To abolish reason would be to abolish our human life with language.

Reason has developed in many ways according to the history of our attempts to understand one another and be responsible for our actions. So it is sensitive to culture, power and privilege, sexual identity, race and so on; even in a fairly homogeneous group there will be areas of disagreement as to what is reasonable. Such disagreements and failures of understanding are part of the texture of human life. Reason is not an absolute belonging to any one person or group; reasons must be shareable. It is not a super-concept which anyone can finalize; it does not depend on super-hard rails that our minds must follow when we are reasoning. There is always the possibility of creating new forms of reason.

It is common in this postmodern age to complain of the violence of reason. But if reason is seen as the human way of understanding one another then it need not be violent but can be a powerful way to peace. Reason is used for violence when a particular group of people who claim to be more rational than the rest of us use it to obtain power. Thus men have claimed to be more rational than women, scientists than ordinary folk, intellectuals than the masses, European culture than Oriental, and so forth. Often the power relation is disguised. Argument, a form of reason, may be used to bully people into submission. Intellectuals may claim to be the spokesmen for what the proletariat 'really' aspire to. Psychoanalysts may claim they know the 'true self' or what lies in the unconscious, which is what people 'really' desire.

Reason and language are intertwined. We tend to ascribe rudimentary reasoning to the higher animals but they cannot justify their behaviour by reference to a reason, they cannot explain their errors by reference to the reasons they thought they had, they cannot reason or argue from one thought to another. A dog can want to go for a walk but it cannot plan to do so next week or intend to go for one on good or bad reasons. A cat may jump on to a table to get at the goldfish but that was its purpose, not its reasons; it cannot justify its action.

Reason and value

Reasons have an evaluative dimension, we speak of good and bad reasons for something. 'Why did you vote Labour?' 'Because their candidate is handsome.' There can be arguments here as to whether this is a good or bad reason to judge who to vote for. Do people's looks necessarily make them good politicians?

Ordinarily, when a person gives a reason for an action he is saying how he understands his action himself. 'Why are you walking down the street?' 'Because I want to buy some bread.' I am the authority on what I am up to. Of course you may have a good reason to disbelieve me: you know I am very secretive, I look furtive, and so forth. But such circumstances are exceptions to the rule. If noone ever had any authority on their reasons for their actions then human life as we know it would cease. When one gives one's reasons sincerely for an action or belief one is giving a justification for them. Our authority over our reasons depends on our being able to say what they are; this requires attention rather than searching for a hypothesis or making an observation. We do not look into our minds and discover a reason; to ask how one knows one's reason for doing something is senseless.

Reason is a power and not a force. Some people are able to respect reason better than others. That is, they are able to acknowledge others reasons for action without resorting to some kind of force. Commonly people claim that their reason is *the* reason, as if they had access to its absolute source rather than it just being *their* reason. The phrase 'it is reasonable to ...' is always suspect as it hides its imperialism in an impersonal form.

Reason always acknowledges the other person as having a right to reason by its insistence on the problematic partiality of any account of knowledge and its respect for the other's reason. It accords a space for the possibility that however stable a current consensus might be there is always the possibility for criticism that might properly upset the consensus. It is committed to the belief that, if others could live a life with very different forms of reason, there would still be the possibility of critical engagement with them, that they might be right to be doing what they do and we wrong – or perhaps we just do things differently as we have different desires and beliefs. What makes judgements of reason objective is the intelligibility of continuing dispute. For freedom is presupposed by reason; our reasons may be ours but they can always be disputed as to whether they are good or not.

Reason is easily confused with rationality. The picture we have of rational people is that they are consistent and their arguments follow a fixed pattern, which is guided by rules that can be codified. It seems as if the rational person, by following rules, is locked on to rails that are there objectively to be followed in a way that transcends the reactions and responses of the people around him. So the rational person is believed to be more in touch with reality than the irrational one.

This picture is profoundly suspect as is argued in Wittgenstein's discussions, in *Philosophical Investigations,* of the concept of following a rule and in the extensive literature on this (see, for example, McDowell 1998, Essays 10 and 11). There is not space to repeat these discussions but they show that reason:

> is a matter of our sharing routes of interest and feeling, modes of response, senses of humour and of significance and of fulfilment, of what is outrageous, of what is similar to what else, what a rebuke, what forgivenesss, of when an utterance is an assertion, when an appeal, when an explanation – all the whirl of organism Wittgenstein calls 'forms of life'. Human speech and activity, sanity and community, rest upon nothing more, but nothing less, than this. It is a vision as simple as it is difficult, and as difficult as it is (and because it is) terrifying. (Cavell, 1976, p. 52)

That reason is not codifiable does not mean that no activity is. If you invite me to play a game of chess then there are codifiable rules that are reasonable to follow if we are to play. If I move the rook diagonally then it would be reasonable for you to protest. However I might reply that it was reasonable for me to do so as I wanted to broaden your mind as to the possibilities of playing with chess pieces. Of course, it would be reasonable of you to walk away. Games, the law, and thousands of activities have codifiable and objective rules that are reasonable to follow if one is to take part in the activities they regulate.

However, a particular version of reason is often generalized as if it was reason, a fixed pattern which we all ought to follow. So we are typically subjected to allegedly authoritative pronouncements by others as to what we really ought to do, feel, mean, want, or intend; what is 'reasonable' and what we should do to be 'liberated'. Children, people who are seen as mentally disturbed, and people from very different cultures are particularly subjected to it. Thus the meaning and mechanisms of homoerotic desire was explained by those whose authority stemmed from their alleged immunity to it. People with very different practices and interests, and so with different notions of intelligibility, were seen as having a 'primitive mentality' and their practices were interpreted in terms of our notions of reason. It was only when these people were able to 'answer back' that these imperialistic theories began to look shaky. However,

infants cannot answer back and so are ideal subjects for theoretical speculation; thus Klein and others assume that they are insane, suffering from
persecutory anxiety, splitting processes and so on. Neurotics and the mad
are scrutinized, pathologized, and exoticized (the Wolf Man, the Rat Man,
and so forth) by those who are considered privileged and so exempt from
such scrutiny. They occupy a position that is assumed to be impersonal
and so objective, 'rational', and 'scientific'.

Freud, for example, believed in the unity of science and that there was
a uniform scientific method, and that psychoanalytic method was part of
it. But this is one of Freud's many pipe dreams; there is no uniform scientific method and the notion of the unity of science is a form of
scientism, a metaphysical belief appropriate to totalitarianism (Dupre,
1993). The roots of reasoning lie in the 'whirl of organism' and not in particular versions of it that may be useful for certain purposes.

As reasons are our human way of understanding each other, they can
be meaningful only if their meaning is shared and actually counts for
others. Reasoning must include 'I' and 'you' rather than the experts' neutral language, which in theory can be spoken by anyone. So there cannot
be experts on reason as there are in the judgement of physical disorders
where most people agree what would be a cure, and so there can be
acknowledged experts in producing it. We need a different approach to
'disorders' of reason than to physical disorders. One might say *the axis of
our examination must be rotated but about the fixed point of our real
need* (Wittgenstein, 1958, p. 108).

If we rotate the axis of our examination we learn to ask different questions, problematize the taken-for-granted, discover something about who
'we' are and our stake in the taken-for-granted. It is a political act in that
politics involves our relations with others, with our history, and the laws
of our society. Politics also involves questioning our real needs – who
decides what they are? Who decides what is reasonable? Who decides who
will liberate us from oppression? Do we have any say in this? A point made
with force by both Laing (1967) and Cooper (1978).

My reasons involve taking myself seriously and this involves recognition of you, of our common humanity. If the reason you do something
does not count as a reason for me in my situation, I can grasp why it is a
reason for you in so far as we are both in the space of reasons. Acting for
a reason commits one to respecting others' reasons because the intelligibility of reasons involves that there is always an other; there is no absolute
reason, they are human.

But as we humans are finite creatures, disputes about reason are not
interminable in practice. Consider the class of judgements as exemplified
by thoughts about whether or not a particular course of action would be
unreasonable or even mad. Is there an objective ground to decide what is

reasonable or not? *If I have exhausted the justifications I have reached bedrock, and my spade is turned. Then I am inclined to say: 'this is simply what I do'* (Wittgenstein, 1958: 217).

Bedrock is not absolute. Our history of initiation into the language games that provide us with our notion of reason provides us with what we consider reasonable. But others may have been initiated into different notions. Such people may be unable to participate with us in reason. Doubt and disaffection may sever them from the community in which their education was intended to initiate them into (Wittgenstein, 1969, §298). Unless they develop a sense of irony they will not find it easy to accept our notions of what is reasonable (Wittgenstein, 1969, §254 and §281).

An example may help. A community of about 15 people, many of whom had been in mental hospital recently, decided by vote to accept a new member who continually wet his trousers. Within a week the living room and kitchen stank of stale urine. This person would also set light to his trousers when he went shopping, but as they were soaking wet they smoked. The shopkeepers strongly protested about this and in the end the community reluctantly had to admit they could not accept him any longer. Bedrock was reached. The only place he could go was back to a mental hospital.

Now I can easily imagine a rational group of people who delighted in the scent of stale urine and were amused at his dramatic appearance when shopping but who strongly objected to someone who refused to do his share in washing up the dishes – a position that was tolerated in this community, especially if that person was a man. In these people, bedrock has shifted.

First-person authority

There is a basic asymmetry between our first person awareness and our knowledge of others; between 'knowing' our own minds and knowing the minds of others. This asymmetry between self and other is fundamental to the idea of a person, and these asymmetries are irreducible. Sartre (1957a) and Wittgenstein (1958) were pioneers in pointing this out and Moran (2001) has developed their work.

Since Descartes it has been commonly believed that self-knowledge is a kind of inner perception. This belief is implicit in most psychoanalytic theorizing. Thus Freud in one of his most important essays, *The Unconscious* (Freud, 1915, p. 170) wrote:

> Consciousness makes each of us aware only of his own states of mind; that other people, too, possess a consciousness is an inference which we draw by analogy from their observable utterances and actions …

If this were true it would mean that self-knowledge would be essentially similar to our knowledge of others, only the latter has to be inferred. Freud frequently emphasized that psychoanalysis is based on careful observation and inferences, so completely blurring the asymmetry between self-knowledge and knowledge of others.

A basic feature of first person awareness is that the credibility of what I say about myself is often not grounded in observation or evidence. Rather it is grounded on my paying attention and that is my authority. So it is not knowledge in the ordinary empirical sense of the term, for knowledge implies evidence for that knowledge – we may be right or wrong about it. Thus we are usually aware of the position of our body without observing but by paying attention to it. If in ordinary circumstances I say I am sitting down it makes little sense to ask me on what evidence I say this. It would be nonsense to say 'I know I am sitting down but only because I have observed it'.

We generally know our own intentions, feelings, thoughts and beliefs without appealing to evidence. There is an immediacy about this aware-ness; we do not need to observe ourselves to know that we are in pain or that we are going to the baker to get bread. Nor do we identify our feel-ings and thoughts; if I feel angry I do not identify the feeling and perhaps misidentify it as being sadness rather than anger. Nor do I need to consult paradigms or authorities – is this anger or an intention? In all these cases knowledge, ignorance, certainty and doubt have no place, only indeci-sion. Thus I may not yet have decided what to think, feel or believe about something and I can change my mind. 'I feel angry'; 'no, he obviously did not mean what he said'. I have changed my mind and am no longer angry.

Now, being angry, feeling pain, intending to go for a walk, are natural expressions for human beings and are prelinguistic in their origins. If a child is angry, or cries when hurt, we do not ask the child if it is angry or hurt or tell it that it has correctly recognized its feelings, but we respond appropriately. If it picks up a toy to play with, we do not ask if the child did this voluntarily or intended to. These are all spontaneous expressions of an ordinary child and are not descriptions of any goings on in a mind. As a child grows up it learns to articulate these expressions and so can say 'I intend to go for a walk', 'I have a throbbing pain in my knee', and so forth. It can then convey, or refuse to convey, information about itself but this sophistication is based on its early spontaneous responses.

Contrast all this with our knowledge of other minds. Knowledge of others, such as whether they are in pain or not, whether they are going to the baker or not, whether they are angry, depends on how well we know them, observing their behaviour, on what they may answer to question-ing, on their culture and so on. And in all this we may be right or wrong. People can feign pain, tell lies about where they are going, pretend not to be angry. In all these cases intimacy, observation, knowledge, and inference play an important part in our understanding of others.

Of course, people may not be right about what they think or believe and may not acknowledge their pain or distress. Thus one may believe oneself to be a moral person but others may see one as being a prig; nevertheless one can say with authority that one believes oneself to be a highly moral being and not acknowledge that one suffers from mental pain and conflict. What one 'really' is may take a lot of painful discussion before it can be acknowledged by both sides.

The authority of first-person awareness of our thoughts and feelings is of great importance, as it is expressive of our relation to the world and to our evaluations of ourselves. How I think of myself will make a far bigger difference to how I live than how I think of others. When I decide what to do, *this* is what it commits me to, it is not the apprehension of a particular thought in my mind. If it were I would have to find a way to make it my own. In other words, having lost my authority I would have to fall back on trying to control myself, which is to treat myself as another. These insights are spelled out in detail by Sartre (1957a, Part 2); what he calls being-for-itself is roughly similar to what I call first person awareness, following Wittgenstein and Moran.

There is a logical difference between first person authority and merely attributing some psychological state to oneself. For an attribution is essentially a third-person stance towards oneself, whereas first-person authority requires attention, deciding, and being responsible, rather than attributing a psychological belief to someone who happens to be me. Thus a person may declare that his analyst has told him he is envious and he may believe her because the observation is empirically well grounded. He weakly acquiesces under cover of being hard headed, believing in the truths of psychoanalysis. But he is acting in bad faith. For what he is aware of empirically, as a facticity, is no substitute for what he is committed to categorically. So he continues to behave enviously; taking envy to be merely an attribution, a quality of himself, rather than a description of his orientation to people. The interpretation has merely helped him to become submerged in his own facticity (Sartre, 1957a, p. 47–70). Freud vaguely saw this problem and tried to account for it in his essay *Negation* (Freud, 1925), but he and other analysts continued to attribute psychological qualities to people, including those they had never even met.

We can 'step back' from our activities and so call into question our current beliefs and desires and reduce their force as we do when we ordinarily deliberate as to what we are going to do. This capacity is exclusively first-personal. It is not a special form of awareness in which we become aware of some mechanism or process in our mind. Rather this 'stepping back' allows us to appraise our beliefs and impulses and decide whether there is a good reason to act on them. Thus, in treating impulsive people, say those who steal impulsively, it is important not merely to tell them to stop stealing. If one does, they take this 'order' impulsively, having no sense of first-person authority in this area of their lives. It is only when they are free to 'step back' from their impulses and enter the space of reasons that they can decide what is reasonable for them to do and show what they value.

Grasping a reason makes the reason inherently intelligible to others as well as to oneself. If my reason is intelligible to them they can see what I value, although they may not value it themselves. The authority of the reason derives from my very own insight into the force of the reason; it is a way of putting myself in charge. This requires the authority of first-person awareness and involves the category of freedom. If a decision is treated as if it is caused by some unconscious process, or as the result of social conditioning, then this is depersonalizing. Of course, a person may pretend to decide and then he may be following a leader or be embroiled in transference phantasies. Nor does a decision depend on psychological facts about myself. These would all be mere attributions to myself and would not involve the category of freedom. Deciding is not a particular mental state or process, nor is it forcing oneself; it is to be freely committed to the world in a certain way; to see and assess the situation I am in.

This is not something that one can do with respect to other people. One may try to persuade them, force them by threats and so on; this may result in them forcing themselves, perhaps attributing psychological states to themselves, but all this would be treating themselves as another. An interpretation can be true only if it is acknowledged to be so, not if it is taken to be some psychic 'given' discovered by the analyst. In the latter case the categories of freedom and decision no longer apply. Mere conformity to a reason must be distinguished from following reason; it is only in the latter case that reason gives one's actions their meaning, character and liveliness.

If the authority of first-person awareness is not recognized in therapy then therapy becomes alienating. The therapist treats what the patient says as merely reports on his state of mind, data for interpretation and inference as to what is going on in the 'unconscious'. The client may well be aware that this is being done and that his words have no authority and are being taken as only saying what he seems to believe or feel. If he expresses uncertainty about all this then this is taken as merely symptomatic and indicative of his state of mind that actually may not be uncertain at all. If he expresses frustration or despair at this, his words are yet again taken as merely gesturing at his own state of mind, not speaking his mind, taking responsibility for what he thinks. The radical abrogation of first-person authority means that people's authority to make up their mind and have their beliefs count for something is lost. This loss cannot be made good by supplementing it with expert knowledge, information about what is 'really' going on in his mind, in the unconscious. If he acquiesces in this he may become a psychoanalyst, but he has lost his own rational authority and freedom to think.

Self-deception

Psychotherapy is largely concerned with problems of self-deception. Here there is a clash between two perspectives. In the case of my beliefs about the natural world I can, of course, be deceived. I may truly believe that the Earth is flat; this is a case of the authority of first-person awareness. But, as has been pointed out, reason does not belong to me, it is a human capacity and does not have to follow fixed patterns. The sentence 'the earth is flat' has a meaning to other people as well as to me so they might well ask me to point out the place where we can jump off it. So if we are interested, a dialogue might follow that might encourage me to deliberate.

Psychotherapy is concerned with the conflicts that occur when the authority of our first person awareness is lost. This collapse creates a conflict between how we actually think, feel and act and how we know objectively and theoretically we should act or how others experience us. Thus I may be aware of feeling anxious on seeing a spider but know that, objectively, they are harmless. I may think I am being reasonable, but others may experience me as being unreasonably persecutory.

Most mental conflict can be understood in this way. Depressed people are aware that it is not reasonable to feel so terrible, they distinguish depression from mourning the actual loss of someone they love. So they have non-evidential awareness of feeling terrible that clashes with how in theory they think they should feel. An obsessional person may know his thoughts are compulsive and unreasonable but be unable to act on this knowledge. In all these cases there is a conflict between two perspectives on oneself, there is the tacit substitution of the objective theoretical point of view for practical understanding and engagement in life, the authority and freedom of first-person awareness is lost.

Freud in his *Psychopathology of Everyday Life* (Freud, 1901) gives numerous examples of this. People may forget a proper name or set of words that their reason tells them they should know. They may make a slip of the tongue or of the pen in which they write or say something they did not intend. In all these cases individuals are non-evidentially aware of their intention but things do not turn out as expected – something is forgotten, said, or done that was not intended. Freud made a very important point in seeing the analogy between these parapraxes and neurosis and dreaming. But he gave a causal explanation for them arguing that they were due to suppressed psychical material. He never made clear the nature of 'suppressed psychical material' and how it can be something that can act as a cause. A mechanical apparatus can be described in causal terms but just what is a mental apparatus? When would saying 'you have a mental apparatus' help me to understand myself? It might, however, help me to see you and treat you as a complicated machine, an entity without freedom.

Approaching these phenomena in terms of reason and its loss rather than as due to causal mechanisms makes sense of them in a different way. It turns attention away from the mind and mythical mechanisms to the person's relations to the world in which he or she lives. Thus awareness of my commitment to the truth of my beliefs transcends any description of my psychological state. Supposing someone is generous; that means he or she acts generously. But generous people may not even be aware that they are generous, they certainly do not have the thought 'I am generous and so I must act generously'. Mean people, on the other hand, may think, 'I must be generous' as a theoretical necessity that may lead them to force themselves into 'generous' behaviour; this may lead to a loss of spontaneity and smug self-satisfaction but not to generosity. The expression of commitment is to be freely and responsibly involved in the world and with others rather than compulsively altering and valuing one's psychological states.

Self-knowledge involves being aware of and taking responsibility for one's thoughts and cravings. In self-deception the sense of first-person responsibility is lost and we become conflicted between what we believe we ought to be and how we are. Self-deception exists when we crave to be something other than what we are; it is marked by anxiety and loss of spontaneity as the person has lost touch with the practices that could make sense of his or her life. It leads to conflict, which is often manifest in the futile effort of trying to be what we believe we ought to be.

From the first-person's point of view, the relation between their belief and the fact believed is not evidential but categorical. That is, to speak of one's beliefs is to speak freely of one's conviction of the facts and not of some piece of evidence that might convince one. We have not obtained reasons for action if we learn of our beliefs only through assessment of the evidence about ourselves. For one has access to one's beliefs in a non-evidential way. There is a difference in category between the sort of thing one may treat as evidence on which to base a judgement and the judgement itself that one arrives at after deliberation. The attribution of attitudes to oneself is no substitute for knowing one's mind as the exercise of deliberation.

The empirical fact that one has a belief say, in one's envy, is not evidence for one's truthfulness. If my belief exists only as an empirical psychological fact about myself that I have obtained through evidence, say in analysis, then that does not mean that I am persuaded of its truth. I might go on seeking more evidence – analysis interminable. Or I might try to change it, treating myself as another as if envy were just an empirical mechanism in someone's mind, perhaps caused by the death instinct. To realize the truth of my envy is to see my commitment to it rather than to be aware of psychological mechanisms. It is to turn from examining my mind and reporting on it as if it were another's, to acknowledging that I am committed to envy, that I express envy in the way I live; I may then come to realize the harm my envy is doing to others and myself and take responsibility for it.

First-person awareness is both our normal condition and part of our rational freedom. It can be disturbed or lost due to trauma or a confusing upbringing. It is authoritative and does not depend on psychological evidence about oneself from any 'expert'.

Theory

Freud made a disastrous mistake by thinking that mental illness is best understood in terms of individual psychology rather than reason. In mental illness people are in conflict with themselves, and often with others; it is a disorder of relationship, a failure of understanding and so of reason. Basing psychoanalysis on a special procedure for the investigation and treatment of individuals with neurotic disorders led him to believe that mental health can be judged by only one group of people who are supremely rational – himself and those who have been properly analysed and taught to apply his procedures. So he developed theories of the mind that depended solely on this special procedure and the information obtained by it, forgetting that any special procedure hides as well as reveals.

A theory that is supposed to be an aid in curing us of our self-deceptions is very different from a theory of natural science (Heaton, 2000). Psychoanalytic theories claim to tell us what is going on or has gone on in our own mind. This is stated very clearly by Freud in his *Introductory Lectures* (Freud, 1916/17) where he claims to have made very important 'discoveries' about our minds by using his particular technique. He emphasizes that the truth of his theories can be verified only by having an analysis oneself by a practised analyst, but that we all have a natural antipathy to the findings of psychoanalytic research.

But he was wrong about people's 'natural antipathy' to his theories. He thought it was due to fear of our sexual instincts; he liked to picture himself as the fearless confronter of the terrible forces lying in our untamed sexual instincts – the Conquistador of the human mind. The antipathy people feel to his huge generalizations is more likely to be due to their instinctive repugnance for Freud's steamrolling language in which he ignores our authority and freedom to speak in our own first-person language, to know our own minds. This critique of psychoanalytic discourse is admirably put by Luce Irigaray (2002) in *To Speak is Never Neutral* and some of her other writing. As Sartre and Wittgenstein have argued, a transcendental relation to the self is ineliminable, our ordinary first-person knowledge proceeds independently of evidence about psychological facts about oneself; rather, it commits us to knowledge beyond our psychological state that cannot be described in language.

A theory about the mind in psychoanalysis is a structure of beliefs initially expressed in first-person language by the believer in the theory. In the case of psychoanalysis it involved Freud's self-analysis, his own self-delusions, especially his ambition, sweeping generalizations from his own conflicts and experience with his patients, and his subsequent ruminations on all this (Breger, 2000). But why should the beliefs and theories Freud developed to understand himself and what went on between his patients and himself apply to all of us? Freud's views were vital to him, they were his and he possessed them; and so was envious of anyone who tried to alter them, for they helped him make sense of his life and his experiences with his patients. But that is no reason to suppose that his beliefs are relevant to everyone. Nevertheless, they are of great interest to psychotherapists as they throw light on many confusions of self-deception in modern Western culture.

Psychoanalysts believe that their theories can capture what is 'really' going on in their clients' minds; they believe that their theories provide so much data about mental life. They assume that deep meaning lies beneath appearances; this leads them to commit the logical fallacy that the earlier something is found the more basic it must be. Freud was a great story teller. 'Once upon a time …' is a powerful way to start a myth, but is not a truth.

The imagery of a deep truth leads analysts to believe that it can be excavated from actual discourse. The real is assumed to be in a mysterious medium – the unconscious – only to be observed by a person trained in the techniques of psychoanalysis. Their theory-making and often their practice nearly always privileges their own first-person perspective over that of the other. They ignore the fundamental asymmetry, basic to the concept of a person, between self-knowledge and knowledge of others (Moran, 2001, p. 152–94).

Their view depends on a dogmatic theory of language. It involves the uncritical belief that all words and sentences work in the same way. That is, that words refer to things, and sentences picture or represent how things stand to one another. Often this appears to be so. We can think of the word 'tree' as standing for the object 'tree', or the name Bill Clinton as standing for the ex-President of the USA. This is the referential view of language.

However when we come to use mental terms such as talk of our thoughts, feelings, desires, then this referential view of how language works breaks down. For language is a way of communication, of being in touch with people, rather than one solely for representation. *My own relation to my words is wholly different from other people's* (Wittgenstein,1958, p. 192). So the words used to describe me by another person will differ from my own use of words that express me. We do not merely describe our feelings, thoughts, and so forth, but we express them. If I say genuinely that I am sad my utterance has a different function from description, I am expressing sadness in words and gesture. There are no such processes as thoughts, feelings, desires, and so forth, that go on in a mind; this is an illusion created by a rigid attachment to the referential view of language. We express our thoughts, feelings, intentions; they are language dependent but not objects we observe (Wittgenstein, 1958; Fogelin in Sluga and Stern, 1996; Sluga in Sluga and Stern, 1996).

The psychoanalytic attachment to the referential theory of language leads to an endless task of analysis and a radical dehumanization as it ignores the authority of first-person expressions in claiming to know what goes on in the mind of others. It is an illusion of privilege to suppose that the mind of others is transparent. For the privileged have easy access to, and live according to, the culturally available narrative structures that they use to make sense of their lives. Psychoanalysis itself is such a structure.

Psychoanalytic theories assume that we know ourselves by means of identification. For psychoanalysis, identification is not simply one psychical mechanism among others, but is the operation itself whereby the human subject is constituted (Laplanche and Pontalis, 1973: Identification). As has been pointed out, first-person awareness does not depend on identification, it is only third-person awareness of other people's states of mind that may involve identification. So according to psychoanalysis our personality is an alien structure.

The results of this alienation can be seen in psychoanalysts' attachment to their own theories; they imagine that theories are things to be possessed! Hence the quarrelling and splits between the various schools; they are unable to reason. It requires dispassion. Consider Freud's and Klein's analysis of their own children. Ordinary common sense tells us that a responsibility for a parent is to nurture the dignity of the first-person stance in their children, especially in adolescence when it can be rather shaky. Respect for the other is surely basic to love, which is not a demand, fuelled by idealization, that a person be in a certain way; but rather a free gift that respects the particularity and authority of the other and does not rush in to correct her supposed deficiencies. Neither Freud nor Klein recognized the primacy of love; they had a purely instrumental attitude to people and a scientific theory of language, idealizing their own theories and using a particular technique derived from them to 'improve' people in the light of their theory.

To make a psychoanalytic theory useful rather than merely idealizing the possessor, to use it to clarify my self-deceptions and so make my life less conflictual, cannot be done by me directly taking it over as I might take possession of a gift of money. It is not merely to agree that the knowledge conveyed by the theory applies to me, for that would be to take an essentially third-person stance to myself. I would be taking it as the correct description of some feature of mental life, just as I assume that a description of the human heart applies to my heart.

In natural science we find out if the theory contains some truth by seeing if its predictions are right, if experiment confirms it or not; we can check it objectively; its validity does not just exist in the mind of the theorist to be handed over to another mind. But in so far as a theory throws some light on my state of mind I have to acknowledge it, to realize my commitment to its truth. This requires a shift of attention from my states of mind to their expression in my activities in the world. I must deliberate in my own way and this will involve a categorical shift in my use of language. I express myself, no longer using language referentially as would an observer describing what he thinks is going on in my mind.

Thus if a psychoanalyst tells me that I am re-experiencing some part of my forgotten life by substituting him for my father then, if I take this as merely a manifestation of transference, an application of the theory and special procedures of psychoanalysis, this would be to take myself as another. It would just be stating a fact about the mental life of people in psychoanalysis. It is only by turning my attention to what I am actually doing, to my muddled thinking and feeling and the way they manifest themselves in my life, rather than to the peculiarities of my mind, that I make his remark mine; that is, I take responsibility for what I am doing.

Supposing I entirely agree with Freud's 'findings' and explanatory theories, or rather with the particular 'findings' and theory that I fancy, because there are many different theories in psychoanalysis and it would be contradictory to believe them all. How do I know that my understanding is correct? After all, I am in analysis because I am self-deceived. How do I know that my beliefs are not due to subtle forms of suggestion? How do I know that I believe in the theory merely because I want to? My analyst confirms that my beliefs are correct but how do I know that she is not deceived?

Supposing I am cured of my neurosis after seeing my analyst for some years. This surely proves her theories are correct. But this would be to fall for an elementary fallacy made frequently by psychotherapists. The fact that a treatment works does not tell us how it works. We cannot assume it works because of the theories the analyst happens to believe. Perhaps what was really important was that the analyst was a kindly lady who listened to me patiently and put up with my tantrums; her theories merely kept her happy and enabled her to remain a member of the psychoanalytic group she depended on for referrals. There is no evidence that any theory held by psychoanalysts makes the slightest difference to their clinical results; it just influences the language they use. What is important is the ability of therapists to help their clients 'step back' from their beliefs and impulses and so deliberate and freely decide their actions; this involves tact, encouragement, and insight.

Freud quite rightly realized the importance of the fact that our ordinary discourse is littered with misrecognitions, forms of nonsense, slips of the tongue; that often a truth about ourselves is revealed in our abortive actions, dream images, and symptoms. And this also applies to our inner speech and thoughts. But his theories contradict this important insight because he modelled them on those of natural science and ignored the truthfulness of first-person awareness. If truth in psychoanalysis emerges from the mistake, as is argued by Lacan (1988, pp. 261–72) then it is difficult to see how if a person believes a theory is true then it necessarily contains a truth about that person. In fact people may disagree entirely with their analysts' theories and interpretations and yet gain considerable benefit. The therapy helped them find where they themselves stood; they were helped to find their own first-person authority because the analyst created a space for reason to grow rather than indoctrinating the person with the theories of the mind that the analyst fancied.

An analysis must fit the form of whatever theoretical framework is being deployed. Theories concerning objects remote from perception use analogy. Thus noone can perceive the internal world and its objects, so psychoanalytic theorists use schemas and models to describe what they imagine to be the structure of the mind. But analogy depends on the concept 'similar'. Thus we classify whales as mammals as we are struck by their similarity to mammals; but it would be equally rational to say they are a peculiar form of fish; it would merely reflect a difference of interest in the society. Freud had a genius for seeing analogies. Parapraxes and dreams are similar to neuroses; there are similarities between the story of *Oedipus Rex* and the loving and hostile wishes a child experiences towards its parents; internal objects are 'similar' in some respects and 'dissimilar' in others to the objects we can see.

But analogy presupposes a taxonomy – a scheme for classifying. It has been pointed out that 'the use of the word "rule" and the use of the word "same" are interwoven.' (Wittgenstein, 1958: 225). So the perplexities surrounding the concept of rule-following dog also that of similarity; similarity does not depend on rails fixed to reality. So no schema or model in psychoanalysis founds a truth; identity and difference depend on our point of view.

Truth

Freud claimed that psychoanalysis was a search for truth, but the only notion of truth he recognized was the empirical scientific one; he never even argued that that can be the only one. For example, few would claim that mathematical truths are empirical. He never recognized the difference between truth and truthfulness; it is the latter that is most relevant in a relationship. Thus psychoanalysts often imply that if an interpretation provokes change then it is true. However, this is not a criterion of truth but one of effectiveness. Thus, if a therapist tells a patient that she must carry on seeing him otherwise she will go mad then this 'advice' may well work and the patient agree. But it is certainly not a criterion for the truth of his assertion.

This distortion of the notion of truth is basic to psychoanalysis. Thus the Freudian notions of wish fulfilment and desire are based on the experience of satisfaction (Laplanche and Pontalis, 1973, p. 156). This primal experience, as postulated by Freud, is based on his assumption of the initial helplesness of human beings, in which the organism can be in a state of tension that can be removed only with the aid of an outside person who brings food and so provides satisfaction. He goes on to assume that satisfaction is thenceforth always associated with the image of the object that has procured it, so when the tension recurs the original object will be hallucinated. Thus real satisfaction and the hallucinatory one constitute the basis of desire. The formation of the ego, the fulfilment of wishes, and reality testing are all based on this picture.

This has profound consequences. It means that noone knows what they really want unless they have been properly analysed. If I want a glass of milk then the psychoanalyst knows that what I 'really' want is my initial experience of satisfaction at my mother's breast. This picture of the nature of desire and its dependence on the expert gave a rationale for consumerism. Edward Bernays, Freud's nephew, the great pioneer of public relations, used it to sell Freud's work in America (Ewin, 1996) and to make many fortunes by helping to create a consumerist society – the technique being not to attend to what people ordinarily say they want, to their truthfulness; but to their subliminal desires, what the expert knows they 'really' want. In psychoanalysis this picture is used to great effect to create the 'need' for psychoanalysis.

Wittgenstein in many places criticized this picture that for thoughts and desires to be true we need three things – the thought, the fact, and satisfaction (Wittgenstein, 1975, §3). This is a mythology of psychology which ignores what everyone knows and must admit. The fulfilment of the expression of a desire, say to eat an apple, does not consist in a third thing happening such as satisfaction or pleasure but is tautologically fulfilled by my being given an apple. Of course, we may then feel pleasure, satisfaction, disappointment, and so forth, but none of these are necessary to make sense of the desire. Freud's theory amounts to: *If I want to eat an apple, and someone punched me in the stomach, taking away my appetite, then it was this punch that I originally wanted* (Wittgenstein, 1975, §3, part 22).

Freud ignored the difference between the grammar of language, which we can disobey and reason about, and the regularities of the facts in the world, which we cannot. We express our desires and wishes in language, whereas tension in an organism is a fact of nature that is beyond reason. There is no evidence that a small baby has such a developed language that it can recognize images. A baby's activities provide the prelinguistic behaviour that founds language; it is not born with a language. As he so often does, Freud projects his own beliefs into people, especially into those who cannot answer back.

The difficulty is that we often find it very difficult to decide what we want, we readily change our minds and want more, and when we get what we asked for we are disappointed. It is this that makes us vulnerable to the siren voices of psychoanalysis and consumerism. But this does not mean that there is a 'real' desire lurking in our unconscious known by a group of experts but that we often cannot decide what we want. As was pointed out most rigorously by Kant, reason itself tends to overstep all possible use in experience, and that is the source of the endless cravings of desire.

Theoreticians of the mind in psychoanalysis are similar to metaphysicians who Voltaire observed: 'are like minuet dancers, who, being dressed to the greatest advantage, make a couple of bows, move through the room in the finest attitudes, display all their graces, are in perpetual motion without advancing a step, and finish at the identical point from which they set out.'

There is no evidence that belief in any metapsychology enables treatment to be more effective. It may reassure the believer, exercise his ingenuity, and make him knowledgeable, but this does not make it true. But it is truth-telling that heals.

Conclusion

The asymmetries between the first-person perspective and the third-person perspective on mental life are basic to the concept of a person. They have a profound influence on how we value and treat ourselves and others, and how we use language in knowing ourselves in contrast to others. The natural sciences seek causes because nature is passive before their investigations and cannot answer back; but humans can, they are free to speak and reason and are not passive objects. This is essential to their nature as persons. Psychoanalysis and many forms of psychotherapy treat the mind, especially when they theorize, as if it were part of nature, just another organ like the brain or liver but more complicated. But by doing this they do not recognize persons as ends in themselves and use language as if its sole use was representational.

Neurosis and psychosis are disorders of reason. The logic of their treatment must be the logic of reasons rather than of causes; questions of sense, meaning, and truthfulness are important rather than truth and the discovery of mental mechanisms. Reason is duplicitous because self-deception as well as self-knowledge can stem from it. Animals cannot be deceived about themselves. So the task is not to create more and more elaborate theories of the mind but rather to understand the nature of reason, pay attention to how we are with one another, and how language deceives and illuminates.

CHAPTER 6

Letting thought happen: language and psychotherapy

BARBARA LATHAM

A.

A.i. You find words beautiful – the right word like a fine stone found at the beach. For me a word is only a bullet.
A bullet shot straight at her as she is, inevitably, condemned.
If any word could be lodged, out of context, a bit of shrapnel, fixed and solid to worry over and always an accusation, what could I say?

A.ii. Your repertoire of words includes 'love' and 'understanding' but they are not in mine. Never presume that is a little drama we might play together. All I know is hate or rage. That or going numb. ('Catatonia is safer than murder', she later says.)

Although psychotherapy is referred to as the 'talking cure', we face many impediments to conversation – making time for difficulties masked in much of our lives.

We may enter a consulting room afraid of ourselves, or afraid for ourselves, or go in and uncover much getting in the way of the hoped-for exchange.

A.iii. I dreamt of my hands reaching out, to be in touch with you but missing – thwarted by fumbling after too many years spent out of touch with anyone.

That dream is truer than this non-stop talk. I prepare all the things to say and fill each session but who am I speaking to when I still can't begin to look at you? [E.v.] [Where several vignettes are taken from one therapy, the section, for example E, and the number, for instance v, are given in brackets so that those who wish can cross-reference.]

A.iv. Even here I'm set on winning over the audience. How are you to place any faith in me when I hear myself ingratiate? [E.iii.]

If what is told in therapy are tales of a self, told for a reason, are they entirely to be believed?

A.v. *Therapy suits me too well. I'm usually at the mercy of misgiving – uncertain as to how I will be found out.*
Here I am the author of myself and who can contradict? [C.ix.]

A.vi. He arrived with sharp, metallic certainties – he was a robot and I the authority.
We appeared to be stuck with the categorical belief that he knew he lacked whatever constitutes humanity and needed an expert. Fixing a faulty object seemed to be my set task.
It was one way to begin.
(His taking ecstasy seemed to make more of a difference to him.)

A.vii. *'My sexual life began at six', she said matter-of-matter-of-factly. 'I see nothing wrong with it. The man was kind to me.'*
Nevertheless she came because she was unraveling over yet another lover treating her badly.
Men used her, she believed and was beside herself. [A.xiii.]

A.viii. *'Don't speak to me as if I was a person!'* [A.i.]

A.ix. She was in trouble and sent to therapy – it was excruciating for her. *'Don't look at me! Whatever you do don't look!'*
She could come only if I promised never to make her speak of herself. It was a year before I knew her father looked on her at birth and, seeing a defect, insisted that she, unlike her siblings, definitely was not his. He never relented over this.
The mother was determined her daughter must struggle on as if the considerable physical disability did not exist – she must contrive to make part of herself invisible at home and school.

A.x. Another woman half hides as I open the door, then keeps her back to me.
She would prefer therapy to be a talking about, rather than a showing, herself.
The complicated past (before her birth and soon after) apparently provides an impenetrable thicket to be cleared. Might she then become more visible? [B.vi.]

A.xi. She comes locked in a legacy – a crucial imperative when growing up was to render herself inaccessible to her father's sexually predatory eyes and intrusive ways. [D.v., C.viii.]

A.xii. She lived in terror. I never doubted that, as she rocked on the couch wrapped about herself, banging her head on the wall.

With no possibility yet for a meeting of minds, I go some of the way with her: although the horrors she insists come from a colleague's room are not what I can share, I can make sure I finish my time with her at 11.15 a.m. while he works on the hour.

It makes a considerable difference that I have taken account of her fears, so she never leaves my room to find him opening his door.

It takes a couple of years before we have woven enough for her to begin to see she might be sealed in old fears that no longer prevail and for me to make more sense of her state.

A.xiii. How can she tell me, when she is lost in a sea of equally unreliable words?

How would what I say be any more reliable?

Where, then, do we begin to find anything meaningful?

Language was used for deceit.

What was actually happening was ignored – including her being left for a year as a small girl.

What was addressed was how things were supposed to be.

Together we slip and slide – sentences pouring out as she arrives at the wrong time or the wrong day.

Slowly the ritual slots into place and the routine holds.

Then a few vivid dreams come to her. Several of them still clear to me 13 years on, these dreams provided something different.

She believed they were important and protected them (as she failed to do with most of herself), looking to wonder if her words to me could convey their power. And she now had a way of listening to hear if my words showed I was seeing enough of what mattered to her.

She'd been a painter with more trust in images, but not all words were equal trickery once they related to clear dreams. [A.vii.]

A.xiv. 'Matilda told such dreadful lies' making others gasp and stretch their eyes, as they saw her fail to grasp the facts family adherence demanded.

'That poem seemed planted in my Christmas book to shame me.'

She was ready to apologize if only she could see what they knew to be obvious. For her, certainties slipped away – dropping her down a chute of doubt. Bewildered by what they insisted was the truth, it wasn't until teenage years that she began seeing their fixed views on everyone outside the family were absurd – that their beliefs on racial difference were not common prejudice but utterly bizarre.

But still she isn't sure if anything she says to me is true.

A.xv. *Children weren't supposed to know. They didn't give us any details so I imagined what might be going on from what my senses told me. Although an active imagination gave me more of the truth, it was suspect. It still is, I'm afraid.* [B.iii., E.i.]

A.xvi. *Their conviction was scary. You are this – you are that – because you are our daughter.*

At school I loved a dressing up box – seeing if I could wear something else.

At home I stared in the mirror, puzzled over how they saw all of what I was. They claimed to have God at their disposal.

'I don't want your interpreting – I want to find for myself.'

She feels a need to keep me gagged until . . . [B.vii.]

A.xvii. We meet to engage week after week. She has been judged the wrong kind of daughter, the wrong kind of child at school, and then the wrong kind of person seeking help.

We hover on the edge of proving this true once again – that I am the wrong kind of listener, or she not the right sort of person to be in therapy.

For her, these categories are clear and it is assumed I share them.

Although most denunciation is reserved for herself, there is fury and contempt for where I fail to get the measure of her despair.

'She is in siege with herself', she says but how to begin finding a way out if it is certain I can only confirm that life-long, harsh indictment that she is destructive and wrong?

Nevertheless we are helped by her unrelenting and scrupulous honesty as well as sincerity of purpose. [A.i., A.viii.]

A.xviii. In her teens she was sent to a mental hospital by a doctor she trusted to listen to her troubled soul and visions of being at Christ's cross.

She recognized that my judgment not carrying any authority to impose a 'medical solution' is what enabled her to come, but remained profoundly wary.

Her getting to my door implied a wish to risk once again sharing her confusions, however, one step inside the room she froze.

'I can't be caught out and exposed – I wouldn't survive it a second time.'

This pattern went on and on. [E.iv.]

A.xix. Her mother was the one who knew.

She came and spoke in tongues and marvelous metaphors.

She had come from hospital where she had yolk all over her head, she said, from reaching up to what she thought was sky and finding she broke blue birds' eggs.

A suicide attempt, the doctor said.

For several years she did to me what might have been done to her – she drowned me out.

I could not be heard until the multitude of entrancing images could be understood and not dismissed as mad. [F.v.]

Some argue that these difficulties in communication arise if you attempt a therapeutic discourse with anyone who wishes to come.

It is implied that if you select only those who can 'make use of an interpretation', language can be used as a tool by therapists and suitable patients (those who are ready and willing to play our game).

But how can language not be problematic?

Psychotherapy itself draws our attention to the complexities of being in language and to what we can, with honesty, say of ourselves.

To wonder at what can be conveyed and what can't be grasped, aren't we attending to being human?

B.

Therapy is not a particular conversation. Some assume it is a telling of their history, so that is their way to begin and, thankfully, exchanges vary enormously with each person. Few arrive expecting us to work directly with symptoms. (In therapy, as in literature, truth is honoured by moving indirectly.) More often people start wanting only to put out their version of events, seeking to have it reinforced (and might be shocked to realize how little they control what is seen).

Some feel they have to obliterate if there is to be space for their understanding to exist.

B.i. *'It has to be your mind or mine!'*

There are therapists who rise to this as a power struggle they ought to win, if they have 'the truth'.

B.ii. Only if I stay 'entirely professional' (not much of a person) can he conceive of a place where he will not be further burdened by responsibility.

It was put on him to look after his deaf and mute sister who took the time and attention.

Others appear oblivious as to how they might be influenced by our responses and silence. But in a context of communication, where meaning unfolds and interconnections spun, how can the therapist not be part of the subtle process?

If we are in the room and present to the person, how is it possible just to observe and monitor?

Once we establish a ritual practice of meeting regularly, setting aside time to be together in silence and with attention to what is said, we become aware of what is keeping things fixed so that nothing else comes into view. The righteous may keep on tracks but so do those convinced they are one thing, whether faulty in some particular way, or much maligned.

As most people come with intention they begin to listen to themselves.

B.iii. *Why am I driven to make a good story of myself as if nothing less will do?* [A.xv., E.i.]

B.iv. *I've been vile – kicking and fighting my way towards the love I'm certain I need.*
Then, despite myself, here we are drawn back to this.
Do you wipe out weeks of nastiness?

B.v. Then: *niggling doubt that nothing you hear is cherished makes me clam up. You get some sense of my life then move on to the next one, as if all this from me had never been.*
Later: *I get so caught in those old demands, which I put on you. What really sustains is what I radiate, yet convince myself I'm barely prepared to live if it can't be guaranteed I'll be important.*

B.vi. Another, who comes to speak but is afraid of being seen, comes with dreams of being sealed in plastic capsules. She can't make any contact.
Gradually what encloses is permeable, until she manages to free one arm through a wardrobe wall to reach towards me.
She can nearly touch me in her dreams. [A.x.]

B.vii. *Maybe that isn't quite accurate: mother would adamantly disagree.*
How do you know if what you say corresponds to what actually happened?
Sometimes what I bring to you briefly takes on substance and conviction, but my shadows of perpetual doubt wait outside your door. [A.xvi.]

B.viii. *Perhaps I erected a folly in the garden of a somewhat barren heart to re-feel all this.*
It kicked me alive but if I'll never leave a second lot of kids, was it ever real?
It wasn't simply ridiculous.
But what is absurd is a man shut up with a woman with sex off the menu – it couldn't happen anywhere else in my life.

B.ix. *I wanted my stories and ideas heard but whenever I began they were quickly snatched up. Mother was a therapist and knew what everything really meant. I can't carry on blaming her. It's me. Before I'm even half sure what I'm trying to tell you, my sense of things is whipped up to some intellectual confection. I see you aren't interested in them – nor am I. Despite their sterility I can't stop.*

Any effort to give voice to what might be meaningful is choked with psychotherapy theory she doesn't resist reading. She also brings a bombardment of short-cut clichés from magazines and ready-made programmes for living in self-help books (also offered to me).

She remains puzzled as to whether what establishes meaning for her is indeed some authority outside herself. She jumps into meta-comments about her thought and behaviour (but so do therapists, unless they reserve this habit for when they are discussing colleagues).

Therapy is not a business of being told about oneself by books or therapists, it is more a learning to recognize something of oneself. If the experience of therapy is partly letting thought happen, our task as therapists cannot be to pass on our own thoughts or speculations about people and their past.

Once we begin talking about things, rather than addressing what is being shown to us, we can only encourage those in therapy to do the same.

Of course, many therapists agree that they address what is manifest in the room, even if it is their own system of belief (often to do with child development) which they are seeking and finding.

It is hard to see how this can help people come more alive to ways of thinking they want for themselves.

B.x. *I used to find it easy to pray. I grew up with it. At school I liked the peace of chapel – emptying myself and finding an idea or image rise in the stillness. I want that back. These days my head is permanently engaged – as if being busy with lists and mending the washing machine is its only track.*

We know that people in therapy who decipher whatever comes their way according to one particular code cannot let the unexpected appear. However, this capacity in language for making constructions, which we then believe, gets in the way for all of us. Even words of wisdom, from our predecessors' thought, are too liable to detach themselves and turn into preconceptions. Yet it is obviously alluring to attach oneself to someone more esteemed, whether Freud or R.D. Laing.

Given our capacity to hold on to beliefs and generally misuse ideas, how can we expect ourselves, or anyone, to have a simple relationship with language?

As we are drawn into the manifold complications of human speech, none of us is to be entirely trusted.

C.

Language is there before us – a particular family and cultural discourse already in play, with a grammar to structure our minds.

If we are to speak at all we can only join, to become suspended in particular conceptions (for example, notions of what constitutes a self are shaped by different languages and then vary considerably with each era).

We can have no foundation for viewing ourselves outside what we inhabit.

How could we have any absolute or pure thought that is not part of the shared language in which we are already immersed?

C.i. She spun for 24 hours with the astonishing force of one in the grip of an eruption which would no longer be denied.

Insisting she was a spinning wheel, her usual strength increased to push off two men who took it upon themselves to insist she rest, she was driven and claimed she would stop only once she'd found the pure thread of herself to spin.

It was a start – it brought her to recognition that there was no way out of a power struggle if she was not going to accept being told what she thought. She'd hoped that, rather than fight, she'd find direct access to herself, but found those she'd expected to help were as quick as most of us to take over her half-formed sense of things and tell her what it meant. [D.vi.]

C.ii. His 4-year-old was fascinated by death and kept asking when granny would be dead.

One night when the boy asked 'where do all the dead people go?' the father began an explanation, only to be cut short with an emphatic 'no, they go back into that light.'

'Where does that come from? What can it possibly mean to him? I'd be more comfortable assuming it's his way of refusing to consider decomposing flesh but he didn't sound defensive, just matter of fact.' [B.x.]

What, of all we might attend to, are we seeing?
The ancient Greeks were looking to see the gods show themselves but who can even speak of such things now?

C.iii. Her parents still think Indian, she says, but she grew up in London. 'If I don't see things as they do, I'll be lost to my family' – and her extended network matters. She has no wish to live 'selfishly, proving I can be an individual, cut off from my community.'

Nevertheless, she came saying she was afraid, *'perhaps I'll become lost to myself if I never express how things are for me.'*

Both literally and figuratively she speaks a different language from her family.

C.iv. *'My daughter'*, she says, *'takes up any words she hears – she is quick and absorbs them accurately – she only has to hear a word once – it's rare she uses any incorrectly. Presumably she fills them with more comprehension over time. She used the word "library" long before she'd ever been in the one we pass on the bus. Do we all take up the same words to suffuse with differing comprehension?'*

The discipline of the practice supposedly holds us back from jumping to conclusions about what is being meant by the use of even familiar words. We keep listening, as we might persevere with poetry (reading and re-reading till we get the feel of it, not reaching for a theoretical commentary on the text).

It is more a matter of capacity to stay with the baffling than going into the consulting room equipped with a system of knowledge for ready interpretations, translating the patient's words into our own. However, if we as therapists are not equipped with superior knowledge, we can only cultivate limited qualities of perceptiveness or discrimination: claiming expertise provides more protection, especially in the face of those who know us all too well!

C.v. She is teaching on a counseling course and says she is *'fully adept at therapy-speak and cynical.'*

'I've always been applauded as highly articulate. Who knows where any of it is connected?'

She no longer attempts speaking in her mother tongue – *'that is when I truly despair at my success.'*

We attempt to meet the person we are with – *'don't speak to me as if I was a person!'* And often go back, over and over the same detail, for either or both to get a better feel of what is being said.

C.vi. She was beginning to gather details and told me a fact.

'I have found out', she says *'that I was 2 when I was sent to boarding school.'*

To get by she learnt to disconnect – whether the mother is dead or alive, whether she is dead or alive to her mother, is a regularly, recurring dream.

One great horror was disintegrating after taking acid, when she became isolated in outer space, eternally unable to make contact.

She sought herself through the accounts of others and wondered, at first, if I might provide her with a story, patched together from theories of child development, telling her what it meant to be sent away at 2.

We had this fact between us but would we ever share much sense of its significance?

We met over many years.

An institution had held her in place growing up – our routine of meeting and the consulting room became another fixture. It was through disruption to this, with holiday breaks and a change of our meeting place, which prompted such disconnection, it was as if we'd barely ever met, that both of us were shown something of what happened to her. Facts – illegitimate and sent away at two – which could only be spoken lightly early in our contact, began to gather weight. [G.ii.]

Together we made more sense of patterns in her life; we did not reach an explanation. Over time people can become more aware of their reasons, or grateful that their behaviour is more comprehensible, but that is the best therapy can do (Heaton, 2000). It is not the same as knowing the causes of human suffering – any such knowledge base would enable prediction, which analysts have been singularly unable to do. Who knows how any life will unfold?

C.vii *'I can't bear to watch her make my mistakes, but what can I do?'*

Her daughter turns away sharply these days if she attempts to mention anything to do with physicality.

'I am beginning to accept I can't just pass on what I know, and nor can you.'

C.viii. *When I agreed to come for three months, I expected to just get things off my chest about my father, as if it would be that easy to make peace with myself and him.*

I supposed I could pass on what hadn't been said, as if it was simply there in waiting. One way of dealing with him was to try and never be properly present. I got proficient at going AWOL while he hit. If I was only half there it's hardly surprising this is difficult. Disconnecting made it seem safer with him but I'm left still semi-absent to myself. [A.xi., D.v.]

C.ix. She writes poetry I can admire. *'At least there were words for making a game with the day – nothing else was my own – with 11 of us and a small place, even my bed was shared.'* [A.v., E.vi.]

She never missed a session but rarely let me finish a sentence, possibly keeping me to my better intentions of saying what is required and only what is required.

D.

Making space to attend to what has not previously been seen, with some-one who can bear to witness our anguish, faults and contradictions, creates strong emotions.

As therapists we listen for the way we are addressed and what might be being assumed in that. Usually it is not explicit.

D.i. *My family keeps its hold – some knotted and steeled frame has a grip, though so much of me falls through the gaps. Unfocused rage at all they were unable to hear, made you seem the incarnation of perfect understanding – as if I could rely on you absolutely.*

Oh well, I can, at least, still bring my dreaming here, while mother continues ringing every day to be petulant about the weather.

We hear the pain of human life and a particular version of it.

Since we have all been involved in story telling from birth, we bring a fundamental sense of narrative intelligibility to what is said.

People claim that it is the first time anyone listened without waiting impatiently to change the subject or to have their say. For some it is time to dare to speak.

D.ii. *What was maddening was not what actually occurred, although that was grisly and terrifying – Dad's eruptions of violence were extreme – but then we had to pretend they'd never happened. She kept away. She could not stand up to him and we weren't allowed to say what he'd done. Not to her – not to anyone. Her only acknowledgement was to offer us sweets I couldn't accept. It was crazy but I'm the one in therapy, not them. I was the one who grew afraid of being mad.*

D.iii. She was suicidal and her doctor 'sent' her.
Then: *I spend my days swamped by nameless miseries so don't expect me to talk.*

She was as good as her word, although she came regularly for months and left her heavy silence in the room.

Later: *I know it's small but to me it's a miracle. I'm learning to stay in the dark opened for whispers I used to miss when I went dead. It is astonishing that something shapes, unseen in the dark, to throw light on things before duly vanishing.*

D.iv. *I never imagined being able to tell him of my frustration. Anyway he fell on to the pillow and into sleep as soon as he was spent.*

Although I smoldered, I bridled my tongue for fear of saying more

than I meant. Since he was the one to kindle sparks in the first place, I was scared of destroying more than I knew.
Thank goodness I took the risk.

Pitfalls in plenty await, as they do everywhere in language.

Some get carried away with what they find to say, insisting on inflicting it on friends or family as 'the truth'.

In the existential novel *I am not Stiller* (Frisch, 1954), the hero writes:

> At times I have the feeling that one emerges from what has been written as a snake emerges from its skin. That's it; you cannot write yourself down, you can only cast your skin. But who is going to be interested in this dead skin?

D.v. *My sister complains that therapy is turning me into an 'emotional flasher'. I can't resist flaunting my bits of story. I still hate being looked at as much as when I started. It sounds absurd but, while I'm doing my emotional peep show, I have the illusion of being in control of what is seen. At least my sister and I talk a bit. A first in the family.* [C.viii., A.xi.]

Equally we therapists can flash our latest reading.

D.vi. A woman who came with a long struggle ahead to think for herself arrives from a previous therapy with an interpretation she's been given and passes it on to me as if it's some truth of herself. In fact its in fashion, though the woman probably doesn't know that: 'Your problem is you fail to recognize the difference between your urethra and your vagina', she is told. She is an experienced nurse in a gynaecology department. [A.ii.]

D.vii. *Will you agree to leave alone my mother, my father and good breasts? I've had a bellyful of those already – not that I understood half what my previous therapist said.*

D.viii. *'Don't talk to me as if I was a person'*, she has to tell me. She might have said you are missing me and merely talking at me.

It isn't easy to speak only to meet the other. When we don't resist temptation to engage people with our notions about them (even though these are likely to be meaningless comments or a serious distraction) they can be mystifying, to play a part in establishing our power, or encouraging a false knowingness.

Since the enterprise is for the patients to connect with themselves, the exchange seems most reliable when it takes on a life of its own in their language.

Sometimes what has been denied bursts forth with disconcerting force.

D.ix. During 'psychotic episodes', language bubbles up in her and over-flows on the bus or with anyone she passes on her way. She speaks volumes and can't hold any of it together. When she is once again man-ageable to herself and housemates she has limited connection to what was said and we are back, trudging slowly towards the startling truths in it.

It can be disconcerting to leave people to find their own solutions if you watch them take serious risks, but we are not there to interfere, 'for their own good'.

People in extremis can still be working out what they need to do, if we don't interrupt (this is one of the crucial points made by R. D. Laing).

D.x. *'Even at my craziest a small corner of me recognized that while I was driven by a frantic search for where he was hidden, I was also work-ing my way to face the fact that I'd never find him. Eventually I sent off for his medical records, half knowing that proof he was dead would arrive in the post. And then the madness would have to end.'*

She'd surfaced, badly injured, from a coma to be told her young hus-band was killed in the crash. Friends and family had been through the initial shock she'd been unable to share. The disjunction was too great and she convinced herself of a conspiracy until she was ready for sorrow.

Unlike presentations of our work, thought in therapy is not linear and does not have systematic coherence. In practice we go over and over the same territory, seeing it differently. We criss-cross in each way that opens up. Main themes recur, are revived, relived and augmented. We may find more mean-ing in what we have previously heard, or clarify what seemed confusing.

The facts of a person's life don't alter – 'sent away to school at 2' – but their way of speaking does. A person who arrives fixed on something, or someone, to blame, including themselves, may let the accusation find a different place, provided it's not too entrenched.

Presenting problems begin to fade from sight if the focus shifts.

Any story of the process is constructed after the event.

D.xi. *I went to where I could be left alone in silence under a sheet. I need-ed to find my way with the enormity of it. I assumed it safe to do so.*

Everything I thought I knew seemed to have been wiped out – proven to be an illusion – so how could I begin to speak while I only had old expressions? Let alone challenge those who came at me complacently with their pre-packed solutions?

'Shock' the doctor said, insisting on pills I didn't want. 'Please leave me. I need to stay with it', – but he knew 'over exposure' from too long in the water and 'shock' at a near drowning.

True, I was exposed to more than I'd faced before and shocked out of previous expectations of myself, to see I was not as I'd presumed.

Why should I ever agree to put it all behind me, as 'a nasty business best forgotten', if I'd been returned to something precious? It seemed the fullness of my life depended on not obliterating this tough gift.

I went under a sheet to stay with what needed absorbing – a subject in waiting, barely aware of being an object of interest. Others in the student hostel had a newspaper grasp of the event and wanted gory details. But I was too immersed to meet where they were shaping up an anecdote of the event. For me it had no form as yet and their words bewildered. What did they mean by 'accident', when all of it made too much sense to be referred to as 'accidental'?

Deep in the sea there'd been an enclosure that felt complete, until life abruptly thrust me out to surface in fragmentation.

There in the water was mother's death and longing to sink with her, yet I was taken up and driven to swim for survival. I could only submit to a force that seemed beyond any will I'd experienced before. And yet ...

I sought a place of refuge to take it in. They could not begin to engage with what it meant to me but were ready to interfere, 'for the best', presupposing to know what was good for me.

It took a long time to find this space, where you don't intrude with any agenda I can spot.

Something in me knows what to do and I can trust that.

Other professionals en route here were too caught up with their own ideas of help. They encouraged me to paths that were approved and in the end I went, just to prove myself to them, and in despair at losing too much of myself.

Friends are puzzled at what I gave up for this and don't see that without an opportunity to relive and articulate – going back to deep water and surfacing to make some sense – I was living shut out of the best of myself. [C.i.]

There are triumphal resting places to stop and look, admiring what can be said, yet words remain a limitless play of no winning.

Pushing oneself to find what can be put into language brings its own follies but so does that too-ready shrug of acceptance at what can't be said.

It is through serious attention to thought we glimpse the inevitability of frustration at being immersed and unable to step outside language to take any overview. In *On the Way to Language* (Heidegger, 1971), Heidegger writes, 'the essential nature of language flatly refuses to express itself in words – in the language, that is, in which we make statements about language.'

E.

Psychoanalytic ideas, like all thought, are also a product of historical forces. Despite intention, these ideas have played out to provide capitalism's requirement for mobile, detachable selves; it generates personal stories and histories to carry and define who we take ourselves to be.

A 'self' may not be an entity we can construct, nevertheless we regularly meet an expectation to cater for those in search of a stronger self-identity.

'I need support. My confidence sometimes goes shaky.' She is in her early twenties, advising the police on race relations and her certainties don't always support her!

There is a prevailing preoccupation with self-worth, self-confidence and self-assertion.

Mobility generates new questions and produces a convention for replying to the unanswerable – who are you? – where do you come from? – what are you doing?

We have become so rational in accounting for ourselves with a tangle of assertion and pride. In tune with advertising, we embark on selling ourselves.

While the Maori would give a long genealogy to place themselves, we are more likely to display how far we consider ourselves self-directed. All our history can never be spoken, but something of how we see ourselves is.

Although therapy is often asked to fortify a self and is, rightly, accused of encouraging an excessive attachment to oneself (whether one's own view of things or one's own desire or emotions), it remains a potentially subversive space. The demand is not what is met and therapy opens the possibility of facing the limits of one's own perspective, or the confines of a mind that cannot take hold of itself, as well as showing how far we are from any mastery of a self.

The subtlety with which what therapists take to be manifest can be addressed depends only partly on the therapist's skill and also on how far patients will take their awareness.

Probably none of us is as thoughtful as we like to believe, but therapy generates frustration and most people paying for the hour begin to hear themselves – even those who started with an assumption that they'd pass the listening to a therapist.

E.i. *As a child I used to dream waking to go to the toilet. All the detail would be accurate and I was sure I'd walked to the bathroom.*
I still behave as if I can imagine the world as I desire it to be. [A.xv., B.iii.]

E.ii. She looks for tiny signs, proving life is fated – that things are meant to be.

She might be able to read omens and predictive dreams but she may be seeking a way to take control rather than submit to what was done long ago over which she had no say.

It isn't easy for her, or me, to distinguish between these two.

E.iii. *He left when I was 8 and didn't say he was going. Mother made no attempt to make sense of it to us.*

I told versions to myself and friends, trying to cover the gaping cracks of uncertainty and to bandage unsightly scar tissue.

Basically I felt so unworthy if he'd left, and my presentations kept me just above that.

In therapy she traced him, only to find he was dead, depriving her of a sustaining hope of eventually getting to the definitive narrative that would finally catch 'it'. His life and desertion of her must always elude any account of it, but 'how do I give up forging illusory connections to feel better about myself?' she asks. [A.iv.]

Therapists also seem driven to illusion in asserting the value of what we do – too readily talking as if it is psychotherapy that has worked out the causes of human suffering or has the answers for it.

E.iv. She comes each week in a state of fury with herself. The hour with me increases it. She bangs her head on the wall trying to force herself back to a place she once knew. The psychiatric treatment has left her shut out of her mind she insists, but also wonders if *'perhaps I put up this barrier to myself? There has to be some way back! You could at least show me where to find the door'* she rages. [A.xviii.]

E.v. *Even if I was to crawl here on bended knee, there can never be forgiveness for some nameless crime, hidden in shame but always there behind me.*

Somewhere the irredeemable was done and never spoken – not once put in words.

I wasn't raised a Catholic, yet beneath any apparent confidence lies this tidal wave in me, beginning in no definite crime and unable to fit any name, yet threatening to overwhelm. [A.iii.]

E.vi. *Life seems to just slip by if I don't keep phrases about it to hold.* [A.v., C.ix.]

Life passes; words, however, can be kept.

Thought shifts and unfolds but we are inclined to give it shape as solid as these letters on a page.

We can say things we barely know.

E.vii. *I failed to take in he was dead. Of course I said he was and used the proper expressions but they would not sink in.*

For some there is the beguiling pull of what we can't put our finger on – perhaps an elusive question we should be asking about our body or mind?

Therapy can play seductively into the necessary uncertainty, with false promising of getting to the bottom of ourselves, or of finding the base for attributing meaning to our lives.

Meaning in history, whether private or public, derives from wide-ranging sources, depending partly on what is in fashion. Where we attribute meaning is a matter of faith.

E.viii. *I seem haunted by a possibility of wholeness I vaguely recall. Or perhaps it's only an idea. It niggles so that even if I came across a tiny bit of illumination, I can't be satisfied – I crave all the lights on full.*

Through being in language, human presence becomes unglued and divided. We become subject to the appearance and concealment of ourselves (Agamben, 1993 and 1999). We unexpectedly find something crucial of ourselves in symbols, dreams or symptoms.

Occasionally words fall into place before us and we find we have moved into them. People speak of finding a poem that affected them profoundly, long before its relevance became visible. Other times, words come much later, bringing to light what has already passed.

A symbol that speaks to us brings a double energy, from that sudden surfacing of what was previously submerged and the delight of recognition. We are taken back as well as forward – making it obvious temporality is peculiar and not linear. The satisfaction and beauty is never diminished any time we are in the presence of one of those rather rare moments, when something simply drops into place between the two of you in the consulting room.

The sense that not just the future is hidden from us takes people to many forms of divination (as well as therapy). If not at Delphi, we still come across occasional oracles to disconcert by revealing a different order of things from the usual rationality. Premonitions and some dreams also disconcert.

The conscious/unconscious split is both a recognition of a profound truth apparently always known to man and, too readily, a corruption of it into decipherment and decoding, as if we are simply a puzzle to ourselves, which could conceivably be worked out by some authoritative grand master.

As soon as we slip towards believing that therapy can decode 'the unconscious' the practice becomes quite different, for we introduce expertise. The symbolic is of an entirely different order in which, as the arts show, there is talent and occasionally impressive ability but never conquest.

F.

Language is what we share (along with an all-too-human propensity for self-deception) yet each of us has a distinctive and recognizable voice. Furthermore, we each draw words idiosyncratically from that collective pool. The variations are fascinating once people become a speaking subject, rather than subject to their 'condition'. What can be difficult in listening to 'victims', or those locked in symptoms, is the degree to which they are reduced to sounding much the same.

Voice, like breath, comes through the body and is easily constricted. A voice at odds with the rest of the person, or not passing freely, raises a question. A whining tone or an effusive, breathy sympathy immediately tells us something, even if we can't specify.

The therapist, as much as the patient, arrives in the room embodied, and the physical presence of each will influence the encounter (despite the best endeavours of believers in the blank screen).

Our tone of voice, expression and general bearing is almost certainly as important as our choice of words. Our background is visible in our voice, as is something of our temperament.

Because we have the language to claim too much, it is hard to keep straight how far we are at the mercy of our own natures and flesh, as well as external events.

We get only glimpses of those orders to which we are subject, but never a hold on them to establish a base.

It is easy to imply that completion, with full clarity, might be a possibility – to tread through the ashes of reason proud to account for ourselves.

F.i. *As my familiar shape returned after the birth so did proper sentences. During the pregnancy I panicked – what I'd taken for granted seemed to have vanished and, although I'd hear myself that some part of the sentence was in the wrong place, it just kept happening.*

F.ii. *Why don't I remember that it is the same each menstrual cycle? I'm convinced everything is just dropping away – love, my life, the lot – and duly record my misery, yet I'm always hopeful again by the end of the week.*

F.iii. *My memory has so many tricks and I'm a sucker for them. Any take on the past generally reflects my current physical state. Whenever the pain comes back everything looks entirely different.*

The atmosphere in the consulting room can be crucial, though usually people refer to it only towards the end of therapy. Just as our impact on the chemistry – whether pleasant or grim expression, or sense of humour and responsiveness – may barely be spelled out. How little of it can be addressed in any account of what is going on?

Nevertheless, vocabulary used by therapists encourages sloppy thought – the term 'pre-verbal' is used as if we can have expressions to hand to speak confidently of what is not in language, and over-used words, like 'containment', imply we know the significance and can speak of what our presence offers.

F.iv. Her smile is irresistible and my features melt into a heartfelt response.
   Who can grasp what passes in our exchange of smiles?
   Is there any need to begin to do so?
   Yet it is undoubtedly an important aspect of what is going on.

F.v. She came back after being abroad for years and didn't say she remembered one word I'd spoken but that she'd never forgotten my laugh. *I dreamt it while I was away and remembered it exactly,* she says with pleasure. [A.ix.]

Long before we speak, we respond to people about us – all our senses alert to gauge situations – and we continue to go by the nose after we add the wonder and confusions of words. Although all of it is drawn on, there can never be coherence in the way we do so. As with any art form that attempts to attribute significance, what comes to mind can surprise – 'where did that come from?' – since we draw on more than we can know and intuit much of our way with what might be happening. Sometimes a wild hunch is apt; equally often it shows more about us than the patient; we learn to hold it till we think we recognize which is which. (Therapists have, rightly, been accused of false certainties over 'child abuse' or over what is claimed to be going on in consulting rooms, and of false promises of expertise, in attempts to gain power and recognition. Listening to one another we constantly hear assumptions of comprehending more than is possible; speculation runs away with us. Then there is the pleasure of presenting therapeutic skills whereby a momentary clarity within a session becomes a knowing account).

We cannot but rely on trying to read what our imperfect bodies tell us.

To assess where the body is shaping thinking, or where notions of the self override, so that whatever the body might show cannot be registered through a haze of assumption, parallels the other difficulties for both therapist and patients in psychotherapy.

How do we speak to what might be happening without misjudging – through believing ourselves too knowing or worthless – in control or a victim? Siegfried Sassoon, writing of his time with Rivers during the First World War, addresses this:

> Even Rivers could not cure me of the youthful habit (which many people never unlearn at all) of being conversationally dishonest. All he could make me do was to make me feel uncomfortable when I thought about it afterwards, which was, anyhow, a step in the right direction. (Sassoon, 1937, p. 72)

Therapists may keep quiet until they believe they have seen clearly and not reveal all their confusions, but we have no way to discard our muddles to go into our work rendered safe for the task.

There is the idea that if you never speak of yourself you leave appropriate space for the patient – as if it is a matter of technique. While it is certainly true that many of us are eager to talk and prefer no interference, the understanding any therapist takes into the room plays its part. How we make sense of what we are offering is integral to the practice. If a therapist believes that the past *is* what it is being played out in the consulting room, or that the hidden and declared meaning of what is said does relate to themselves, their belief is likely to shape much of what unfolds.

It is not just any illusions we have of ourselves, it is whatever pictures we've made of what therapy can do, or did for us, that come into the room if we do.

Submitting to the limits of what can be said and of what we can know of another, as well as judging straight what it is that we are seeing rather than what we are believing, is a great difficulty for all of us.

G.

Although questioning the language used in the way we speak of our work and in the training of psychotherapists has been addressed more systematically by other contributors (Gordon, 1999), I conclude with a few points about preparing ourselves and others to practise psychotherapy.

Helping someone to see what has, hitherto, been imperceptible requires discernment and, there, none of us has cracked it.

Paul Klee: 'art does not reproduce the visible but makes visible' (Klee, 1961, p. 76).

A good artist shows us something more of the order of things – therapists, more modestly, have only to be midwives to patients seeing more of themselves.

We take responsibility for the frame that usually stimulates a discourse. The practice cannot reveal final truths about the patient, or human nature, but with experience we hopefully acquire greater ability to make space for others, very different from ourselves.

To take up the place of therapist is to trust oneself to speak honestly to what seems to be happening in the room. Few of us are perceptive enough to appreciate how often we fail to do so.

Our own experience of listening to ourselves in the presence of another is fundamental preparation. However, only some of our masked motives, or plays for sympathy, will have been faced – only part of our self-inflation is likely to have been unravelled.

As we meet strong emotions, many therapists vaguely hope their good hearts are more important than clear heads, as if the human heart was ever a reliable instrument.

G.i. He came with vivid dreams that were powerful and strange.
  When he left the room, part of his sad story stayed stirring me.
  All of it seemed more than could be digested.
  It grew more difficult to speak as the room, at moments, filled with surges of unspoken longing.
  I didn't doubt some of it was his, but what if it was also my own?

We put ourselves in extreme situations with some people and, of course, we make mistakes, especially when we are too quick to think we know what is being shown. Although, thankfully, people hold us back – *'don't speak to me as if I am a person'* – we can't rely on that, and many are seducible into the exchange we stimulate from ideas of our own. Notions we have taken up in training of the direction the conversation 'should' go almost inevitably foreclose.

G.ii. She was extremely ill with a recurrence of cancer, but announced, *'I can't die before I know who has lived!'*
  She wanted long-term psychoanalysis, although this seemed highly unlikely and against all medical odds. After some months I decided we 'should' address her deterioration – otherwise I might be 'colluding in a denial' of the illness, which she did not mention after the initial session.
  I asked if she'd given any consideration to arrangements she might want with me if she could no longer get to my room, as it was already problematic.
  With a ferocity I'd not seen, she snapped she didn't come to me for her cancer, everyone else was interested in that.
  Twelve astonishing years later, as we spoke freely of her death, she could tell me how nearly she came to giving up in despair at that moment, when she heard I did not share the possibility she had found for herself in my consulting room.

She had, she said, felt expectant, knowing she planted bulbs of herself in the room and felt certain she'd stay alive to see the flowering. Which is what she did.

'I felt I was finished, if even you were saying to me your illness is all there is.'

That dogged determination of hers, to reconnect to herself before she died, could be obliterated, she realized. At the time her rebuke was sufficient for me to give way. Maybe she knew better and, besides, my heart went out to her on first meeting; I thought she would soon die so was prepared to break whatever 'rules' I was still carrying with me from various supervisors.

As I stopped blocking her path, she got on with what she'd come to do. [C.vi.]

If we set up a power struggle to dictate the shape of what should be seen, we slip into dogma – the very thing therapy attempts to shift.

Given that human beings are not reducible to one system which attributes meaning, what sort of training best equips us to make space for another's attempt to make more sense of this life?

The biggest problem in preparing students for the work is to hold them back long enough to get a proper gauge of its intricacy, without erecting false hoops to put them through. (During training we were told it takes at least 10 years to make a half way decent therapist and probably longer to find one's own style. However it was only all those years later I began to experience what Laing was trying to convey.)

Perhaps the best we can do is challenge assumptions. It is, however, easier to give students new beliefs than to challenge the many that already clutter them.

In training, as in therapy, those taking on responsibility lead the way. If we stimulate students to think, instead of passing down the finished form of theories, they are more likely to be able to do the same.

The teaching faculty demonstrates the extent to which each is serving understanding more than themselves and whether they can provide a serious challenge to those in training, or are presenting, for agreement, some completion of beliefs about their work.

If a range of exchanges is possible, is it our nature or training that makes us tune into certain rhythms or patterns?

There seems to be a question of whether therapists can trust that a healing discourse will unfold without a theory suggesting what should take our attention. (At the start of my practice I was more comfortable with personal history, but have seen enough people come and find the basic view of themselves and their situation shift without discussing their childhood.)

The opening up of vision to a fuller span of the generative force of life may be a noble possibility in therapy, as in art (Klee, 1961), but what qualities help us in this endeavour?

Ordinary abilities such as perspicacity and sense probably cannot be taught, whereas any clarity over our place in the scheme of things, or the limits of personal perception, come under wisdom rather than any academic study. Although it is possible that some therapists grow more thoughtful in certain respects, we maintain the specificity of our history, nature and body and keep our blind spots and drawbacks, as family and colleagues will be quick to spot!

How we do justice to the complexity of what goes on in therapy is an obvious conundrum. Exchanges about the practice tend to degenerate into the merely anecdotal, or resort to jargon and meta-statements.

Just as the living tradition of literature has frequently and shamelessly been reduced to an object of analytic knowledge – a means for it to be displayed – so, sadly, is the practice of psychotherapy becoming subsumed by endless papers and books, which, rather than preparing us for the work of being with one another, appear to inform, giving knowledge of patients as objects.

The value for someone of being able to shift a perspective that seemed locked, cannot be conveyed to answer a challenge for evidence or proof. The urge to make more sense for oneself of what is going on, which is what brings most of us to therapy, must remain not just at the heart of the practice but in the ways we speak of that practice.

Acknowledgments

I have drawn on experience, mostly but not always, from the context of therapy, (my own as well as from those who come to work with me). There is one comment from a cousin.

I have not attempted an account of anyone's therapy but have drawn out single comments, or aspects, to illustrate an issue for the purposes of this chapter.

Except where I made notes for myself at the time, to think over what was said, the vignettes are in my words, from memory and from my sense of things.

I have not taken from the therapy what was necessarily of interest to the other person; the therapy is theirs, this presentation is a different work.

The longer passages are included with the permission of the subject. One is now dead; however we talked over the themes used here and she gave me license to speak of what is written in (C.vi.) and (G.ii.).

Although most of the short pieces are not taken from encounters in progress, any that are have been discussed. Where recurring themes are addressed, in several cases what is represented is an amalgam. In others, details have been omitted or slightly altered to protect identity. One is imagined to capture something of what seems often repeated.

I wish to acknowledge appreciation for the range of influences during my training at the Philadelphia Association – in particular the late Hugh Crawford, as my first supervisor, whose distinct pleasure in language and etymology encouraged me in my own, and R.D. Laing who drew me to the P.A. with the hope that I might be helped to think without being told what to believe and who, later, showed one way it might be done.

I also have to thank the late Hugh Crawford for giving me the experience of watching him work in one of the P.A. households and for helping me to see that what confounds eventually can be elucidated.

Above all, I am grateful to John Heaton who, over many hours of conversation, brings his rigorous mind and philosophical reading as a foil for my different way into thinking.

The work, thankfully, constantly confronts me with questions and ways to see I am still making too many assumptions.

CHAPTER 7
Wonder and the loss of wonder

PETER LOMAS

> I veer between a vision of the human race rather like Jonathan Swift's, dark
> and embittered and satirical, and a kind of idealism that maybe there are
> just enough wonderful people in the world to make us feel thrilled with the
> possibilities of the human.
>
> Joyce Carol Oates, *Middle Age*

Sentiments can never be encapsulated in discursive writing; they elude
precise definition. The sense of wonder is among those that are particularly difficult to describe; it has affinities with joy, amazement, awe, love,
beauty, ecstasy, and intensity. It can also be used in quite a different sense
as an alternative to speculation – for example, 'I wonder if there are any
cornflakes left'. But I am not concerned with this mundane sense. In what
follows, I aim to focus on the spontaneous wonder of life of which the
ordinary person is capable. At times I shall draw on my own memories of
wonder, believing that these are typical.

Wonder has much in common with love. Both states of mind are served
better by poets than philosophers. And both, I believe, bring us closer to
life, whether the feeling is directed towards life in general or to a particular thing or person. When we are aware of the wonder of life we become
more fully enmeshed within it; it is close to us, all around us; we are at
one with it, we feel a love for it. Such experiences, however, can be
ambiguous.

I have the habit, mid-morning, of walking across Jesus Green to the
town (Cambridge) to have a cup of coffee. One morning not long ago I
suddenly found myself feeling that I was approaching a strange town
about which I knew relatively nothing – probably a foreign town. I looked
at people as if they were simply people and not identifiable as shoppers
or workmen. It was an exhilarating feeling, a release. In one sense I was
detached: this was no longer the Cambridge I knew yet the world felt
closer than usual. For some reason (unknown to me) I had succeeded in
freeing myself from the defences, the conditioning, the routine, the

worried preoccupations that so beset me that I had seen an aspect of the world that normally eludes me.

Shortly after writing the above I came across an essay by Charles Simic on the poetry of Adam Zagajewski: Simic quotes an extract from a poem that, to me, gives voice, in words I cannot match, to such moments of wonder.

> The city comes to a standstill and life turns into still life, it is as brittle as plants in a herbarium, you ride a bicycle which doesn't move, only the houses wheel by, slowly, sharing their noses, brows, and pouting lips, the evening becomes a still life, it doesn't feel like existing, therefore it glistens like a Chinese Lantern in a peaceful garden. (Simic, 2002)

Simic writes: 'Poetry and thinking for Zagajewski have to do with learning how to see clearly. His poems celebrate those rare moments when we catch a glimpse of a world from which all labels have been unpeeled.'

Baudelaire describes the state of mind of the artistic genius, who is a 'man-child' or 'convalescent':

> The crowd is his domain, just as the air is the bird's, and water that of the fish. His passion and his profession is to merge with the crowd. For the perfect idler, for the passionate observer it becomes an immense source of enjoyment to establish his dwelling in the throng, in the ebb and flow, the bustle, the fleeting and the infinite. To be away from home and yet to feel at home anywhere; to see the world, to be at the very centre of the world, and yet to be unseen of the world, such are some of the minor pleasures of those independent, intense and impartial spirits, who do not lend themselves easily to linguistic definitions. The observer is a prince enjoying his incognito wherever he goes. (Baudelaire, 1981)

I have so far dwelt on experiences that occur to most of us only rarely and are sometimes referred to as 'transcendental'. But there are, I believe, experiences unremoved from daily life – in fact, deeply enmeshed in it – which could also be described as wonder.

In her novel *Your Blue Eyed Boy,* Helen Dunmore describes a scene in which a mother is on an outing with her two children:

> Once I saw them walking towards me out of a sunset. The air was dusty with harvest, the light thick. They had their arms slung around one anothers shoulders, and their hair was spiked with sweat from running. They were rimmed with gold. Then they came close and they were my boys again, squabbling, jostling for attention. (Dunmore, 1998)

The change from the transcendental to the everyday is sharply contrasted. There is no difficulty in attaching the word 'wonder' to the former experience, but what of the latter? One can well imagine that the mother loves the children with an intensity of feeling that is comparable to the previous vision. They are 'my boys'. She may well feel, at times, something like: 'How can it be that these precious beings have come, out of nowhere, into my life and are here, and they love me as I love them?' Would this not be wonder – a feeling so intense that no words can convey it? It is perhaps unrealistic to make an absolute distinction between the two states. The situation is comparable to that of emotion and reason, often considered to be quite separate entities but which we increasingly realize cannot be clearly separated.

> It is an essential element in wonder that we recognise what we see as something we did not make, cannot fully understand, and acknowledge as containing something greater than ourselves. (Midgely, 1989)

In order to match up to Midgely's formulation – which to me, is a satisfying one – the mother in the novel quoted above would need to have a capacity to love her children without the corruption of narcissistic possessiveness. The capacity for wonder in everyday life is, I believe, part and parcel of a healthy and realistic attitude to living: the world around us is accepted as mysterious and unavailable to an omnipotent desire to control it.

When we have been away from a loved person we are likely to see them afresh and with delight on our return. This feeling can also be intense when we have been, in a sense, away from the world, separated from it by serious illness or depression. The wonder that accompanies such a return is movingly described in George Herbert's poem *The Flower*.

> How fresh, O Lord, how sweet and clean,
> Are thy returns! Even as the flowers in spring,
> To which, besides their own demean,
> The late-past frosts tributes of pleasure bring Grief melts away
> Like snow in May,
> As if there were no such cold thing.
> Who would have thought my shrivelled heart
> Could have recovered greenness? It was gone
> Quite underground; as flowers depart
> To see their mother-root, when they have blown;
> Where they together
> All the hard weather,
> Dead to the world, keep house unknown.

Although Herbert is a deeply religious man he is not describing an otherworldly phenomenon, a visitation from God, but the renewal of a perception of the wonder of ordinary life which he has lost but which is now intensified by its recovery.

We can, even in health, all too easily lose this perception, worn down by routine demands, disappointments and inner constraints. Certain occurrences have the potential, if given the chance, of jolting us out of our dullness of spirits. One of these is the birth of a child, to which I shall return later.

Whatever else we might think about wonder, most of us would agree on the fact that it diminishes with the growth of experience. We know this from our own memories; we see it in the eyes of children; and poets, most notably Wordsworth, remind us painfully of the glories we can no longer see. This loss is usually attributed to the gradual erosion of the child's innocent belief in a benign world as he or she gradually loses the comforting protection of the parents and comes up against a harsh reality. Freud incorporated this view into his theory of child development and it became a pivotal theme: the pleasure principle is replaced, if only shakily, by the reality principle; the child no longer feels omnipotent.

Winnicott elaborated this hypothesis with the notion that the child believes that he has created the world. However this theme is put, the implication is that the baby enters the world by means of the Garden of Eden. But is this really so?

This world is not always kind to babies. Massacres and hunger exist in large areas of the earth; babies of most cultures are subjected to some very weird practices. And we in Western civilization, although fortunate, do not always escape unscathed. The factors that inhibit wonder do not necessarily correlate well with the degree of obvious disruption or material hardship that a child undergoes.

I do not know how much I have lost my own sense of wonder compared with most people, nor why it became lost; I can only make some guesses. My entry into life can hardly have been paradise. The birth was by means of a protracted labour and a forceps delivery. My mother's father, to whom she was devoted, was killed four days before my birth. I am told that she was in such a disturbed state that an aunt had to find a name for me. Like most babies at that time in our society I was bottle fed on a strict Truby King four-hourly schedule. Yet I have a photograph of myself at around a year old in which the eyes are full of wonder and interest in the world. One of my first memories is of being taken to a concert at my sister's school and hearing music so enthralling to me that it stayed in my head and seemed to come from another world. I now know it to have been the Polovstian Dances.

By the age of 6 or so the photographs show that the glow in my eyes had faded. Is this the inevitable loss of innocence? The child has now learned caution, scepticism, pretence and found the art of manipulation that gives protection from the manipulation of others. Or was it, in my case, a consequence of a change for the worse in the family atmosphere at that time, with which, for whatever reason, I could not cope.

The child's sense of wonder is often dismissed as a state of illusion.

This, I believe, is mistaken. Under the influence of illusion we are deceived by appearances; we believe that something is other than it is. The word usually implies that a deliberate, although not necessarily conscious, misrepresentation has taken place, either by the person himself or by somebody else. We may, on the other hand, be simply mistaken about how things stand because of our ignorance. We once believed that the world is flat: can we today be sure that our claims to understand the universe amount to so very much? And the child's ignorance of the world is in many ways even greater than ours, but this is no reason to dismiss her view as invalid.

The tendency to confuse wonder with illusion incorporates the particular form of illusion that we call idealization. Idealization defensively selects those aspects of the object that appear to be good, exalting it above all rivals, and denies the existence of any flaws.

Although a baby may well indulge in idealization of the mother, we are not justified in assuming that her feelings of wonder towards her are, on the whole, unrealistic. The baby does not know or care whether the mother is compulsively promiscuous and has a propensity for shop-lifting. If the mother stirs in her a wonder of life she is seeing an aspect of her that is real, although it may not be perceived by the local magistrate.

In my brief description of childhood memories I said that I could not be sure that the loss of wonder was due to particular circumstances or was the inevitable consequences of growth. This is probably a question we can never answer in any particular case. The former is the focus of much of the psychotherapist's work; here I am more interested in the latter. One question to ask is whether the simple acquisition of knowledge of the world leads to a deadening of our feelings. In his book *Be My Knife*, the novelist David Grossman writes:

> I don't have to tell you of my joy when he began to speak; you probably remember the wonder of a child first naming things. Although every time he learned a new word, one that is a little 'theirs', everybody's, even the first word, a beautiful word like 'light' my heart curdled about the edges, because I thought, who knows what he is losing in this moment, how many infinite kinds of glamour he left and saw, tasted and smelt, before he pressurised them into this little box, 'light' with a t at the end like a switch clicking off. (Grossman, 2002)

This is beautifully put, and, I believe, very true. The writer is quite aware of the richness that language adds to our lives but he notes the price that we may have to pay for it. The disenchantment described is one of the disadvantages of our increased capacity to gain certain kinds of knowledge and is not necessarily related to whether the knowledge is itself dismaying. Perhaps, as Charles Simic suggests, our innocent sense of wonder is lost except for moments when we 'catch a glimpse of a world from which all labels have been unpeeled'.

What is true of words is true of the impressions that precede words; the child articulates the world, in however primitive a way, from the beginning. She learns that people are not all the same; one of them, for example, lets her cling to and feed from the breast. Although we still don't know much about how a baby experiences the world, the observations of experimental psychologists increasingly reveal her early sophistication. We have to make informed guesses about the baby's experience. The guesses of psychoanalysts, which command such respect, are often bizarre and the distinctions they make too rigid. It would seem likely that the process by which the baby becomes able to deal with the world are gradual and complex. There is a continual gain and loss of her hold on the truth. She will be likely to realize that the world is not as joined up to her as closely as she thought. But this is a matter of degree. In time she will learn to make more distinctions, and, indeed, to accept the average adult's certainty of these distinctions. However, there can be doubt as to whether this is simply a passage from illusion to truth. May she not be leaving behind a truth largely unknown to the adult? There are many thinkers, such as Bohm, who assert that we compartmentalize our perception of the world to a degree that seriously distorts our comprehension (Bohm,1980). If, in so doing, we lose our sense of wholeness it is no surprise that we thereby lose our sense of wonder.

The degree to which a child is likely to lose her sense of wonder depends in part on the culture in which she lives. In the past our own society appears to have achieved a greater sense of wholeness than at present. This is a consequence of the progressive dominance of the objective mode of functioning to which Max Weber gave the name 'rationalization':   .

> Rationalisation is the product of the scientific specialisation and technical differentiation peculiar to western culture ... It might be defined as the organisation of life through an exact study of men's relations with each other, with their tools and their environment for the purpose of achieving greater efficiency and productivity. (Weber, in Freund, 1968)

This process, Weber believed, resulted in 'disenchantment'. In other words it diminished our capacity for wonder. The process has accelerated and today we are in its grip with no foreseeable path of escape.

One source of disenchantment is a pervading suspicion. We could well be called the *Age of Distrust*. Each one of us, however meagre our area of responsibility, is watched, assessed, monitored and examined. It is not the person as a whole who is assessed but a particular aspect of them; the methods of investigation are applicable (or thought to be applicable) to specific functions. Up to a point this makes sense. We need, for example, to know if someone can drive a car safely, and we need to monitor dangerous driving. But this reasonable approach to finding out who can be trusted to do what has acquired a momentum and prestige of its own that goes far beyond common sense. We are measured piecemeal and often crudely and our degree of spontaneity is as threatened as that of a child whose every movement is watched by a nervous and controlling mother.

A notable example of disenchantment with an area of life in modern society is that of childbirth. For several years I worked as a general practitioner. I did not, on the whole, enjoy the work for I lacked the necessary interest in physical medicine. But one kind of experience stands out. On the occasions of a successful home birth there was a sense of wonder in the room. I felt it to be not only in myself but in the others present. I am not speaking of success, satisfaction, accomplishment or pride, although these feelings were no doubt there, but of a sense that something had occurred that I can only describe as magic.

I can look back now, detached from the experience, and think: 'What was the future of those babies, and their mothers? Were we denying the harsh realities of life and living a while in a fool's paradise?' But I do not think so. We were living in the moment, our defences down, especially those of the mother. Wonder, however, is a dangerous state of mind. If something untoward and unexpected occurs we are not ready to withstand it. I suspect that this may be a factor in post-natal depression.

That such experiences are possible in childbirth is a poignant reminder of the fact that, under the influence of modern technological medicine, such experiences are more difficult to achieve. I wrote about this subject before conditions in labour wards changed for the better (Lomas, 1966). But the process is still controlled by technology; the statistics for caesareans, episiotomies, epidurals, inductions and sedation are frightening; home births are a tiny minority.

The movement for a natural form of childbirth, so long the subject of distrust, is gaining influence. Because my daughter teaches active childbirth I have had the opportunity to watch quite a number of prenatal and postnatal sessions, some of which take place in a swimming pool. It would take me too far away from the theme of this chapter to give an account of the work. What is relevant, however, is the manifest state of mind of those taking part: it is a mood of happiness. Quite apart from the freedom of bodily movement, there is an atmosphere of relaxed mutual support and perhaps most notably, a bonding between mother and baby in the classes in which babies go in the swimming pool as early as at 2 months old. It is an atmosphere in which any potential for wonder is likely to be aroused. The movement has, I believe, much to teach psychiatry; and perhaps psychotherapy too. It is significant that RD Laing took an interest in and made a contribution to natural childbirth.

Where is the place of wonder in psychotherapy? Let us plunge into the deep end. I imagine writing a book on *How to Practise Psychotherapy*. I begin something like this.

> Before meeting the patient you should compose yourself into a frame of mind in which to be receptive to wonder. There in front of you is someone who is unique and mysterious. There is no replica. Here is a person who has lived on this strange earth and tried, as far as he or she can, to survive it, to make sense of it and to maintain their original passion. What piece of work is a man. And this person is coming to me with whatever trust they can muster and whatever hope is left in them.

The opening words of my imaginary book are, I think, no more bizarre than Bion's suggestion that we approach the patient 'without memory or desire'. And, indeed, there is an element in common, shared in Freud's advice that we engage with 'free-floating attention'. We are not prejudiced towards the patient in a particular way. We do not think 'I must first make a diagnosis. Is the patient hysterical or obsessive or what?' But there is a notable difference. Bion's admonition is in keeping with the psychoanalytic tradition of emotional detachment and is not an encouragement to closeness. Wonder, I believe, is.

Psychotherapy is still deeply entrenched in the scientific tradition and the philosophy of the Enlightenment, however much individual therapists may feel deeply and passionately about their patients and however much the subject matter is unsuited to this kind of thinking. The Enlightenment is still all around us and is nowhere more incongruent than in the field of psychotherapy.

For this reason I find it difficult to write the imaginary opening words of my book. They do not describe a technique to follow. They are an exhortation to take up a certain kind of moral attitude – and most people do not usually take kindly to such exhortations. Moreover, if it were not to be taken as the view of a starry-eyed simpleton I would have to be quick in modifying it by acknowledging that we cannot cast aside our shrewdness, our scepticism, or our capacity to spot inauthenticity and to perceive evil when it is there and deal with it appropriately.

I shall have to put the matter less extravagantly. What I have in mind is less the occasionally exhilarating and moving moment in therapy than a more low-key attitude of spontaneous appreciation of the other's presence in the room. It is the kind of experience that I described earlier as ordinary wonder. If this is a good attitude to have, how does one cultivate it?

I have not myself ever consciously tried to acquire such an attitude, yet I am sure that I possess it more than I did in my early years as a therapist. The explanation is no doubt complicated but I think it has more to do with the removal (if only partial) of harmful ways of thinking and feeling that has enabled me to be more spontaneous. Some of this change is due to the influence of certain writings and certain people who have enabled me to be more open. Some of it, I believe, is a consequence of the fact that I have gradually found myself, perhaps with the increasing confidence that comes with experience, to be less distracted than I once was when practising therapy by anxiety, greed, ambition and many other untoward emotions. In case this seems an immodest view, let me hasten to say that I am comparing my present self with how I was and that I am not assessing myself in relation to other therapists, many of whom may well have a more natural bent than I for the kind of approach that I have in mind.

I have assumed, without explanation, that an attitude that contains an element of wonder is therapeutic. It is, in fact, rather difficult to give logical reasons for the beneficial effects of sentiments because they are not techniques designed for a specific purpose. Wonder is akin to that illusive concept, wholeness. It is easier to describe the parts than the whole that is more than the sum of the parts. We know, however, from our everyday experience, that when others respond to us with respect, recognizing our intrinsic value as unique beings rather than compartmentalizing us, it has a therapeutic effect.

The suggestions I make above do not require us to dismiss the immeasurable insights we gain from psychoanalysis. But what is important, I believe, is to be wary of an approach that, as its name implies, involves a dissection of the whole into parts; and, in particular, a focus on what is wrong rather than what is valuable. Freud's advice to adopt an attitude of free-floating attention directs us to the whole but, paradoxically, his emphasis on theory and technique distract us from a free attention.

Those who come to a psychotherapist for help have become, to a greater or lesser extent, disenchanted with life; they have lost their sense of wonder. One way of conceiving the therapist's task is to say that the aim should be to restore, as far as possible, this sense of wonder. To achieve this requires us, amongst other things, to try to ensure that we do not ourselves adopt a stance that enables wonder to slip out of the room.

CHAPTER 8
A backward glance

ROSALIND MAYO

Western culture as we know and live it today was built on several foundations, one of which was theological – specifically Judaeo-Christian traditions and beliefs.

Religious stories, like psychoanalytic ones, are enormously influential and seductive, whether one believes them or not.

This chapter is about some stories, psychoanalytic and religious, woven around human origins and human embodiment.

Specifically, those stories are about male and female bodies and some of the meanings attributed to them.

The subject of this chapter might also be 'Woman what hast thou to do with me?' From the Gospel of John, it is Jesus' question to his mother, Mary who, by her words and actions, initiates the first miracle in Cana and shows the divinity of her son.

Freud's analysis of religious art was shaped by the cultural and intellectual currents and questions of his time. Encounters in the present with such 'works of art' similarly have their own questions, which may be completely irrelevant and spurious to the artist's or patron's intentions and meanings.

I have taken up Freud's engagement with the figure/symbol of the Virgin Mary.

An apotropaic concept or figure is one that displaces another, or turns away as in looking elsewhere.

A shewing or shewen is a letting be seen, or a put in sight.

In my name

Heavy with child
Belly
an arc
of black moon

I squat over
dry plantain leaves
and command the earth
to receive you

in my name
in my blood

my tainted

perfect child
my bastard fruit
my seedling
my sea grape
my strange mulatto
my little bloodling

let the snake slipping in deep grass
be dumb before you. (Nichols, 1998)

Quite probably there has been no time in human history when the physical and biological connectedness of the mother to a child has been in doubt.

Paternity, on the other hand, the biological relationship between a child and its father, has until quite recently been of uncertain origin. Whilst Augustine observed with some disgust that being born in urine and blood was enough to expel anyone into the world, Hegel noted and worried that the male organ had a double function; the paternal issue confused with a waste product, paternity clouded by uncertainty and chance.

The Judaic Christian bible and tradition is in part, at least, a story about these human origins. More specifically, it narrates the meanings that have been attributed to and constructed around human embodiment, and this relationship to God, particularly the meanings associated with female embodiment.

There is a story in the Old Testament of a woman who is turned to a pillar of salt for looking back. (Genesis 19:15–17). On the way to Sodom and

Gomorrah, three angels call in on Abraham and Sarah, now in old age and without a child. Abraham greets his guests, offering them hospitality. Sarah is sent away to bake cakes and fetch water. Whilst she is gone Abraham also provides food for the guests, who sit and eat. One of the angels asks where Sarah is. Abraham replies that she is in the tent. The angels say they will visit him again the next year, by which time Sarah will have given birth to their son. Sarah, we are told, was listening at the door of the tent behind him. Some translations suggest that she was in the tent with the third angel.

The text raises a number of questions; there are clearly allusions to the paternity of the expected child. And then there is Sarah's absence during the angel's announcement. It is not clear if Sarah knew that God had already told Abraham that she would have a son to be called Isaac. God has made a covenant with Abraham, and the promise that Abraham's seed will be fruitful and multiply, and that Sarah and Abraham, although very old, will have a child, who will become the father of generations. The sign of this covenant is to be circumcision, a cut to the body, signified, and sealed in blood.

Abraham becomes the spiritual and cultural guardian of the alliance between God and Israel. Sarah's inclusion in the covenant is at best indirect, (is it possible to be included indirectly?) the shedding of her blood, the cut in her body through childbirth overlaid with the rite of circumcision.

Later, when Abraham is called by God to sacrifice Isaac, Sarah is again absent.

Abraham, as a son of God, is prepared to sacrifice his own son in an act of faith and responsibility. This story of ethics and faith takes place between fathers and sons. Does Abraham act on behalf of Sarah? Can he, can someone else, take upon himself the other's leap of faith? Would it still be Sarah's act of faith? What Sarah thinks or feels we never know, except that the child is hers also. It is Abraham's story (Genesis 12–22).

Etymologically, religion means that which binds, which holds together. Is Sarah bound also in this binding? Is she held in this holding together? Are women under the law?

Because this is a story of origins, written during exile, to give hope to those in exile, and to reaffirm faith and history, it is presented as a linear narrative, disrupted only by God's intervention; a story of 'beginnings' of origins, written when humans have found their endings, and have sought God there.

In this retroactive history it is a long wait to hear the cry of the mother at the court of King Solomon.

Leaving the land of Canaan the angels continue on to Sodom, arriving outside the house of Lot, who presses the angels to take shelter in his house. During the night men come from the town telling Lot to send his guests out so 'that we may abuse them' (Genesis 19: 8).

Besides confirming the wickedness of Sodom, and pointing to the reason for exile, the story also acts as a foil for Abraham's goodness, he has tried to plead with God to spare the people of Sodom.

However it is also a lesson about offering hospitality and protection to the stranger, the 'foreigner'. All the more striking, then, when Lot offers his virgin daughters to be abused instead of his guests.

In the morning the angels lead Lot and his wife and family out of the town. They are instructed not to look back, but Lot's wife looks back.

This nameless woman, absent when the angels appear, absent when her husband offers up her daughters for rape, is turned into a pillar of salt.

For a moment, Lot's wife, as she is called, makes a re-appearance in history. The Gospel of Luke has Jesus saying, 'Remember Lot's wife.' It is given as a warning to all those who might want to make their lives secure in this world (Luke 17: 32–37). The context is apocalyptic, looking towards the end of the world. This most conservative of the Evangelists uses 'Lot's wife' as a punitive instrument, as an example of someone, a woman, who lacked faith and trust.

In the New Testament, despite the fact that Jesus violates the taboos of unclean flesh – a woman's sinful flesh, blood and death – there is still a question hanging over a woman's capacity to show faith. The question of her carnality.

Where women in Pauline Christianity appear to transcend this, it is usually because they are 'high born' Romans, and/or 'matrons' – women past childbearing age who are 'included' in the symbolization of virginity.

St Paul, caught up in his vision of the the end of the world, concedes that he has no word from the Lord concerning virgins (Corinthians 7:1).

And angels, absent from the scene for many years, make another appearance, to a virgin!

In *The Gift of Death*, Jacques Derrida takes up Jan Patocka's *Heretical Essays on the Philosophy of History*. From this Derrida concludes that 'the history of the responsible self is built upon the heritage and patrimony of secrecy, through a chain reaction of ruptures and repressions that assure the very tradition they punctuate with their interruptions' (Derrida, 1995).

Patocka says that the secret is the mystery of orgiastic practices, that are repressed and incorporated into or by philosophy, and the secret or mystery itself is maternal. This new thinking, inaugurated by Plato, involves the desire to forsake the lap of the earth mother in order to set out upon the path of pure light.

Freud wrote about religion throughout his psychoanalytic life, his interest and publications increasing as he grew older, beginning with *Obsessive Actions and Religious Practices*, originally published in 1907, and concluding with *Moses and Monotheism: Three Essays*, published in 1939, the year he died.

As a subject, *The Interpretation of Dreams* (Freud 1900) has deep roots in the Judaeo-Christian tradition. But he also worried about how his religious writings might affect psychoanalysis, and he took measures to distance himself from some of his own work by having it published anonymously, or intending to publish it posthumously.

In this regard, Freud was doing no more than following current, similar ideas and attitudes towards religion.

Since the eighteenth century religion had become the last taboo for modern thought. Religion is the other that cannot be assimilated, but only at best correlated, and more usually simply ignored or dismissed. 'Like the Jesuits of Voltaire's imagination, religion usually enters the rooms of modernity and leaves without regret' (Tracy 1999)

Marx and Feuerbach had set out to defeat religion; Hegel attempts to colonize it. Freud took the view that religion was an anthropomorphic creation, providing solace in a world that more often than not gives us too much to bear (*Civilization and Its Discontents*).

He hoped that science would and should replace it, but he doubted that the majority of people would be able to rise above religion's comforting illusions.

Freud's view of religion was complex. Writings such as *Mourning and Melancholia, The Theme of the Three Caskets*, and *The Uncanny*, provide another aspect of Freud's views on religion.

His attitude to works of religious art tended to be more favourable, partly because he thought the artist would be less conventional in his attitude to religion, and also because art (like science), according to Freud, tends to reflect the son's triumph over the father, and not, as in religion, a submission to the father.

The conclusion for Christoph Haizmann in *A Seventeenth Century Demonological Neurosis* (Freud, 1923) contrasts, for example, with Leonardo da Vinci, and for Freud confirms his view: Leonardo through his art triumphs over his father, whereas Haizmann takes refuge in the cloisters of a religious community of the 'pious fathers'.

The concept of postmodernity may be likened to the current medical thinking on irritable bowel syndrome – a ragbag of definitions that are difficult to localize.

Could it be that following the death of God and the subject (male) there is little left to interest us, other than how to stay alive now, and the nostalgia and mourning for what we have lost?

In some postmodern thought and texts, this has occasioned some to return to the repressed other of religion, in the shape of Gnosticism, the Christian mystics, the apophatic thinkers, and the saints and martyrs of early and medieval Christianity.

There seems to be an almost pre-Lapsarian desire to this nostalgia, as there may indeed be to all nostalgia, a return to a world before Descartes, a return to the body.

Can a return to early Greek and Christian texts be more than a return to particular bodies, in other words, an apotropaic turn?

The title of Freud's essay, *Leonardo da Vinci and a Memory of His Childhood*, seems to divert attention from the scene. For the focus of Freud's discussion is Leonardo's painting of the *Madonna and Child with St Anne* (1508–1518, Louvre, Paris).

Freud has been here before, and so it is surprising, therefore, that he proceeds to construct a history, a miniature biographical reconstruction of Leonardo's life that turns upon a smile.

A smile that evokes something else – a memory, an image, a mother.

Beginning from the smile of the Mona Lisa, Freud weaves his way back to the childhood of Leonard da Vinci.

Leonardo was separated from his own mother whilst still young, around the age of 3 to 5 years.

He was taken to live with a paternal grandmother and a stepmother. Freud suggests that the three women have become condensed in the composition.

St Anne the grandmother represents Leonardo's own mother, Caterina, guarding the other woman who mothers her son.

Perhaps it is not easy to access, there is no direct route, the way (in) is not obvious or clear, where to begin? In the Beginning: Prelapsarian, a mother and a child. Two women, a mother and her daughter and a child. They are coiled around each other, shimmering, iridescent flesh, arms and legs entwined. Anne looks at her daughter, Mary looks at her son; they are bound in their gazes.

There is something solid here, connecting, and connected with each other in a tenderness that seems to extend and grace everything beyond them in a mysterious light and shadow, into an infinitely extended landscape.

What intimacy, an offering of disclosure, to look, to wonder, but there is something impenetrable here, beyond the grasp and gaze of the eyes, unnameable.

It seems an awkward composition: St Anne, older, but with no sign of ageing, softly imposing, sitting in the background, her face and eyes gaze lovingly at her daughter. And Mary sits almost within her mother's lap! Her head gently resting on her mother's shoulder.

Leaning toward the child, her arms outstretched holding him, and he is positioned almost between his mother's legs!

Are we to see in this, his human, and embodied birth into the world, and that moment to come enfolded within this, like the petals of a rose, when she will hold him again, cradle this same body in her lap, now crucified, the *pieta*.

And the child with his plump dimpled body, his hands clutching the ears of a lamb, seems to be in a movement, or a flight away from his mother, on his way into the world! She looks at him; His faced turned towards her, for a moment, a backward glance.

The Renaissance painters treated this devotional narrative of St Anne with Mary and Child many times – Leonardo at least three.

An earlier composition included St John the Baptist as a child.

In his notebooks Leonardo defined his purpose, explaining that the best figures are those whose actions clearly express their emotions so that the beholder can understand them.

'Painted figures must be done in such a way that the spectators are able with ease to recognise through their attitudes the thoughts of their minds (*il concetto dell'anima*)' (Goffen, 2002, p. 33).

Traditional depictions of the Virgin Mary, whilst honouring her as a beautiful and loving mother, were careful not to arouse an inappropriate sexualized response.

In maintaining a balance between her loveliness and her purity, both were protected – the Virgin Mother and the beholder.

Leonardo was unconcerned with the spiritual dangers inherent for the viewer, or the possible impropriety in the conception of the image.

It is precisely the power of the image to inflame and arouse that interests him.

He has no difficulty in conceiving divinity or the sacred, in the erotic and indwelling in human flesh, and frequently this is a 'feminized' flesh, or embodiment.

Michelangelo's interpretations of the Madonna have little in common with any of Leonardo's creations.

Michelangelo's Mary is masculinized, her body and face are large and muscular for a woman of the sixteenth century, and this is in order to give her a spiritual virility that is her *virtu*.

Along with his male contemporaries, Michelangelo intended to honour Mary by making her male.

When philosophers and theologians praised women they often did so by ascribing to them male characteristics of mind.

Michelangelo studied Leonardo's works but with the intention of rejecting them, that is to offer another very different conception of the Mother and child, an almost thesis/antithesis.

Leonardo's tenderness and emotional and 'psychological' connection is absent from Michelangelo's treatment. Here the mother looks elsewhere, and is distant, if not almost alienated, even when the Child looks at her; Mary's face is turned away.

Leonardo's interpretations take us into another world, the sublime: an exquisite intimacy exists between the mother and child, and she is a graceful and an unmistakably 'feminine maternal'.

Theologically, Leonardo has condensed the Immaculate Conception and the Incarnation into something that offers a startling alternative to the Classical idea of the Trinity as Father Son and Holy Spirit, represented as male.

This is an Incarnational theology, which creates for the Christ child a family centred upon an embodied and maternal Trinity.

This creation emphasizes the female bodily origin of Christ's body and life, whereas the classical Trinity emphasizes the origin of his soul.

The parents of Mary – Anne and Joachim, first appear in the Second Century apocryphal text, the Protoevangleium of James, which tells the story of Mary's early life in a way that parallels the early life of Jesus.

Like John the Baptist, Mary was a miracle child born to parents in old age. Dante (an enormous influence upon Leonardo) mentions her in his description of Paradise.

> Opposite Peter I saw Anna sitting,
> So content to be gazing at her daughter
> That she did not move her eyes to sing Hosanna.
> (Dante, Paradiso XXXII, 133, in Divine Comedy)

In popular belief, far from the intrigue and theological contortions of the official church and its theologians, Mary, Anne and Joachim, formed part of a beloved and familiar story.

Its message and its belief are unclear, belonging as it did in the main to the piety of the 'ordinary man and woman', until it reached the ears and minds of the medieval scholastics; here story, custom, iconography and myth began to be translated into doctrine, the material changed into the spiritual.

The idea of instituting a feast day for the Immaculate Conception grew out of Mary's popularity with the laity in Italy France and Spain, and presented the Church with the question of whether or not to ignore the growing power and veneration accorded to Mary, or harness its potential to the Church.

Arguments raged for years between clerics, often on behalf of the laity, theologians and the Church. The question hangs upon whether or not the Virgin was free from Original Sin. If so, at what point did this start – conception, or birth.

Augustine had already spoken on this – well, almost; whilst rebutting the Pelagian heresy he insisted that all men were born in sin, adding that he wished to make an exception regarding the mother of our saviour. Thus far, he committed himself no farther.

The angelic Thomas Aquinas, who strove to articulate the comparability of faith and reason, pointed to the heart of the matter. Mary could not have been free of original sin at her conception because no one could have been redeemed before the Redemption!

It was Duns Scotus who neatly contrived a solution, for a time anyway: a *praeredemptio*. The Virgin had been preserved from sin, until the Redemption of the cross. If Christ saves us through his redemption, the Virgin who bears him 'must' be included in a backhand manner, beginning from her own conception.

In other words, *she* is the bearer of a pre-redemption, hence an Immaculate Conception, neat and skilful, but precarious.

The Russian and Greek Orthodox Church held back from commitment to this concept for very good reasons. If Mary is granted freedom from original sin, she is set apart from the rest of the human race; in other words, there is no human earthly bond that unites her with the rest of humanity.

The danger recognized by those who refused the dogma of the Immaculate Conception, then and now, is an ancient enemy – Gnostic dualism.

The lesson is that the ideal cannot be incarnate in a creature who is like everyone else. For a woman, the punishment for the Fall was the pain of childbirth, from menstruation to lactation. If Mary was spared all of this through her special exemption then the doctrine opens on to an abyss, for the full humanity of Jesus becomes questionable.

The Assumption of Mary proclaimed by Pope Pius XII in 1950 is a logical step from the Immaculate Conception. Free from the taint of original sin, Mary is also free from death and decay in the grave.

Eventually the iconography of the Immaculate Conception, which was centred upon Anne and Mary expressing an embodied relationship to each other and to the lineage of the Christ child, is superseded by representations of idealized masculine fantasies of seventeenth-century art.

One composition shows Mary kneeling in the skies before God the Father, surrounded by doctors of theology who debate her function and role, supporting their arguments with their writings.

By this point she has become absorbed into Christian practice, a patriarchal instrument for belief. In place of Mary as the one who bodies Christ into the flesh and the world, there is Mary transcendent, disembodied, a remote, a solitary figure who has lost her connection to her mother, her child and the earth (Kovachevski, 1991).

An Ethiopian manuscript believed to date from between the fifteenth and eighteenth centuries, entitled *Legends of our Lady Mary the Perpetual Virgin and Her Mother Hanna,* contains a lament by Mary when she receives news of her mother's death.

Words that speak of dereliction and abandonment, left alone in the Father's house (symbolic order) built of brass.

Woe is me! Woe is me! My mother has left me a sorrowful woman … mother who will be like you to me? To whom have you left me? Woe is me O my mother! Oh daughters of Israel, come and weep for me and cast me not away, for I am an only daughter, and I have no one to take her place … and I am alone in the house of brass. (Budge, 1900)

I place my hope on the water
In this little boat
Of the language, the way a body might put
An infant

in a basket of intertwined
Iris leaves
Its underside proofed
with bitumen and pitch,

then set the whole thing down amidst
the sedge
and bulrushes by the edge
of a river

only to have it borne hither and thither,
not knowing where it might end up;
in the lap, perhaps,
of some Pharaoh's daughter. (Dhomhnaill,1990)

For each of us destiny takes the form of a woman. (Freud, 1913).

In 1900 Freud wrote the case history of Dora. During her analysis, Dora mentions her first visit to Dresden, and Freud recounts, 'not failing, of course, to visit the famous picture gallery', that Dora remained two hours in front of the Raphael's Sistine Madonna, rapt in silent admiration (Kovachevski, 1991).

Freud asked her what she had found so pleasing about the painting. She could make no clear to answer, eventually saying, 'The Madonna'.

Freud makes two references to this, one in the notes, where he expressed his future intention to investigate the theme of the virgin mother.

In a footnote Freud adds what he calls a supplementary interpretation, that Dora is the Madonna.

According to Freud, young girls often feels themselves oppressed by imputations of sexual guilt, and the notion of the Madonna is a favourite counter idea. Freud goes on to say that, had the analysis continued, Dora's maternal longing for a child would have been revealed as an obscure though powerful motivation in her behaviour.

Why does Freud make only two brief notes regarding something that he seems to sense, something around Dora staying for two hours looking at a painting of the Virgin Mary and child?

Female virginity is a subject that does not yet exist; on the threshold of being. A 'condition' (Hippocrates, Charcot and Freud) that requires a rupturing, a puncturing, a penetrating of the hymen to – reveal being.

The Virgin Mary is a 'closed gate', a 'spring shut up', 'A fountain sealed' (early Church Fathers).

As Françoise Meltzer observes, female virginity is like a metaphor for female subjectivity (Meltzer, 1999). Its value is its state of non-being!

In early Christianity, female virginity becomes a symbol of holiness, revered and respected, a symbol of power.

Virginity meaning in part integrity, and autonomy becomes a proof of spiritual purity and virtue, an image of wholeness, and wholeness is equated with holiness, usually achievable only by a man.

A woman's body is by definition the impossibility of the state of holiness. Virginity offers escape.

There are many stories of women who, to prove their spiritual and physical virtue adopted a life of chastity, often accompanied by the most tortuous denial of their bodies.

Many of the Church Fathers – Cyprian, Jerome, Augustine and Tertullian – fervently believed that for a woman to enter heaven she would have to become a male.

The Gospel of Thomas has Jesus and his disciples debating the place of Mary in their group. Simon Peter argues that Mary should leave because 'women are not worthy of life'. Jesus replies, 'I myself shall lead her so as to make her male ... For every woman who makes herself male will enter the kingdom of heaven' (Apocryphal Acts of the Apostles – Miles, 1989).

A paradox: It was common in third- and fourth-century communities, often consisting of both sexes, to see men dressed as women, symbolizing their betrothal as the virgin brides of Christ.

However this in no way cancelled out that, for a woman who wanted to lead a life of chastity and celibacy, to follow a path towards 'the spiritual', she had to become male. Those chosen by God are ultimately male, even if they are born female.

Although male virginity has long been prized and desired in Western philosophy, literature and art, there is of course no comparable physical 'image-symbol' where the male virgin body could be perceived as whole and integral in the same way.

Christian female martyrs and saints frequently demanded their accusers to uncover upon their death the evidence of their spiritual and physical purity (an unbroken hymen) (Clark, 1983).

Derrida picks up the ambivalence inherent in the word hymen as a signifier of both marriage and virginity, to expose the unstable position of the subject in relation to the alliance with language and the social contract (Oliver, 1997).

An undecidable concept that calls any alliance into question, a sign of ambiguity and irresolution. The hymen functions as an elusive signifier that does not mean one thing, but neither does it mean nothing.

It therefore has a subversive or, in theological terms, a redemptive reading, used in association with the Virgin Mary (or Dora) as a symbol of freedom and grace which resists phallic domination.

Dora comes to Freud with her aphonia, an absence of subjectivity, of agency – on the brink of being.

She stands for two hours before this image of a virgin mother who stands on a billow of clouds, with her child in her arms, two cupids gazing at her adoringly, and St Barbara kneeling at the side – St Barbara who defied her father and died by his hand rather than recant the faith he hated.

(Dora also wants to defy her father who is trying to trade her off to the husband of his mistress. Where does Freud's silence stand in this matter?)

Freud's analysis begins and ends with his Oedipal drama. Dora tells him that what interested her in the painting was 'the Madonna'. So, reasons Freud, Dora would like a baby.

But there is no Father here, no earthly mother to get in the way, a virgin mother with a child, conceived through the ear with the co-operation of the Holy Spirit. She experiences none of the female bodiliness of other women, none of the pain of childbirth; after giving birth she is still a virgin. She does not die (unlike her son) but goes straight to heaven, where with her tears, she constantly intercedes with God on behalf of those who are left in their humanity-flesh. A woman like no other (Warner, 1985).

In his notes Freud first mentions the virgin, equating it with sexuality: a young woman's guilt because of sexual thoughts.

Later, his reference to the Madonna assumes Dora's desire for a child.

Dora may have wanted to be the Madonna, or the child in the Madonna's arms, or to love or be loved by the Madonna! What Dora might have seen in the painting Freud could not see – his mind was made up.

Was there a moment then, when the Freudian maternal was loosened from the knot of femininity?

Freud could not see the possibility for a femininity unconnected to the maternal. Freud did say that he hadn't mastered Dora's, 'deepest rooted' feelings. Peter Gay (1988) observes that, for reasons known only to him, Freud did not build on what he had begun to understand.

In *Motherhood According to Giovanni Bellini,* Julia Kristeva claims that the art of Bellini and Leonardo da Vinci represent two different faces of the Western psyche and the differences follow from their different relation to the mother.

Bellini's art reveals his separation from the maternal. Bellini, like Michelangelo, portrays the mother as preoccupied, elsewhere, deep in thought, inward looking, sometimes daydreaming. In earlier Madonna paintings Bellini paints an absent mother, with a split in her body; her body is there, she is not. She seems to have a life outside and beyond the child, her son. She is there to facilitate something, she is an origin but points away from herself, beyond herself.

Leonardo paints the son's desire for the mother, the paternal function. Here is the beloved child of a beloved mother who exists for him alone. According to Kristeva, Leonardo's Madonna represents the other half of the Western psyche, 'thraldom' to the maternal (Kristeva, 1980).

'A mother is only brought unlimited satisfaction by her relation to a son, this is altogether the most free from ambivalence of all human relationships', Freud said (Appignanesi, 1993, p. 15).

We know of course this idea had more to do with Freud's wishful fantasies of his relationship to his mother and his own childhood.

According to Freud, then, a mother's desire is always for a boy. So motherhood is always the paternal desire. And the 'child' of psychoanalytic theory is always a son. Freud's interpretation of Leonardo's painting, expresses this same sentiment, and he attributes the same desires to Leonardo.

Freud claims that da Vinci has overcome his Father through his art, but there is the constant evocation of the maternal in his paintings.

Freud could not make his way about with Dora's response to Raphael's Madonna in that Minoan-Mycenean ground before Oedipus brought language down even unto the belly of the mother, that place where the daughter loves the mother. But here where the son loves the mother and the mother's desire is undividedly and completely for her son, Freud was at home!

There is no mark to inscribe a sigh.

There is a Wedding in Cana of Galilee; Jesus and his disciples are present. Mary the mother of Jesus is there; she goes to her son and tells him there is no wine left for the guests. Jesus replies with a question, 'Woman, what have you to do with me?' (John 2: 4)

How do you write a lump in the throat?

What has happened here in this encounter between the Greek world of pagan ritual and practice and monotheistic Judaism, in the move from the Eastern shores of Christianity to the West? Between a punitive patriarchal God, whose love required a renouncing of sensuality and embodiment, and an imaginary pre-oedipal world of a maternal goddess, a state very difficult to reconcile with the complexities, responsibilities and relations of adult living?

Mary: assimilated but unbaptized, within the Christian narrative, this woman with the symbolic power to reconnect once again divinity with human intimacy, touch and tenderness. In her the word made flesh, and (it) was good!

In *Moses and Monotheism,* Freud (1939) wrote that he understood Christianity to be a compromise between Judaic monotheism and paganism. By compromise Freud was pointing at the partial reconciliation between the two faiths: Christianity's absorption of the maternal flesh of the goddess religions, and Christ's inversion of the Judaic laws of purification and defilement, 'the condition for another opening up to true symbolic relations, the true outcome of the Christic journey' (Kristeva, 1982, p. 115).

Christianity has failed to realize the full possibility of what was opened up. The maternal body and flesh is only partly assumed in Christ, subsumed in the Eucharist, *his* body and *his* blood. Christ alone represents perfect heterogeneity between the divine law and the maternal flesh of the pagan world (Kristeva,1982).

The codes and rules of purity and impurity associated with the 'old order' of being have been internalized as sin and grace, a function of language and speech, a source of abjection, hate and impurity within the self. A hate of self, a deep suspicion of goodness and an unnameable fear of maternal contamination, continued by psychoanalysis.

Tina Beattie (1999, p. 151) suggests that neither 'ethical monotheism nor pagan philosophy ever became fully reconciled to the maternal flesh through Christianity, despite the best efforts of early writers such as Tertullian, (and to some extent) Augustine, writing as the last voice of hope for the theological representation of the goodness of the female body' (Beattie, 1999, p. 151).

For two thousand years the figure of Mary the Virgin Mother has infused Christianity. A saturated symbol twisted in the service of patriarchy. And yet, outside motherhood no situation exists in human experience that so radically and so simply brings us face to face with the emergence of the other.

there was the angel … the intermediary

In Fra Angelico's painting, *The Annunciation,* the Angel returns to the world again. A book lies open on Mary's lap, its text of the law-lifeless letters, without breath, words – waiting to be reawakened in the vulnerability and risk of human flesh, of the maternal body. The way is open again – waiting – her body the opening into the world – the gift (Fra Beato Angelico Da Fiesole, 1386/7, Vicchio di Mugello-1455, Roma, Madrid).

He returns in an unexpected place in an unexpected guise. In the womb of a woman. Is she the only one left who still has some understanding of the divine? Who still listens silently and gives new flesh to what she has perceived in those messages that other people cannot perceive. Can she alone feel the music of the air trembling between the wings of the angels, and make or remake a body from it (Irigaray, 1997)?

Mary's fiat, is *'yes* here I am'.

Selected bibliography

Appignanesi L, Forrester J (1993) Freud's Women. London: Virago.

Atkinson C, Buchanan CH, Miles. M (eds) (1987) Immaculate and Powerful: The Female in Sacred Image and Social Reality. Boston Mass: Beacon Press.

Beattie T (1999) God's Mother, Eve's Advocate: A Gynocentric Refiguration of Marian Symbolism in Engagement with Luce Irigaray. Bristol: Centre for Comparative Studies in Religion and Gender.

Brown P (1989) The Body and Society: Men and Women and Sexual Renunciation in Early Christianity. London, Boston: Faber & Faber.

Budge, W. (1900) The Miracles of the Blessed Virgin Mary and the Life of Hanna (Saint Anne) and the Magical Prayers of Aheta Mikael. Lady Meux Manuscripts, Limited ed. 286/300. London: W Griggs.

Capps D (ed.) (2001) Freud and Freudians on Religion. New Haven and London: Yale University Press.

Caputo JD, Scanlon MJ (eds) (1999) God The Gift and Postmodernism. Bloomington: Indiana University Press.

Clark E (1986) 'Acts of Paul and Thecla', in Ascetic Piety and Women's Faith. Lewiston Me: Edward Mellon.

Clement C, Kristeva J (2001) The Feminine and the Sacred. Palgrave: Colombia University Press.

Derrida J (1995) The Gift of Death. Trans. David Wills. Chicago Ill: University of Chicago Press.

Dhomhnaill Nuala Ni (1990) Pharaoh's Daughter. In Jouve NW (ed) (1998) Female Genesis: Creativity, Self and Gender. Cambridge: Polity Press.

Eliot TS (1979) Four Quartets. London: Faber & Faber.

Freud S (n.d.) The Standard Edition of the Complete Psychological Works of Sigmund Freud. 24 Volumes. Ed. and trans. James Strachey. London: Hogarth.

Freud S (1905) A Fragment of the Analysis of the Case of Hysteria. SE vol. 11. (From Five Lectures on Psycho-analysis). London: Hogarth.

Freud S (1911) Leonardo da Vinci and a Memory of his Childhood. SE vol. 11. London: Hogarth.

Freud S (1923) A Seventeenth-Century Demonological Neurosis. SE vol. 19. London: Hogarth.

Freud S (1927) The Future of an Illusion. SE 21. London: Hogarth, pp. 1–56.

Freud S (1930) 1929 Civilization and Its Discontents. SE vol. 21. London: Hogarth, pp. 57–145.

Freud S (1931) Female Sexuality. SE vol. 21: London: Hogarth, pp. 215–20.

Freud S (1933) Femininity, in New Introductory Lectures on Psycho-Analysis. SE vol. 23. London: Hogarth.

Freud S (1939) Moses and Monotheism: Three Essays. SE vol. 23. London: Hogarth.

Gay P (1998) Freud: A Life for our Time. New York: WW Norton.

Girard R (1977) Violence and the Sacred. Trans. Patrick Gregory. Baltimore: Johns Hopkins University Press.

Goffen R (1989) Giovanni Bellini. London: Yale University Press.

Goffen R (2002) Renaissance Rivals. Michelangelo, Leonardo, Raphael, Titian. London: Yale University Press.

Irigaray L (1991) Marine Lover of Friedrich Nietzsche. Trans. Gillian Gill. New York: Colombia University Press.

Irigaray L (1997) Women-Mothers. The Silent Substratum of the Social Order. In Whitford M (ed.) The Irigaray Reader. Oxford: Blackwell.

Jouve NW (1998) Female Genesis: Creativity Self and Gender. Cambridge: Polity Press.

Kovachevski C (1991) The Madonna in Western Paintings. Trans, Nicola Georgiev. London: Cromwell Editions.

Kristeva J (1980) Desire and Language. Oxford: Blackwell.

Kristeva J (1980) Powers of Horror – An Essay in Abjection. Trans Leon Roudiez. New York: Colombia University Press.

Kristeva J (1987) Tales of Love. Trans. Leon S Roudiez. New York: Colombia University Press.

Laqueur T (1992) Making Sex: Body and Gender from the Greeks to Freud. Cambridge Mass and London: Harvard University Press.

Louth A (1981) The Origins of the Christian Mystical Tradition. Oxford: OUP.
Meltzer F (1999) Re-embodying: virginity secularised. In Caputo JD, Scanlon MJ (eds) God, The Gift and Postmodernism. Bloomington: Indiana University Press.
Miles M (1989) Carnal Knowing: Female Nakedness and Religious Meaning in the Christian West. London: Burns & Oates.
Miles M (1992) Desire and Delight. A New Reading of Augustine's Confessions. New York: Crossroads Publishing Company.
Moller VS (1999) Philosophy Without Women. London: Continuum.
Nichols G (1983) In my name. In Jouve NW (ed.) (1993) Female Genesis: Creativity, Self and Gender. Cambridge: Polity Press.
Oliver K. (ed.) (1997) The Portable Kristeva – European Perspectives. New York: Colombia University Press.
Rieff P (ed.) (1963) Dora: An Analysis of a Case History. New York: Collier.
Tracy D (1999) Fragments: The Spiritual Situation of our Times. In Caputo JD, Scanlon MJ (eds) (1999) God, The Gift and Postmodernism. Bloomington: Indiana University Press.
Warner M (2000) Alone of All Her Sex – The Myth and Cult of the Virgin Mary. London: Vintage.
Whitford M (ed.) (1994) The Irigaray Reader. Oxford: Blackwell.
Wiles M (1977) The Christian Fathers. London: SCM.

Paintings

Leonardo da Vinci
Madonna and Child and Saint Anne. Paris, Louvre.

Michelangelo
Madonna of the Stairs, (marble) Florence.
Madonna of the Doni Tondo. Florence.
Madonna of the Pitti Tondo. (marble) Florence

Diego Valasquez
The Immaculate Conception.
Coronation of The Virgin

Raphael.
Sistine Madonna

Giovanni Bellini.
Coronation Of The Virgin.
Madonna With Two Trees. Venice.
Lochis Madonna.

Piero della Francesca.
Madonna della Misericordia.

Fra Beato Angelico Da Fiesole.
The Annunciation.

CHAPTER 9

Psychotherapy and the making of subjectivity

DAVID SMAIL

Psychotherapy has won the battle for recognition and respect that it fought for most of the twentieth century. And yet, I fear, the victory is empty and, indeed, we may have achieved no more than to replace one form of oppressive intellectual domination with another.

When they came to considering the life – and more particularly the health – of the mind, the psychological and psychiatric orthodoxies of the last century relied upon the crushing power of a dogmatic authority almost totalitarian in its scope and its claims. The intent was to make out of science an indisputable methodology whose mechanical application could stifle dissent and set up a ruling élite able to pronounce upon objective truth with a certainty as infallible as that of any pope.

The result of this approach was, of course, to dehumanize the subject such that he or she came to be seen as nothing more than a biological or behavioural automaton, devoid of meaning or purpose other than that instilled by, on the one hand, biochemistry and genes and, on the other, mechanical reaction to processes of conditioning. Infuriatingly for those who dissented from this view (and entirely inconsistent with any rational perspective), the high priests of orthodoxy placed themselves conceptually outside the bleak world thus created for their puppets, pulling their strings as if from within another universe.

There were throughout, of course, critics of this intellectual thuggery, the most effective of whom – the debate having moved on – are now largely forgotten. I think particularly, here, of Michael Polanyi (1958), who almost single-handedly reduced the embattled monolith of scientism to rubble. Apart from the behaviour therapists (and subsequently 'cognitive-behavioural practitioners') who allied themselves strongly with the bogus authority of 'science', psychotherapists of many persuasions were prominent among those who saw in behaviourism, positivism and the 'medical model', threats to human freedom and dignity that demanded vigorous resistance. Psychoanalysis, analytical psychology and object relations theory had throughout offered a home to those with a deeper and wider (if not necessarily more accurate) view of human nature, and the feeling of excitement and relief generated in clinical psychology by the mid-century challenges of people like Carl Rogers, Fritz Perls and George Kelly may be hard to imagine for those who weren't there to experience it. The force of scientism was not, after all, irresistible.

In retrospect, there was more than a touch of naivety about our enthusiasm. In our celebration of the demise of the positivist-behaviourist dragon, we failed to see that other menaces were lurking in the forest – not least the invitation to self-deception brought about by our own professional interest. Furthermore, so traumatized had we been by the years of our subjugation that many of us failed to recognize that the beast was indeed slain, and even now raise the battle cry against a non-existent foe. For example, in advocating in his recent book (House, 2003) the adoption of a 'new paradigm' that sweeps away all the old modernist prejudices of hegemonic science, Richard House rather overlooks the fact that the 'new paradigm' is already here, looking just about as comfortable and confident as the old. 'Qualitative research' and 'grounded theory', 'discursive' and 'narrative', 'constructivist' as well as 'deconstructionist' approaches are well ensconced in mainstream psychology and psychotherapy journals and taught as the new orthodoxy on the countless psychotherapy and counselling courses that have mushroomed over the past couple of decades.

In this way we seem to have picked up and elaborated those aspects of psychological and therapeutic thought that focus on the person's autonomy, responsibility, 'self-actualization' and powers of self-reinterpretation, while overlooking the significance of those contributions (like, in particular, RD Laing's) that saw that subjectivity is intelligible only within a social context. In our excitement at having escaped, over the past 40 years or so, from the dominance of a disciplinary scientism, we have, it seems to me, come to prefer the constructions of our imagination to those of what I want to call, unashamedly, reality. What threatens the accuracy of our understanding now is not the imposition of a brutally impersonal objectivity, but a rampant subjectivism that seeks to disconnect us entirely from the world.

In this way, so-called 'postmodernist' approaches in psychology that adopt what one might call a naïve social constructionism, or privilege 'narrative' above history in psychotherapy, seem to me, rather than advancing our understanding, to stand in danger of pointing us backward towards pre-scientific notions of a world in which the substance of what is is inseparable from the stuff of our fears, hopes and desires. Psychotherapists' embrace of such accounts may stem from a laudable desire to dissociate themselves from the intellectual dishonesty of any claim to a special relationship with 'the real world', but in hoping to set the human spirit free, we stand in danger of cutting our ties with enlightened reason altogether. In proclaiming our contempt for science, we lose a necessary respect for empirical enquiry such that we inevitably find ourselves authoring just another theology. This just adds to the impression that the history of psychotherapy is much more understandable as a history of competing cults than as any kind of progression, however halting, of scientific insight.

As Susanne Langer struggled to document in her compendious and vastly ambitious three-volume *Mind: An Essay on Human Feeling* (Langer, 1963–1982), human beings' understanding of their world has taken shape over millennia, emerging hesitantly out of dream and religious mystery. Gradually the world has taken on the lineaments of a reality from which we can stand apart just a little, even though, of course, it will always be a world formed and appreciated by and through our own interests and embodied nature.

In my view, psychotherapy would much better concern itself with our place in and relations with our world, rather than reinforcing the idea that somehow we create reality. For the latter idea is, essentially, a magical one. I don't think it would be stretching matters too far to characterize the unifying philosophy of the plethora of psychotherapies that the past hundred years has spawned as one of 'magical voluntarism'. By this I mean, of course, the idea that individuals can, in crucial ways, change themselves from the inside out, essentially by acts of will following upon 'insight'.

I have written quite a lot about what I see as the strict limitations of this kind of view (for example, Smail, 2001) and I do not want to elaborate upon them further here. What I should like to do, though, is try to say something – I hope rather more positively – about what I see as a more valid and intellectually justifiable role for psychology and psychotherapy in relation to emotional distress.

Contrary to what many psychotherapies claim, or at least imply, people are in my view not self-creating, self-choosing entities able, once they have seen the need, to adjust themselves through an act of will. Like the rest of nature, we are held in place within a world (in our case, in particular, a social world) and the extent to which we can change our situation within the world is dependent on the powers and resources available to us to do so. To understand the causes of emotional distress, we need to look beyond 'individuals and their families' to the society that encapsulates us all, patients and therapists alike.

It is necessary to stress, however, that this position does not just empty out into some kind of impersonal socio-political stance. Important though both sociological and political questions are to our understanding of and response to distress, for practitioners whose concern is with personal suffering our focus must be on the character and formation of individual subjectivity (for that is where our suffering takes place). I don't think that, on the whole, therapeutic psychology has dealt terribly well with subjectivity; for the most part it has sought to constrain rather than liberate it. (This process has a long history: Freud's account in *The Interpretation of Dreams* (1954 edition) of Scherner's (1861) treatment of imagination and dreaming bristles with disapproval at his (Scherner's) unbridled enthusiasm for the scope and freedom of the imagination. One can almost see Freud reaching for the shackles of the 'Superego' which he was later to think so necessary for the development of 'civilization'.)

Subjectively, each of us lives at the centre of a private world of thoughts, feelings and experiences that is quite unique as well as, in present-day society, exquisitely vulnerable. When, as inevitably we must, we compare this world with the world in which those around us appear to live their lives, our sense of our own vulnerability may become so acute as to be almost unbearable, for their world may seem to reflect a certainty and solidity that is entirely lacking in ours. Within the secret depths of our personal experience are packed a seemingly infinite range of hopes, fears and fantasies, desires we hardly dare to recognize and shames that are anguish to contemplate. From the moment of birth, and indeed before, we are exposed to an unremitting tempest of sensation – pleasures as well as pains – to which, as we mature, becomes attached a framework of judgement that buzzes with justifications, condemnations and self-deceptions to the point where any kind of self-certainty seems impossible.

What gives form to this subjective world, makes it intelligible and bearable, is the social space in which we find ourselves located and that confers meaning on our experience. Subjectivity as a possibility arises out of our nature as embodied beings, but it achieves a coherent shape through social interaction. Our bodies, to be sure, give us knowledge of the world, but we can only truly articulate and make sense of that knowledge through the structures of meaning that are provided through our congress with others.

But that does not mean that our embodied knowledge of the world is infinitely malleable, or can be made to conform to whatever stories we choose to tell ourselves. Those stories may be true or they may be false; they may guide us towards an intelligible world that answers faithfully to our embodied understanding, or they may obscure it from us in a blanket of mystery that renders our actions tentative, fearful, dangerous.

Where the public world is painstakingly shaped to accommodate, appreciate, elaborate and civilize our private experience, to take proper account of the way we understand the promptings of our bodies and put them to use, a kind of harmony may be given to our lives that, while certainly not erasing all possibility of tragedy, at least gives us a chance to live, as selves, in accord with others about the nature of the world into which we have been thrown. There comes to be a kind of satisfaction in being a subject in social space.

Where, on the other hand, the public world is shaped to exploit our subjectivity, to mystify, obscure or distort the wordless knowledge our bodies give us of the world, no such harmony will be possible. Either we may accept and attempt to live within the distortions, surrendering to a disciplinary orthodoxy at the cost of our souls, or we may be driven to live out our subjectivity in a constant state of uncertainty and apprehension, scurrying in the cracks which show through make-believe like woodlice in a rotten wall. Very rarely, some people seem to have, from the start, a confidence in their embodied experience that no amount of bullying and deception can shake, but even so they nearly always find themselves in a rebellious minority split off in many ways from the social mainstream.

In comparison with the centuries of art, literature, philosophy, religion and science that have, at their best, strained to dignify our subjective experience of life by building a worthy public framework for it, the stance taken by psychotherapy has been deeply ambivalent and for the most part extremely superficial. Indeed, it is hard to avoid the judgement that, in most of its official theorizing, therapy has throughout been developed as one of the principal means of discipline whereby the subject is forced into line with dominant ideology – with the ruling dogmas of power. Very few approaches to therapy explicitly reject at least a covert form of 'normativeness' in which certain moral and/or aesthetic standards of human being are specified not in the subject's interest but in the interests of power. In this kind of approach subjectivity is, as I suggested earlier, constrained rather than liberated, and patients' fearful expectations of being judged are only too quickly confirmed. If we are to help to free people from the kind of disciplinary therapeutic regimen that Foucault criticized so effectively (for example, Foucault, 1979), I suggest that it might be a good idea to switch our 'clinical gaze' from people to the environment in which they find themselves.

I wish we could get rid of the term 'therapy': there is so much that is misleading about it. But even if we're stuck with it, there's no reason to equate 'therapy' with an individualistic struggle to change 'selves'. The focal concern of psychology with the making of individual subjectivity in no way implies that subjectivity is necessarily self-made. In order to understand subjectivity, in other words, we have to look beyond it. If personhood, along with the subjective awareness of it, is the outcome of an interaction of a body with a world, it surely becomes the psychologist's business to pay careful attention to the constraints and influences of both.

I have no quarrel at all with the observation that, to a significant extent, human beings are socially constructed. Indeed, it would be simply absurd to deny it. What does strike me as false, however, is where what I call naïve social constructionism imports chunks of the therapeutic philosophy of magical voluntarism to suggest or imply that social constructions can be reconstructed, or indeed deconstructed, at will. This kind of ill-considered notion, often derived (with what justification it is hard to say) from rarefied 'postmodernist' philosophical discourse, contributes, as intellectual justification, to a pervasive cultural preference for make-believe over reality.

The idea of 'choice', so crucial to the limitless expansionist programme of consumer capitalism, finds its psychological form in the belief that, along with consumer goods and lifestyles, we can also choose our selves. Indeed, reality itself becomes something to be managed, truth a construct to be spun according to the needs and requirements of the market. If people are to be persuaded to respond satisfactorily to the economic and political necessities of the times, they have to be made to believe in 'realities' that are almost entirely artificial. The apparatuses that have been perfected to this end are truly awe-inspiring. We are right to observe that such realities are indeed artificial constructions, but wrong to conclude that this is the only kind of reality there is.

Paradoxically, perhaps, the existence of make-believe proclaims the importance of truth. Notwithstanding the best arguments of naïve constructionism, make-believe is not the outcome of an ultimate relativity but derives its importance from its ability to be taken for the truth. The possibility of truth lies behind make-believe, just as a covert truth-claim lies behind every avowedly relativist account of how things are. In this way make-believe is subservient to truth; it seeks to stand in for truth, but is always at risk of being undermined by it.

Make-believe (spin) is essential to politics precisely because politics is vulnerable, even in today's depleted democracy, to dreaded 'public opinion'. For public opinion is what people believe to be true and as long as political power is contingent on what people think, it will be essential to control what they think. Hence the enormous effort that is put politically into maintaining ideological power, to controlling the formation and reception of meaning in every sphere and at every level.

But truth is still not sovereign, for behind truth lies power.

It really doesn't matter to politicians how blatant and absurd the (mis)representation of truth becomes (to the more discerning consumers of the 'safety-valve' media like the *Guardian* and Channel 4) just so long as mass opinion continues to be controlled. Such control is necessary because what people take to be true still, just, has the propensity to undermine power by providing a focus for solidary action. If power should ever manage to find a way of subverting this last vestige of democratic influence, it will cease immediately to bother with spin and abandon with huge relief all the apparatus of make-believe, for truth will no longer be important. (At the time of writing this can be seen particularly clearly in the unconcealed indifference of the US and UK governments to what people think as they prepare their military assault on Iraq.)

The corporate plutocracy that dominates our lives still depends to an extent on a depleted democracy and must therefore sustain a notion of the 'truth', but this is a severely debased form of truth: truth as virtually synonymous with public opinion and purveyed by the public relations and advertising industries. Precisely because it has become so debased, so transparently fabricated and manipulated, 'truth' may be mistakenly represented (perhaps, indeed, in good faith) by the intellectuals of 'postmodernity' as an outmoded construction of the discredited 'grand narratives' of former times. But rather than the exposure of the, so to speak, conceptual impossibility of truth, what we are witnessing is the disempowerment of truth, its cynical reduction to technologies of spin in which there is a tacit acknowledgement that truth is on the way to not mattering at all.

Truth, and its parasite make believe, thus matter only as long as there is a possibility of popular solidarity forming around a common understanding of what is the case (for example, how the world works to immiserate us) and destabilizing the structures of global corporate plutocracy.

In this state of affairs, in my view, the philosophical task becomes that of rehabilitating the concept of truth, which in turn means deconstructing constructionism (in its naïve form)! We can't do this without considering the role of language.

There can be no doubt that language is of the first importance in the formation of human conduct and society. But this does not mean that language is generative of reality itself. The over-excited embrace (and often only rudimentary understanding) in broadly 'therapeutic' circles of notions of 'discourse', 'narrative', and so forth, having their origin mainly in the writings of French post-structuralists such as Foucault, Derrida and Lyotard, has resulted in an almost psychotic disregard of the real circumstances of people's lives. Foucault spoke, after all, of the 'discourse of power', not the power of discourse, and yet it is this misconstruction that seems to have gripped the imagination of the 'naïve constructionists', 'narrative therapists', among others (for example, Gergen, 1994; Parker, 1999).

Of course words do not directly reflect an incontrovertible reality or 'hold a mirror up to Nature'; *of course* language can never give direct access to Truth. And *of course* language is absolutely essential to our understanding of and interaction with the world and each other. But this does not invest language with some kind of magical power of creation through which it brings worlds into being. Certainly, language is the principal medium of persuasion, but it persuades by pointing to something other than itself, something that *is the case* rather than something that is merely *said*.

Language allows us to place our experience at a distance from us, to hypostatize and manipulate it. Otherwise, we could only *live* our experience – or be lived by it, rather in the manner of dreaming. Inevitably, we are constantly tempted to believe in the actuality of our imaginings precisely because we can clothe them in words. This, after all, is why scientific enquiry has to be so sceptical and so painstaking. But when we take imagination as *definitive* of reality (or alternative realities), we have sunk into collective madness.

While we may unite in criticism of a too heavy-handed positivist authority that attempted in the past to establish a direct line to Truth such that a suitably refined and specialized language could indeed be used to *describe* an independent reality, we need to recapture a view of language as *articulating* our relations with the world *as best we can*. We can in this way acknowledge that any form of 'ultimate' reality must always remain a mystery beyond our grasp, but that that does not mean there is *no such thing* as reality. Some things are more real, some statements more true, than others. Reality is sensed in embodied experience before it is articulated in words, and what we *say* needs always to be checked against other kinds of evidence including, where necessary, every other possible intimation we may have of our living existence in material reality. In this respect, neuroscientists seem to have their feet more firmly on the ground than most psychotherapeutic thinkers: Antonio Damasio's (2000) *The Feeling of What Happens*, for example, gives a very thoughtful account of the relations between subjective experience, consciousness and world.

Nothing could suit corporate plutocracy more than for people to believe that the real satisfactions of life have nothing to do with a shared material reality, but stem ultimately from the cultivation of privacy; that subjective well-being, that is to say, is a matter of 'personal growth' *from the inside*. One-dimensional business culture in fact closes down public space such that the 'real' world' (the world of the market economy) becomes simply a given that people have to accept without question: 'resistance is useless'. If the many can be persuaded that they have no say in the shaping of material reality, and that personal satisfaction is purely a matter of self-doctoring and private consumption, the world is left wide open for exploitation by the few.

When the only public meanings available are the grim and unassailable 'realities' of the market, people are left to scrabble together for themselves makeshift ways of sharing experiences that actually cannot be accommodated within the business model (an example might be the rituals of grief that have developed rapidly in recent times – impromptu roadside shrines, greater emotional demonstrativeness, and so forth). Quite apart from feeling politically impotent (and demonstrating our alienation by shunning the 'democratic' process in unprecedented numbers) we have to cast around for ways of making *communal* sense of experiences that inevitably arise from our existence as embodied beings but are no longer served by abandoned – and often discredited – traditions.

However, because we are social beings, individual subjectivity cannot develop and flourish in a virtual vacuum. The structures of public space necessarily supply a kind of exoskeleton for our feeling and understanding of what it is to be human, and where those structures are drastically reduced, our subjectivity becomes fractured and incomplete. At its most grotesque, people may become stripped of public identity altogether: nameless automata at the end of a telephone without powers of reason or judgement, able only to reiterate a handful of stock phrases.

It is of course understandable for people to feel that one answer to the heartlessness of the outside world is to retire into the realm, if not of the inner self, at least of the private life of home and family, and so forth. However, I suspect that this kind of strategy (already thoroughly considered, of course, by Christopher Lasch, (1977)) is built on the false premiss that inner space, privacy, is somehow independent of public structure. In fact, if anything, the opposite seems to me to be the case. For individual people, hell is more often to be experienced within the confines of the family (or indeed the agonies of introspection) than it is in the spaces beyond, and public structures of meaning – what one might broadly call cultures – that have evolved over time to accommodate the concerns of embodied human beings may offer an escape from privacy that actually lends meaning and significance to suffering. A decent, caring, multidimensional public world makes *use* as well as *sense* of private pain and confusion. One of the most tormented and abused (and admirable) people I ever met was rescued as child from total perdition by films and books, which, among other things, uncovered, to her amazement, the possibility of love.

The way to rescue subjectivity, then, is not to sink further into our 'inner worlds', but to struggle to open up public space and build within it structures that are adequate to giving meaning and purpose to our lives. The relentless business onslaught over the past couple of decades has stripped away practically every way we had of understanding ourselves outside the debased and stupefying vocabulary of the market economy. Deeply hostile to social, intellectual, artistic, spiritual and what Ivan Illich (1975) called convivial ways of thinking, being and experiencing (not least because they give subjects the possibility of criticizing their condition), business, where it cannot undermine them directly, invades them parasitically, like one of those wasps that lays its eggs on the pupae of other creatures. Intellectual life gives way to a kind of managerially authorized posturing, intelligence to the bureaucratized application of mindless rules, history to fashion. Even ordinary conversation, via the media, takes on the tones of hyperbolic advertising gibberish.

Every nook and cranny of existence is turned to commercial use and the apparatus of consumerism is everywhere. Taxation is replaced by sponsorship. Every article for sale is laden with the 'added value' of ever more contrived and crazy exercises in branding. Sport becomes big business. Thought, feeling, relating and understanding become standard, iterative rituals in which people no longer know what they think, or what to think, unless it is prescribed by commercial logic, or the crude dogmas of political correctness that have come to replace ethical reflection.

In this kind of situation, what we need rather more than individual therapy, I think, is the reconstruction of society. The task of the therapist becomes that of helping the person understand how he or she has been shaped by the world. This process carries with it no guarantee that individual action can make much, if any, difference to the causes of distress, either now or in the past. We have to do without the magic of reinterpretation. There may, of course, be possibilities for those with the necessary powers and resources – money, education, a sustaining social network – to shift their position in the world a little to their advantage, but they will always be a privileged few.

Nearly everything worth saying has been said before. I suggest that psychotherapists could do worse than see – and develop – their role as contributing to 'liberal education' of the kind advocated by C. Wright Mills (1956):

> The knowledgeable man in the genuine public is able to turn his personal troubles into social issues, to see their relevance for his community and his community's relevance for them. He understands that what he thinks and feels as personal troubles are very often not only that but problems shared by others and indeed not subject to solution by any one individual but only by modifications of the structure of the groups in which he lives and sometimes the structure of the entire society.
>
> Men in masses are gripped by personal troubles, but they are not aware of their true meaning and source. Men in public confront issues, and they are aware of their terms. It is the task of the liberal institution, as of the liberally educated man, continually to translate troubles into issues and issues into the terms of their human meaning for the individual. In the absence of deep and wide political debate, schools for adults and adolescents could perhaps become hospitable frameworks for just such debate. In a community of publics the task of liberal would be: to keep the public from being

overwhelmed; to help produce the disciplined and informed mind that cannot be overwhelmed; to help develop the bold and sensible individual that cannot be sunk by the burdens of mass life. But educational practice has not made knowledge directly relevant to the human need of the troubled person of the twentieth century or to the social practices of the citizen. The citizen cannot now see the roots of his own biases and frustrations, nor think clearly about himself, nor for that matter about anything else. He does not see the frustration of idea, of intellect, by the present organization of society, and he is not able to meet the tasks now confronting 'the intelligent citizen'.

These words were conceived at the middle of the last century. We've got some catching up to do.

CHAPTER 10

Is the unconscious really all that unconscious?[1]

M. GUY THOMPSON

There is little question in the minds of every psychoanalytic practitioner that Freud's conception of the unconscious is the pivot around which psychoanalysis orbits, even if the particulars as to what the unconscious comprises have been debated by every psychoanalytic school that has followed in his wake. Despite the controversial nature of this concept, there is a pervasive agreement among analysts that whatever the unconscious is, it is certainly not a form of *consciousness.* That being said, this is precisely the dilemma that philosophers have found most troubling about the psychoanalytic conception of the unconscious and the reason why so many have questioned its efficacy. In a recent book, Grotstein (1999) addressed a fundamental and as yet unresolved difficulty in prevailing conceptions of the unconscious, which follows when we attempt to assign the very core of our being to a hypothesized unconscious agent that we can never know directly, and whose existence we must infer and, hence, *believe* to be so, as an article of faith. Grotstein concluded that we are still, after 100 years of trying, unable to account for this persistent yet obstinate contradiction: that the unconscious knows all, but is 'known' by no one.

Like many, I have been haunted by this anomaly over the course of my analytic career. For the purposes of this chapter, however, my concern is not a theoretical one but one of approaching the problem phenomenologically, which is to say from the perspective of the psychoanalyst's *lived experience,* what has been depicted by the interpersonal school as an experience-near paradigm. Therefore, I do not intend to offer a new theory about the nature of the unconscious but rather to explore the relationship between the alleged existence of the unconscious and one's experience of it. In the course of my exploration of this problem I shall address a number of critical questions: Does it make sense, for example, to speak in terms of one's capacity to 'experience' the unconscious if the very concept of the unconscious refers to that which is beyond experience? Moreover, does it make sense to talk in terms of suffering 'unconscious experiences' if one is not *aware* of the experiences one is presumed to be suffering? And finally, allowing that experience is, at its margins, tentative and ambiguous, how does one account for those phenomena on the periphery of experience, whether such phenomena are characterized as unconscious (Freud), ambiguous (Merleau-Ponty), mysterious (Heidegger), unformulated (Sullivan), or simply hidden?

I do not claim to have found the answers to these questions or even to have taken a preliminary step in that direction. Instead, I merely seek to explore some of the problematics that the psychoanalytic conception of the unconscious has obliged us to live with ever since Freud formulated it one century ago. To this end I shall focus the bulk of my attention on Freud's conception of the unconscious, as this is the one that all psychoanalysts, no matter what school or perspective they adhere to, have inherited, with all the attendant doubts and misgivings it has fostered. First, I shall review Freud's depiction of the unconscious in relation to his conception of psychic reality, and then turn to some of the philosophical problems that derive from his characterization of the 'two types' of mental functioning, primary and secondary thought processes. Finally, I shall review some of the implications that derive from the psychoanalytic conception of the unconscious by employing a phenomenological critique of its presuppositions, emphasizing the role of Being and experience in the psychoanalytic encounter.

My aim is not a theoretical one but it is nonetheless relevant to theoretical concerns because the questions raised are of a philosophical nature. I am aware that numerous psychoanalysts since Freud have endeavored to situate his conception of the unconscious in light of subsequent theoretical developments, but my purpose is not to assess these developments with a view to contrasting them with Freud's. Instead, I shall review the problematics of Freud's thesis in the light of those philosophers whose perspective is at odds with the very notion of an 'unconscious' portion of the mind and who endeavour to situate the phenomena that Freud deemed unconscious in the context of consciousness itself, or in the case of Heidegger one that dispenses with the conscious/unconscious controversy altogether. To this end I shall propose that the unconscious is a form of sentient, nascent 'consciousness' – implied in Freud's own depiction of it – but a form of consciousness that is unavailable to *experience*. Hence I shall characterize the purpose of the psychoanalytic endeavour as one of bringing those aspects of consciousness that lie on the periphery of experience to experience, to the degree that is feasible in each case.

Freud's conception of psychic reality

Freud's first topography for demarcating the distinction between conscious and unconscious aspects of the mind concerned the nature of fantasy and the role it plays in the life of the neurotic. As a consequence of his experiments with hypnotism Freud surmised that every individual is driven by two kinds of fantasies, of one of which they are aware and the other of which they are unaware. Freud chose to term those of which one is unaware 'unconscious' because we have no conscious experience of them, but are nonetheless capable of discerning their existence when hypnotized. Such so-called unconscious fantasies have been repressed, but because they reside 'in' the unconscious they engender psychic conflict, the manifestation of which accounts for psychopathology, dream formation, and parapraxes.

Thus Freud's first, topographical, model of the unconscious was relatively simple: one portion of the mind is conscious and the thoughts it contains are in the forefront of awareness (or *conscious experience*), whereas another portion of the mind is unconscious and is composed of fantasies that have suffered repression (or more primitive defence mechanisms). Freud also included a third element in this topography, the 'preconscious', which contains thoughts and memories that, although not immediately conscious, are nonetheless available to consciousness in principle. Freud's earlier topography is essentially an outline of the vicissitudes of the individual's psychic life, what Freud termed 'psychic reality'. Freud's depiction of psychic reality is not, however, predicated on the kind of factual reality that is investigated by the empirical sciences, because it is a kind of 'reality' that one *experiences* in the form of fantasy, delusion, or hallucination. Quoting Freud (1913, p. 159):

> What lie behind the sense of guilt of neurotics [for example] are always *psychical* realities and never *factual* ones. What characterizes neurotics is that they prefer psychical to factual reality and react just as seriously to thoughts as normal people do to realities. [emphases in original]

Yet, in what sense can one treat such fantasies as 'realities' when they are not real? Freud recognized that fantasies can be *experienced* as real in the same way that objective reality – which is to say, that which is not our invention – is typically experienced. In other words, fantasies, although not literal depictions of the past, nevertheless convey meaning, and such meanings are capable of telling us more about our patients than the so-called facts of their history. By *interpreting* both fantasies and symptoms as meaningful, Freud was able to obtain truths about his patients that were otherwise hidden. His opposition between 'psychic' and 'external' realities served to juxtapose an inherently *personal* reality with a more literal one. This isn't to say that literal, or objective, reality is necessarily false but it was Freud's genius to see that the truth about one's history can be derived from the communication of otherwise innocuous musings, by interpreting a patient's fantasies as disguised messages. The recognition that fantasies could be conceived as messages suggested there was something 'hidden' in them that the patient neither recognized nor appreciated.

Hence, fantasies serve a purpose: they disclose the intentional structure of the individual's deepest longings and aspirations. But Freud lacked a conception of intentionality that could explain how his patients were able to convey truths they didn't 'know' in a disguised and indirect manner. In other words, his patients *unconsciously intended* their symptoms and the attendant fantasies that explained them – they weren't 'caused' by their unconscious. Freud nevertheless suspected the existence of an unconscious form of subjectivity that was capable of intending symptoms when he coined the term 'counter-will' in one of his earliest papers. Leavy (1988) brought attention to Freud's difficulty in grappling with the notion of an 'unconscious subject' in a study of the development of Freud's psychoanalytic theories.

> One of Freud's earliest ways of presenting the idea of unconscious motivation was as 'counter-will' (Gegenwille), a word that is worth keeping in mind whenever we say 'the unconscious'. Will, so rich in philosophical overtones, has been played down by psychoanalysis. Being a verb as well as a noun, the word will always implies a subject. When I do something that I claim I didn't want to do . . . it does no good to plead that blind, impersonal, unconscious forces 'did' the act: *they* are *me*. (p. 8) [emphases added]

Leavy's use of the term 'will' is not, of course, limited to the conventional usage of *conscious* will, any more than Freud's expression 'counter-will' is. The term 'will' refers to an intentional act that often alludes to *pre-reflective* (or 'unconscious') sources of motivation. Freud (1892) first used the term 'counter-will' in a paper on hypnotism where he referred to an idea of which the patient is unaware, but was brought to conscious awareness under hypnosis. Freud continued to use the term in a variety of contexts for some 20 years. The last time he apparently used it was in a paper on love and sexual impotence that was published in 1912. Leavy notes that the term seems to have disappeared thereafter. According to Leavy:

> Probably the generalization fell apart into concepts like resistance, repression, unconscious conflict, and ultimately, drive. But the gain in specificity was accompanied by the loss of the implication of a personal 'will.' (p. 12n)

As Freud pursued his project of establishing the empirical 'causes' of symptoms, his earlier notion of the unconscious as a subtle agent, or anonymous ego, or counter-will, receded into the background. Yet the tendency to depersonalize the unconscious into impersonal drives, forces, and instincts has not met with universal acceptance, even in psychoanalytic circles. The terms 'instinct' and 'drive' were scarcely used before 1905, although the concepts were there under other guises. Yet, expressions like 'affective ideas' and 'wishful impulses' clearly convey more subjective nuances than the terms 'instinct,' 'drive,' or 'excitations,' for example. With all the current debate over Strachey's translation of Freud into English – especially the translation of *trieb* into either 'drive' or 'instinct' – neither the use of *trieb* nor drive alters Freud's understanding of the concept.

Whichever term one prefers, whether drive or instinct, psychoanalysts, with few exceptions, find it agreeable to use a term in which the *impersonal* aspect of the unconscious predominates. One of those exceptions, in addition to Leavy, was Hans Loewald, who took considerable care to explain how his use of the term 'instinct' was intended to convey a human quality. According to Loewald (1980, pp. 152–3):

> When I speak of instinctual forces and of instincts or instinctual drives, I define them as motivational, i.e., both motivated and motivating ... [For me] instincts remain relational phenomena, rather than being considered energies within a closed system.

Terms such as 'motive' and 'relational' lend a clearly personal nuance to the term 'instinct', and even the word 'phenomena' sounds more personal than 'forces'. If Freud's shift from counter-will to instinct lent credence to his claim that psychoanalysis, at least in appearance, deserved the status of a science, it is nevertheless a science more similar to that of academic psychologists who 'study' rats or physicists who 'measure' energies. However much some analysts may strive to measure the psychoanalytic experience in specifically scientific terms, the legitimacy of one's fantasy life can be grasped only metaphorically and experientially, in terms that remain personal in nature.[2]

Freud's formulation of two types of mental functioning

After Freud formulated his theory of the structural model in 1923, his earlier allusions to the unconscious as a 'second subject' that behaved as a 'counter-will' gradually disappeared. The precedent for this revision was predetermined even earlier by Freud's distinction between primary and secondary thought processes. Indeed, the publication of Freud's (1911) *Formulations on the two principles of mental functioning* roughly coincided with his final reference to the unconscious as 'counter-will' in 1912.

In this formulation, Freud conceived the primary thought processes as essentially unconscious. Hence they were deemed to account for such psychic phenomena as displacement, condensation, the ability to symbolize and to apprehend time and syntax, as well as dreaming. Since the primary thought processes are supposed to be governed by the pleasure principle, they are responsible for that portion of the mind that, 'strives toward gaining pleasure' and withdraws from 'any event that might arouse [pain]' (Freud, 1911, p. 219). More to the point, Freud held that unconscious processes were 'the older, primary processes [and] the residues of a phase of development in which they were the only kind of mental process' that was available to the infant (p. 219). Thus, whatever the infant wished for, says Freud, 'was simply presented in a hallucinatory manner, just as still happens today with our dream-thoughts each night' (p. 219).

However primitive the primary thought processes may seem, they are nonetheless perfectly capable of sensing that when the infant's hallucinatory anticipation of pleasure fails to materialize another means of obtaining gratification must be substituted in its place. Moreover, the primary thought processes are also presumed to be capable of 'experiencing' disappointment, leading to the necessity for another means of engaging the world. Quoting Freud:

> It was ... the non-occurrence of the expected satisfaction, the disappointment *experienced,* that led to the abandonment of this attempt at satisfaction by means of hallucination. Instead of it, the psychical apparatus *had to decide* to form a conception of the real circumstances in the external world and to endeavor to make a real alteration in them. A new principle of mental functioning was thus introduced; what was presented in the mind was no longer what was agreeable but what was real, even if it happened to be disagreeable, [thus paving the way for] setting up the reality principle ... (p. 219) [emphases added]

Freud's conception of the unconscious is based more or less entirely on the distinction between these two principles of thinking. Now the secondary thought processes, governed by the reality principle, assume responsibility for the individual's relationship with the social world, including the capacity for rationality, logic, grammar, and verbalization. It does not take much reflection to see that there is something unwieldy, even contradictory, about the way Freud unceremoniously divides facets of the mind between these two principles of mental functioning. For example, if the primary thought processes are capable only of striving toward pleasure and avoiding unpleasure, and the secondary thought processes are in turn responsible for delaying gratification while formulating plans in pursuit of one's goals, to *what* or *whom* is Freud referring when he suggests that it is the 'psychical apparatus' that 'decides to form a conception of the real circumstances' encountered, and then 'endeavors to make a real alteration in them' (p. 219)? Is the so-called 'psychical apparatus' the primary, or the secondary, thought processes?

We can presumably eliminate the secondary thought processes from this logical conundrum because Freud had just explained that the *psychical apparatus* (whatever that is) was obliged to bring these very processes *into being* in the first place. On the other hand, we can also eliminate the primary thought processes from contention because Freud proposes the need for *a more realistic mode of thinking* than already existed, precisely because the primary processes are, by definition, incapable of executing them.

Many of the questions that Grotstein raises in response to Freud's formulation of the two types of mental functioning are devoted to the need to find a resolution to this problem, and there has been no shortage of subsequent analysts who have raised this point. For example, Charles Rycroft (1968) questioned Freud's conception of the two types of thinking in his 1962 paper, 'Beyond the reality principle' (pp. 102–13). There he questioned whether it makes sense to insist that the primary thought processes necessarily precede the secondary ones. Rycroft notes that even Freud doubted it, because according to a footnote in his paper on the 'Two principles of mental functioning', Freud himself admitted that

> It will rightly be objected that an organization which was a slave to the pleasure-principle and neglected the reality of the external world could not maintain itself alive for the shortest time, so that it could not come into existence at all. The employment of a fiction like this is, however, justified when one considers that the infant – provided that one includes with it the care it receives from its mother – does almost realize a psychical system of this kind. (quoted in Rycroft, 1968, pp. 102–3)

Freud might have added to this 'fiction' the notion that the infant is as helpless as Freud suggests before it elicits the protection of its developing ego. Rycroft (1968, p. 103) observes, 'Freud's notion that the primary processes precede the secondary in individual development was dependent on … the helplessness of the infant and his having therefore assumed that the mother–infant relationship … was one in which the mother was in touch with reality while the infant only had wishes.' Again, we cannot help being struck by the notion that the infant needs somebody else (in this case, the mother or, later, an ego) to grapple with the social world on its behalf. Rycroft concurs with the view of many child analysts that infants aren't as helpless as Freud supposed. According to Rycroft (1968, p. 101):

> If one starts from the assumption that the mother is the infant's external reality and that the mother–infant relationship is from the very beginning a process of mental adaptation, to which the infant contributes by actions such as crying, clinging, and sucking, which evoke maternal responses in the mother, one is forced to conclude that the infant engages in realistic and adaptive behavior [from the very start].

Rycroft concludes that the secondary thought processes probably operate earlier than Freud suspected and that they even coincide with primary process thinking. Even if Freud was right in proposing that infants are indeed ruled by primary thought processes, what if those processes happen to include those very qualities he attributed to the secondary, such as rationality, judgement and decision-making – even an acute grasp of reality? Wouldn't such a scenario, in turn, negate the utility of the ego's so-called synthetic powers? If Freud's *original* formulation of the ego is retained – that it is essentially defensive in nature – then the so-called 'unconscious' id, which is governed by the primary thought processes, could be conceived as *a form of consciousness*. Freud's wish to distinguish between two types of thinking could be retained, but only after remodelling their capacities and functions. Paradoxically, what I am proposing would in many ways reverse Freud's schema. The primary thought processes – which I propose are 'conscious' but *pre-reflective* and, hence, not 'experienced' – enjoy a spontaneous relationship with the social world, while the secondary thought processes – those employing the tasks of *reflective consciousness* – determine the individual's relationship with himself or herself.

The nature of subjectivity has always puzzled philosophers and psychologists alike. Freud's depiction of an unconscious agency whose designs need to be interpreted in order to be understood was his singular contribution to our age. But his theories could never explain what his intuition was capable of perceiving. Freud hypothesized some sort of self, or agency, prior to the formation of the ego. This was supported by his theory of primary thought processes and, in another context, by his conception of primary narcissism. We know that the id is capable of thought because, after all, it decided to form an extension of itself – the ego – in order to insulate itself against the anxiety of being in the world.

In practical terms, the division between the id and the ego is a false one. As Freud himself acknowledged, the ego is merely an 'outer layer' of the id; it was never conceived as a separate entity. If we expect to be consistent with the ego's origins, then that ego – following even Freud's reasoning – is nothing more than a 'reservoir' of anxiety; in fact, our experience of anxiety itself.

Sartre's critique of the unconscious

Given all the attendant problems that Freud's conception of the unconscious has elicited, it is surprising that there is little, if any, attention paid to the prevailing conception of consciousness it presupposes. Whereas Freud depicted psychoanalysis as essentially a science of the *unconscious*, it is impossible to escape the observation that it is also a science – if we can call it that – that is preoccupied with *consciousness* itself, if only implicitly. Terms like truth, epistemology, knowledge, understanding, and comprehension pervade virtually every psychoanalytic paper that is devoted to the unconscious as a concept. But isn't our fascination about the unconscious and our failure to resolve questions about its nature a consequence of our obsession with consciousness and the epistemological bias it engenders?

These are among the questions that phenomenologists such as Jean-Paul Sartre, Maurice Merleau-Ponty, Martin Heidegger, and Paul Ricoeur devoted the bulk of their philosophical writings to: what is the importance of knowledge and what role does it serve in our everyday lives? Of all the phenomenologists, it was perhaps Sartre (1981) who took psychoanalysis the most seriously, even conceiving his own brand of 'existential psychoanalysis'. Fascinated with Freud, the man as well as his project, Sartre was also a Frenchman and, like all French philosophers, was preoccupied with the nature of rationality, a legacy of Descartes. Yet Sartre's fascination with Freud alerted him at a very early stage of his intellectual development to the problems I have summarized above.

Sartre (1962, pp. 48–55; 1981, pp. 153–71) rejected Freud's topographical model for similar reasons that Freud did. In Freud's earlier topographical model the only thing separating the system-conscious from the system-unconscious is the so-called 'censor', which serves to regulate what is permitted into consciousness and, contrariwise, what is repressed into the unconscious. Hence the censor is aware of everything, that which is conscious and unconscious alike. Yet because the ego is *unaware* of the censor, this model posits a 'second consciousness' (the censor) that is both unknown and unknowable to the ego in principle. Sartre's problem with this model is obvious: the so-called censor is the *de facto* 'person' who is being analysed and who disclaims knowledge of all the shannanigans he employs to disguise what he is up to, 'bad faith' in its essence. As we saw earlier, Freud also had problems with the implications of a 'second thinking subject,' and decided to discard this model for one that contained only one subject that *knows*, the conscious portion of the ego, and not one but *three* subjects that do not know: the id, the superego, and that portion of the ego that is responsible for defence mechanisms.

Freud's subsequent revision of his earlier model, however, fares little better in Sartre's opinion. The topographical model is replaced with one that is less concerned with demarcating conscious and unconscious portions of the psyche than with determining the complex nature of psychic 'agency,' or subjectivity. Although the two models are not entirely complementary, it is easy to recognize those elements of the second model that were intended to remedy the problems engendered by the first. Now the id more or less assumes the role of the system-unconscious, whereas the ego more or less assumes the tasks of the system-conscious. Ironically, the system-preconscious does not enjoy a direct parallel with the third agency in Freud's new apparatus, the superego; instead, the superego adopts some of the functions of the now-abandoned *censor*, due to its ability to prohibit those wishes and desires it deems unacceptable. Sartre's principal complaint with the new model is that it still fails to resolve the problem of bad faith, the problem of a 'lie without a liar'. If anything, the new model moves even further away from Sartre's efforts to *personalize* the unconscious, by instituting three psychic agencies that protect the conscious ego from any responsibility for its actions. How would Sartre propose to remedy this situation, to account for those actions that Freud claimed the 'conscious' patient is 'unconscious' of devising, while holding the conscious patient responsible for performing them?

Sartre accomplishes this by introducing two sets of critical distinctions into the prevailing psychoanalytic vocabulary. The first is a distinction between *pre-reflective* consciousness and *reflective* consciousness, and the second is between *consciousness* and *knowledge*. Sartre summarizes the basic dilemma in Freud's conception of the unconscious – contained in both the topographical and structural models – with the following questions: how can the subject (a divided 'subject' notwithstanding) not know that he is possessed of a feeling or sentiment that he is in possession of? And if, indeed, the unconscious is just another word for *consciousness* (Sartre's position), how can the subject, even by Sartre's reckoning, not know what he is 'conscious' of? Sartre's thesis of 'pre-reflective' consciousness is his effort to solve this riddle. Following Husserl's thesis, Sartre saw consciousness as *intentional*, which means it is always conscious *of something*. Hence there is no such thing as 'empty' consciousness; nor is there such a thing as a 'container' or 'receptacle' that houses consciousness – a formulation that rejects not only Freud's thesis but Melanie Klein's 'part-objects' hypothesis as well. Rather, consciousness is always 'outside' itself and 'in' the things that constitute it as consciousness-of something. In Sartre's (1957b, pp. 48–9) words:

> Intentionality is not the way in which a subject tries to make 'contact' with an object that exists beside it. *Intentionality is what makes up the very subjectivity of subjects.* [emphasis in original]

In other words, the concept of intentionality renders subjectivity as already and in its essence a *theory of intersubjectivity,* because to be a subject is, by necessity, to be engaged with some thing 'other' than one's self – even if this other something is just an idea. Sartre elaborates how this thesis would be applied to the social world specifically:

> When I run after a streetcar, when I look at the time, when I am absorbed in contemplating a portrait, there is no I (or 'ego'). There is [only] consciousness *of the streetcar-having-to-be-overtaken,* etc … In fact, I am then plunged into the world of objects; it is they which constitute the unity of my consciousness; it is they which present themselves with values, with attractive and repellent qualities – but *me* – I have disappeared; I have annihilated myself [in the moment of conscious apprehension]. (Sartre, 1957b, pp. 48–9)

Thus, when I experience a rock, a tree, a feeling of sadness, or the object of my desire in the bedroom, I experience them just where they are: beside a hill, in the meadow, in my heart, in relation to myself and my beloved. Consciousness and the object-of-consciousness are given at one stroke. These things constitute my consciousness of them just as I constitute their existence as things through the act in which I perceive them and give them a name. And because naming things is a purely human activity, these things do not exist as rocks, trees, or emotions in the absence of a human consciousness that is capable of apprehending them through the constitutive power of language.

However, such acts of apprehension do not necessarily imply 'knowledge' of what I am conscious of. Sartre makes a distinction between the *pre-reflective* apprehension of an object and our *reflective* 'witnessing' of the act. Ordinarily when I am pre-reflectively conscious of a feeling, for example, I intuit the feeling of sadness and, in turn, reflectively acknowledge this feeling as sadness: I feel sad and experience myself as a sad individual more or less simultaneously. But I am also capable of feeling sadness, or anger, or envy without *knowing* I am sad, or angry, or envious, as such. When such a state is pointed out to me by my analyst I am surprised to be alerted to this observation. Of course, I may resist the analyst's intervention and reject it, but I may also admit it because, on being alerted to this possibility, I am also capable of recognizing this feeling *as mine.* Sartre argues that I would be incapable of recognizing thoughts or ideas of which I claim no awareness *unless I had been conscious of these feelings in the first place on a pre-reflective level.*

In other words, what Freud labels consciousness, Sartre designates 'reflective consciousness' (knowing that I am conscious of it) and what Freud labels the unconscious (or preconscious) Sartre designates as that moment of pre-reflective consciousness that, due to resistance, *has not yielded to reflective awareness* and, hence, to 'knowledge' of it, after the fact. This is why I can be conscious of something that I have no immediate knowledge of, and why I can become knowledgeable about something that I am, so to speak, 'unconscious' of, but am subsequently able to recognize as mine when a timely interpretation alerts me to it. Thus, I can only *experience* something I have knowledge of, but not what I am merely 'conscious' of. The power of analysis, according to Sartre, lies in its capacity to 'arrest' time for the patient, by allowing the neurotic (or psychotic) the opportunity to slow the pace of his anxiety-ridden experience in order to ponder what his experience is, in its immediacy.

Of course, the decisive difference between Sartre's and Freud's respective formulations isn't that it merely substitutes Freud's terminology with Sartre's; on a more radical level it eliminates a need for the notion of a 'second thinking subject' *behind* or *beneath* consciousness, and ultimately offers a means for personalizing the unconscious in a manner that Freud was unable to. There are still problems, however, even with Sartre's formulation. Because Sartre shared with Freud an obsession with the nature of consciousness he went even further than Freud and eliminated the need for an 'unconscious' altogether, replacing Freud's formulation with a model that was rooted solely in a theory of consciousness, a solution that was even more rationalistic than Freud's. Sartre even acknowledged late in life that his earlier project had been too indebted to Descartes and suffered from being infused with rationalism, as though 'comprehension' is the final arbiter to psychic liberation.

Ironically, despite Freud's preoccupation with epistemology he moved away from his earlier bent toward intellectualism and subsequently adopted the more sceptical position that knowledge, per se, plays a limited role in the psychoanalytic experience. The move away from interpretative schemes toward transference (and more recently, relational) conceptualizations of psychoanalysis reflects the growing influence of phenomenology, scepticism, and hermeneutics on psychoanalytic practice. If we want to find a philosophical model that can integrate all these influences, however, we shall not find it in Sartre but in someone who was a mentor to him in the earliest days of his intellectual development: Martin Heidegger. I shall now review those elements of Heidegger's philosophy that appear to solve the problem of the unconscious that neither Freud or Sartre was able to solve.

Heidegger's conception of being and experience

Although he was never all that interested in psychoanalysis, and what little he knew of it dismayed him, there are many aspects of Heidegger's philosophy that are sympathetic to it. Unlike Sartre and Freud, Heidegger was not interested in the nature of consciousness *per se*, because he thought it tended to psychologize our conception of human experience instead of getting to its roots. Heidegger's reasons for taking this position were complex, but at the heart of them was a conviction that epistemology is not a viable means for getting to the bottom of what our suffering is about. Of all the phenomenologists of his generation, Heidegger was alone in conceiving philosophy as a therapy whose purpose is to heal the human soul. This made Heidegger unpopular with academic philosophers but a valuable resource to a group of European psychiatrists and psychoanalysts who saw in his work a humanistic alternative to Freud's penchant for theory. Ironically, many of them, including Medard Boss, Ludwig Binswanger, Eugene Minkowski, and Viktor Frankl, threw out the baby with the bathwater in their haste to separate themselves from the psychoanalytic *zeitgeist* by replacing it with Heidegger as the basis for their clinical theories. This culminated in the impoverishment of both traditions, and only a handful of psychoanalysts (such as Hans Loewald, Stanley Leavy, Paul Federn, and RD Laing) sought to integrate elements of Heidegger's philosophy into Freud's conception of psychoanalysis.

Heidegger is probably most famous for his decision to root his philosophy in ontology, the study of Being, instead of epistemology, the study of knowledge. This is irritating to philosophers and psychologists alike because it discards epistemological questions in favour of a fundamental critique of what human existence is about. This is a topic that most people would prefer to leave alone, for why question the 'why' of our existence when it is patently obvious that we, in fact, exist? But Heidegger was not simply interested in why we exist but how and to what end. For example, when I pause to take stock of myself by asking, 'who am I?', I am asking the question about the *meaning of Being*. In fact, we submit to Being all the time but without knowing it. Whenever we are engaged in writing a paper, painting a picture, driving a car or riding a bicycle, we 'let go' of our rational and conscious control of the world and in that letting-go we submit to Being, an experience that, by its nature, we cannot think our way through. Arguably the most radical critic of Descartes' rationalistic constitution of subjectivity, Heidegger countered that we live our lives in an everyday sort of way *without* thinking about what we are doing and, more importantly, without having to think our way through our activities as a matter of course. The place he assigned to reason is, in effect, an after-the-fact operation that is not primary to our engagement with the world, but secondary; it is only when our involvement with the world breaks down that we take the time to divorce ourselves from it for the purpose of pondering what has happened and why.

Contrary to both Husserl and Sartre, who believed it is possible to employ the conscious portion of the mind in order to fathom the bedrock of who I am in tandem with the choices that determine my subjectivity, Heidegger countered that it is impossible ever to get 'behind' our constitutive acts in such a way that we can determine the acts we intend to embark on *before* committing them. Whereas Sartre argued that I 'choose' the person that I am and can always change who I am by choosing to be someone else, Heidegger observed that my ability to comprehend the choices I make necessarily occurs *after* the fact, so that I am always endeavouring to 'discover' (or disclose) the acts I have *already* made in a world that is not my construction, but is in significant measure 'other' than my intent or volition. This is because I am always embedded in a situation that is imbued with moods and feelings that conspire to 'determine' my choices before I am ever conscious of having made them. Thus my experience of myself is one of having been 'thrown' into the situation I find myself in, and then collecting myself in order to fathom how I got here and what my motives have been, in hindsight.

Hence, more important for Heidegger than the comprehension of the world (Descartes), the search for pleasure (Freud), or management of anxiety (Klein), is the *need to orient* ourselves at every moment in time, by asking ourselves, where are we, what are we doing here, to what do we belong? It is my sense of who I am to ask this question that constitutes me in my existence. Although the question of who-ness is the foundation of Heidegger's philosophy, it is important to understand that this is not a psychological question of identity, as per Erikson, but an ontological question of Being, because it is bigger than the psyche or the self. At bottom, this question is presupposed when we query the role of the unconscious, but it replaces Freud's psychologization of this question with an existential one. If one removes these questions from a strictly philosophical context and inserts them into one that is specifically clinical, one readily recognizes that Heidegger is raising the same questions that our analytic patients are struggling with, only they lack the the means with which to consider them.

Because Heidegger rejected epistemology, his philosophy is inherently sceptical,[3] not in the sense of doubting that I can know anything but because knowledge doesn't get to the heart of what my life is about. Moreover, this attitude is easily adapted for the purposes of psychoanalytic inquiry, as any number of contemporary psychoanalysts have recognized. The novelty of this perspective has also insinuated its way into the thinking of many disparate (including 'classical' as well as contemporary) psychoanalytic practitioners, some by virtue of their acquaintance with Heidegger's philosophy (Leavy, 1980, 1988; Laing, 1960, 1969), some by virtue of Sullivan's interpersonal theory (Levenson,

1972, 1983, 1991), Stern (1997), Bromberg (1998), Langan (1993), and others through the influence of classical psychoanalysts such as Hans Loewald (1980), a self-identified Freudian analyst who studied with Heidegger in his youth. What holds such disparate theoretical outlooks together is their respective conceptions of experience. Heidegger's movement from epistemology toward ontology led to his abandoning concepts like consciousness and even intentionality (as it was conceived by Husserl) in favour of a critique of our relationship with Being and the manner it is disclosed to us in the immediacy of everyday experience.

How, then, does Heidegger conceive of experience and why is this an ontological question instead of an epistemological or psychological one? From a strictly Heideggerian perspective, psychoanalysis is already concerned with our manner of Being and has been from the start. People go into analysis because they are not satisfied with the manner of Being they are in and want to change it. But in order to determine what our manner of Being is about we have to give ourselves to it, through our experience of it. In its essence, psychoanalysis gives us the opportunity to give thought to our experience by taking the time that is needed to ponder it. Heidegger would have agreed with Freud that there are indeed 'two types' of thinking that we typically employ, although he wouldn't formulate them in the way that either Freud or Sartre proposed. Heidegger not only rejected Freud's conception of the unconscious but also avoided employing the term 'consciousness' in the convoluted manner that Sartre did, opting instead to focus his attention on two types of 'thinking': calculative and meditative. Basically, Heidegger believed that the nature of consciousness is so inherently mysterious that it is misleading to equate it with synonyms like 'awareness' or 'knowledge'. We have seen from the thicket of contradictions that both Freud and Sartre entertained about the distinction between a conscious and unconscious portion of the mind that such a distinction ultimately dissolves into a well of confusion.

Whereas all analysts are familiar with situations when their patients resist thinking about certain topics because they are distressing to them and because they prefer thinking about topics that are more pleasing or interesting, Heidegger observed that one manner of thinking (whatever the topic happens to be) is inherently comforting whereas the other is more liable to elicit anxiety or dread (*angst*). We tend to avoid thinking the thoughts that make us anxious and abandon ourselves to thoughts, speculations, and fantasies that are soporific. The prospect of enduring the kind of anxiety that genuine thought entails is distressing and the tactics we employ to avoid it are universal. The task of analysis is to nudge our thinking into those areas we typically avoid so that we can access a region of our existence that we are loath to explore, but which lies at the heart of our humanity. This is effected by *experiencing what our suffering is about,* and allowing such experiences to change us; not by virtue of knowing more than we already do about ourselves, but by helping us accommodate a dimension of our experience that we avoid at every turn. When we succumb to such experiences we are thrown into a different manner of experiencing ourselves and what we, as 'selves', are about.

If the foregoing is to make any sense we must first understand why Heidegger insists on depicting the manner of Being he is concerned about with a capital 'B', a distinction that Heidegger calls 'the ontological difference'. The word 'being' (with a little 'b') is an 'entity,' as such, and is the object of scientific investigation as well as our everyday ordinary perceptions: trees, houses, tables, feelings, and so on. In other words, it refers to things as they seem at first blush. Heidegger, however, transforms these 'things' (beings, or entities) into Being by recognizing their *temporal* dimension. Hence 'beings' necessarily exist *in time,* in a temporal flux of past-present-future (what we ordinarily call 'now'). This temporalization of beings into Being, however, can be achieved only by a *human* being who is privy to a relationship with objects of reflection by virtue of the capacity to think about them and interpret what they mean. Hence, our relationship with time reveals what the Being of 'beings' shares in common: the world as it is disclosed or 'illuminated' *to a person* by virtue of his or her capacity to experience the object in question. In other words, beings (things, objects, perceptions) are transformed into Being when they are experienced by virtue of my capacity to interpret their significance for *me.* This observation sheds light on what psychoanalysts are already doing whenever they employ interpretations for the purpose of helping their patients appreciate that everything they experience is unique to them alone. This is because everything they are capable of experiencing contains an historical component, and only they have lived the history that is theirs. Where Heidegger parts company with most analysts, however, is that such realizations are not intended to merely help patients 'understand' themselves better but to experience who and what they are, fundamentally. Like Heidegger, the analyst 'temporalizes' the patient's *experience* by interpreting its historical antecedents, and in the act of temporalization helps the patient's world come alive. This is what Heidegger calls doing 'fundamental ontology'.

Thought – and the *experience* of thinking

As noted earlier, in Heidegger's later thought he emphasized a form of thinking he characterized as meditative, a kind of thought that is usually dismissed as irrelevant by scientists and academics who employ a manner of thinking Heidegger calls calculative. What kind of thought does meditative thinking entail? J Glenn Gray (1968, pp. x–xi) suggests it is helpful first to understand what Heidegger does not mean by meditative thinking:

> Thinking is, in the first place, not what we call having an opinion or a notion. Second, it is not representing or having an idea (*vorstellen*) about something or a state of affairs ... Third, thinking is not ratiocination, developing a chain of premises which lead to a valid conclusion ... [Meditative] thinking is not so much an act as a way of living or dwelling – as we in America would put it, a way of life.

Offering a different perspective on this enigmatic proposition, Macquarrie (1994, pp. 77–8) proposes that

> 'Meditation' suggests a kind of thought in which the mind is docile and receptive to whatever it is thinking about. Such thought may be contrasted [for example] with the active investigative thought of the natural sciences.

In comparison, Heidegger characterizes calculative thinking as the conventional norm and a by-product of the technological age in which we live. Its roots go all the way back to Plato, but its impact on culture was not fully formed until the scientific revolution that was inspired by Descartes in the sixteenth century. The tendency to perceive the world in the abstract and conceptual manner that calculative thinking entails took an even sharper turn in the twentieth century with the birth of the computer era and the amazing gains that technology has enjoyed over the past century, evidenced in the development of housing, transportation, medicine, and so on. But have these gains made us any happier? The question of technology is a complicated one and remained the focus of Heidegger's attention throughout his lifetime. It would be extreme to suggest Heidegger was opposed to science, but he believed that science has overtaken our lives to such a degree that we have now forgotten how to think in a non-scientific manner. One of Heidegger's most infamous statements about the status of science is that 'science does not *think*' and that the thinking science employs is an impoverished variation of it, epitomized by the credence given to scientific 'research' and the like, which Heidegger dismisses as thoughtless and thought-poor.

Indeed, one of the consequences of the technological age is what has recently been depicted as the 'postmodern condition', the ultimate expression of our contemporary obsession with technology and the technology culture it has spawned. This is a culture that, from Heidegger's perspective, is fundamentally ill in the sense of being 'ill at ease' with itself, a product of the pervasive emptiness that characterizes the twentieth-century neurosis. Heidegger saw psychoanalysis as the inevitable response to the malaise in which postmodern Man is imprisoned, because once we created this dire situation it was necessary that we fashion a cure for it. What, in Heidegger's opinion, is the cure for such malaise? To simply remember how to think in the manner that we have forgotten. In fact, this is the kind of thinking that Freud, despite his penchant for science, stumbled upon on his own, not by engaging in scientific research but by examining his own condition. His efforts culminated in the radical treatment scheme that lies at the heart of the psychoanalytic endeavour, epitomized by the free association method and its complement, the analyst's 'free-floating attentiveness' (neutrality – or what Keats (Leavy, 1970) termed 'negative capability') that he counselled analytic practitioners to adopt.[4]

Whereas in Heidegger's earlier period he was concerned with the region of our everyday activities that we perform as a matter of course without having to think our way through them, the later period of his development, in which he focused on calculative and meditative thinking, entailed a 'turn' in his thinking that emphasized the kind of experience we are capable of obtaining when we have been cured of our obsession for knowledge. Although Heidegger abandoned terms such as 'intentionality' and 'consciousness' in this later period, he then emphasized to an even greater degree the importance of *attending to experience* and even argued that the only means we have of 'touching Being' is by pondering what our experience may elicit from this novel perspective. Thus, for Heidegger, experience, properly speaking, is ontological – one does not genuinely experience with one's feelings or one's mind, but with *one's Being*. Hence one cannot 'feel' or 'think' one's way to experience – one must *submit* to it.

To summarize, whereas Sartre distinguishes between pre-reflective and reflective modes of consciousness, Heidegger distinguishes between a region of our existence that is unavailable to experience and the capacity we have to access it by submitting to it. Whereas Freud's conception of the unconscious conceives it as an 'underworld' of hidden aims, intentions, and conspiracies that shadow the world of consciousness (the world in which we live), Heidegger inverts this thesis into one that dispenses with the psychoanalytic notion of the unconscious altogether. Instead, Heidegger sees a cleavage between the acts we commit *without* thinking (of which we have no knowledge at the moment we commit them) and the acts that become available to experience by giving thought to them. Conversely, it is the world I inhabit without thinking where I reside, not the one (as per Freud) of which I am momentarily conscious. Moreover, this is the world I attend to when free associating in analysis, but a world I shall never, no matter how much I try, be fully conscious of.

Laing's critique of 'unconscious experience'

Much of this, I imagine, is no doubt familiar to you, not because you have studied Heidegger but because, with enough experience of your own, you have already adopted a phenomenological perspective, but without 'knowing' it. This is one of the virtues of phenomenology: because we are capable of grasping it only intuitively, many people stumble upon it on their own, as Freud did, without formal instruction. In a manner of speaking, despite his protestations to the contrary, Freud was a closet phenomenologist and many of his ideas about psychoanalysis, including the bulk of his technical recommendations, were faithful to the phenomenological perspective. As noted earlier, Heidegger recognized that Freud's conception of free association and the analyst's endeavour to effect a state of free-floating attentiveness was compatible with the kind of meditative thinking Heidegger advocated.[5]

Given the parallels between Heidegger's and Freud's respective conceptions of meditative thinking and the analytic attitude (free association, neutrality)[6] it is all the more surprising that Heidegger's influence has not been more evident in psychoanalytic circles. Despite his influence on a generation of Continental psychiatrists following the Second World War, there has been little effort among psychoanalysts to critique Freud's conception of the unconscious from a Heideggerian perspective. A singular exception is the work of RD Laing, who studied Heidegger before he trained as a psychoanalyst in the 1950s. Laing's first two books, *The Divided Self* (1960) and *Self and Others* (1969 [1961]), were inspired attempts to apply some of Heidegger's insights to the psychoanalytic conception of the unconscious in terms of what is given to experience.[7]

In Laing's *Self and Others*, he confronts some of the problems with Freud's conception of the unconscious (noted earlier) in a critique of a paper by Susan Isaacs, a follower of Melanie Klein. Although Isaacs's paper is mostly related to Klein's technical vocabulary, one of the themes in Isaacs's study originated with Freud and has been adopted by virtually every psychoanalyst since: the notion of 'unconscious experience', a contradiction in terms for the reasons we reviewed earlier. Indeed, Laing (1969, p. 8) avers:

> It is a contradiction in terms to speak of 'unconscious experience,' [because] a person's experience comprises anything that 'he' or 'any part of him' is aware of, whether 'he' or every part of him is aware of every level of his awareness or not.

Laing's thesis is that the psychoanalytic notion of unconscious experience alludes to a more fundamental contradiction that began with Freud's conception of the unconscious: that there is such a thing as an unconscious portion of the mind that one is capable of experiencing 'unconsciously' (see above). Indeed, Freud's decision to conceive a separate portion of the mind of which the (conscious) mind has no awareness sets up a series of false theoretical dualities between inner experience and outer reality that land one, in the words of Juliet Mitchell (1974, p. 254), 'in a welter of contradictions such as the notion that "mind" is a reality outside experience – yet is the "place" from which experience comes.' Mitchell observes that 'This problem is peculiar to psychoanalysis … because the 'object' of the science … experiences the investigation of the scientists' (p. 254).

The heart of Laing's argument revolves around the difficulty that every psychoanalyst faces if he or she believes that the psychoanalyst is in a position to know more about the patient's experience (conscious or unconscious) than the patient does:

> My impression is that most adult Europeans and North Americans would subscribe to the following: the other person's experience is not directly experienced by self. For the present it does not matter whether this is necessarily so, is so elsewhere on the planet, or has always been the case. But if we agree that you do not experience my experience, [then] we agree that we rely on our communications to give us our clues as to how or what we are thinking, feeling, imagining, dreaming, and so forth. Things are going to be difficult if you tell me that I am *experiencing* something which I am not experiencing. If that is what I think you mean by unconscious experience. (Laing, 1969, pp. 12–13)

Even if one allows that the psychoanalyst's principal function is that of investigating the experience of the analysand, the analyst must remember that he has no direct access to the patient's experience other than what the patient tells him, whether the patient's account of his experience is reliable, and to what degree. Yet it seems that the analyst is not content with the limitations of the situation that is imposed on him and prefers to engage in fanciful speculations and inferences as to what he 'supposes' is going on in the patient's mind, of which the patient is presumed to be unaware:

> Beyond the mere attribution of agency, motive, intention, experiences that the patient disclaims, there is an extraordinary exfoliation of forces, energies, dynamics, economics, processes, structures to explain the 'unconscious.' Psychoanalytic concepts of this doubly chimerical order include concepts of mental structures, economics, dynamisms, death and life instincts, internal objects, etc. They are postulated as principles of regularity, governing or underlying forces, governing or underlying experience that Jack thinks Jill has, but does not know she has, as inferred by Jack from Jack's experience of Jill's behaviour. In the meantime, what is Jack's experience of Jill, Jill's experience of herself, or Jill's experience of Jack? (Laing, 1969, pp. 14–15)

Indeed, this subtle interplay of how one's experience of other affects one and, in turn, how one's reaction to this effect elicits behaviour that affects others' experience as well was a major theme in Laing's writings throughout his career. The book in which Laing's critique of Isaacs' paper appeared was a full-scale examination of the effect that human beings have on each other in the etiology of severe psychological disturbance, fueled by acts of deception and self-deception that characterize our most seemingly innocent exchanges with one another. Heidegger's influence on Laing's clinical outlook was explicitly acknowledged by Laing when citing Heidegger's essay, 'On the essence of truth' (1977) in that work. Noting Heidegger's adoption of the pre-Socratic term for truth, *aletheia* (which conceives truth as that which emerges from concealment), Laing put his own twist on Heidegger's thesis by emphasizing the interdependency between candour and secrecy in the way that one's personal truth emerges and recedes in every conversation with others, an innovation that owes just as much to Sartre and Freud as to Heidegger's ontological preoccupations.

Many of the terms Laing introduced in that book for the first time – such as collusion, mystification, attribution, injunction, untenable positions – were coined for the purpose of providing a conceptual vocabulary that could help explain how human beings, in their everyday interactions with others, are able to distort the truth so effectively that they are able to affect each other's reality, and hence their sanity as well. It was just this vocabulary that Laing suggested was missing in Freud's psychoanalytic nomenclature. In the language of psychic conflict, Laing agreed with Freud that people who suffer conflicts are essentially of *two minds:* they struggle against the intrusion of a reality that is too painful to accept, on the one hand, and harbour a fantasy that is incapable of being acknowledged on the other. Consequently, their lives are held in abeyance until they are able to speak of their experience to someone who is willing to hear it with benign acceptance, without a vested interest in what their experience ought to be.

Like Heidegger, Laing avoided employing terms such as 'consciousness' and 'unconscious' and situated his thinking instead in the language of experience and how experience determines our perception of the world and ourselves. Instead of characterizing what we do not know as that which has been repressed into one's unconscious, Laing was more apt to depict such phenomena descriptively, as that which I am unconscious of; or better, as that which is not available, or given, to experience, even if in the depths of my Being I intuitively sense that I am harbouring a truth too painful or elusive to grasp. Laing also adhered to Heidegger's thesis that my experience of the world is dependent on what I interpret the world to be, so that if I want to change my experience of the world I have to reconsider my interpretation of it (Laing, Phillipson and Lee, 1966, pp. 10–11).

An apt example of how Laing incorporated the basic tenets of phenomenology into his psychoanalytic perspective was his treatment of the psychoanalytic conception of defence mechanisms. According to Laing (1967):

> Under the heading of 'defence mechanism,' psychoanalysis describes a number of ways in which a person becomes alienated from himself. For example, repression, denial, splitting, projection, introjection. These 'mechanisms' are often described in psychoanalytic terms as themselves 'unconscious', that is, the person himself appears to be unaware that he is doing this to himself. Even when a person develops sufficient insight to see that 'splitting', for example, is going on, he usually *experiences* this splitting as indeed a mechanism, an impersonal process, *so to speak,* which has taken over and which he can observe but cannot control or stop. [Hence] there is some phenomenological validity in referring to such 'defences' by the term 'mechanism.' (p. 17) [emphases added]

Note that Laing uses phenomenology for the purpose of emphasizing what the patient *actually experiences* in relation to the analyst, not what the analyst believes, supposes, or imagines is going on in the patient's (unconscious) mind. Analytic patients, Laing allows, may indeed have a sense of themselves as living 'in a fog', 'out of it', 'going through the numbers', 'on automatic pilot', and so on. Hence, when the analyst suggests that such experience (or non-experience) may be construed as a mechanism, the patient is perfectly capable of appreciating the metaphoric quality of this terminology. Laing's point, however, is that psychoanalysts tend to take this notion not metaphorically, but literally, as though there are indeed mechanisms and the like controlling our behaviour, the nature of which we are unaware and may never become aware, no matter how much analysis we have had.

Laing emphasizes the importance of extending this notion further by examining the ways in which so-called unconscious aspects of a person's behaviour (and experience) must be accounted for *in terms of* what one experiences and how, instead of speculating about what a patient may be said to be experiencing when his experience is inaccessible to both himself and his analyst, alike. Laing suggests, for example, that the patient's defences 'have this mechanical quality because the person, as he experiences himself, is dissociated from them,' and because he is alienated from his own experience and, hence, himself (p. 17). Laing asks, what are defences if they are not *protective manoeuvres employed to keep one's experience at bay?* Phenomenologically speaking, repression characterizes the patient's capacity to forget painful experience, just as denial provides a means of simply ignoring one's experience. Similarly, projection provides a means of attributing self's experience to other, just as splitting characterizes the person's ability to 'divide' experience into two isolated worlds, wherein the existence of the one is kept in abeyance from the existence of the other, and so on.

Consequently, experiences don't 'just happen' in a random, haphazard fashion; I am also capable of resisting experiences, avoiding them, and even forgetting painful experiences I have suffered in the past. In turn, the degree to which I am able fundamentally to experience something – whether eating a meal, falling in love, even undergoing a psychoanalysis – is determined by how willing I am to submit (give myself over) to the experience in question. Hence, there are degrees to experience – it isn't all or nothing. These considerations about the nature of experience offer enormous implications for the role of the psychoanalyst and the means by which interpretations may be used to transform what the patient experiences, and how. Laing noted that Heidegger's conception of experience already presupposes an act of interpretation that, in turn, elicits the possibility of experience in the first place. According to Laing (Laing, Phillipson and Lee, 1966, pp. 10–11):

> Our experience of another entails a particular interpretation of his behaviour. To feel loved is to perceive and interpret, that is, to experience, the actions of the other as loving . . . [Hence] in order for the other's behaviour to become part of self's experience, self must perceive it. *The very act of perception [and hence experience] entails interpretation.* [emphasis added]

According to Laing, everything a patient in analysis experiences is the end result of 'interpretations' the patient has already, surreptitiously given to all that he is capable of experiencing throughout the course of the therapy relationship. Hence what the analyst says is never actually 'heard' in the way the analyst necessarily intends it, because it is *unceremoniously and unconsciously interpreted* by the patient according to his or her interpretative schema, a culmination of everything the patient has previously experienced (and understood by those experiences) in the course of a lifetime. In other words, every analytic patient experiences the world according to a personal bias that is inherently resistant to anything that contradicts it. The dogmatic nature of the patient's views, held together by a lifetime of neurotic impasse manoeuvres, accounts for the resistances that analysts invariably encounter when employing their interpretations. Since both the analyst and patient are always, already ('unconsciously') interpreting everything the other says, what is actually heard by each and in turn experienced is impossible to communicate directly, because every account of one's experience entails the use of words that, when uttered, are *de facto* 'interpretations' of that experience. This constantly changing interplay of speech, recognition, and misunderstanding accounts for the extraordinary difficulty that analysts encounter in their endeavour to effect change, because the change they aspire to effect is at the mercy of the patient's originary experience, the nature of which is impossible to predict, or even finally determine.

Hence, the analyst should resist the temptation to offer interpretations blindly with the hope that some will simply 'stick', but should endeavour instead to learn the means by which his interpretations actually *affect* the patient (transference) and, in turn, why the patient's responses affect him (countertransference) the way they do. In every communication with the patient, the analyst aims to: 1) *learn* what the patient's interpretative framework is; 2) determine the means by which that interpretative framework constructs a 'world' (the transference neurosis) that is attributed to the analyst; and 3) offer the patient a wider range of interpretations to consider, with a view to helping the patient overcome his innate resistance to experiencing something new, or foreign, but also *forgotten*. In his resistance to this process the patient employs alternative 'interpretations' of his own that serve to distance him from painful experiences while eliciting other, more manageable experiences in their place. Should an unanticipated experience slip through the patient's carefully wrought net of defences, he will nevertheless instinctively limit the degree to which he is ready to permit the experience to affect him and, hence, transform his view of the world.

Heidegger concluded that experience never simply 'transpires', in the abstract, but is necessarily *suffered*, in the existential sense. Because we always have a hand in what we experience and the degree to which we permit our experience to affect us, no one can ever actually impose an experience on another person. It is nevertheless possible, through coercion, intimidation, or seduction, to engender an experience that the other person may, in hindsight, wish *not* to have experienced. Such 'experiences' can, in turn, be forgotten and *appear* to have been repressed and, hence, harboured in the unconscious. In fact, 'experiences' are never actually repressed, as such – only those thoughts or discoveries that elicit such unsupportable anxiety that the individual is unable to take in, and hence, experience (integrate) the thought in question. This is because experience is an ontological phenomenon, not a psychological one. I am perfectly capable of entertaining thoughts or ideas without permitting them to affect me. Indeed, we typically attribute such instances to 'intellectualization', a neurotic defence commonly employed by obsessionals. Similarly, a person is just as capable of feeling anger, sadness, even pleasure, but without truly experiencing such affects wholeheartedly, a common occurrence in hysteria. Many people are simply dissociated from their experience characterologically (for example, obsessive-compulsive or histrionic character type), but we are also capable of employing such forms of dissociation selectively, engendering blind spots in what we are capable of experiencing, and how.

But what happens to 'forgotten' experiences, ones we have experienced in the past but now have no recollection of having done so? Do they become stored 'in' the unconscious as Freud implies? In fact, experiences are not 'entities' (and hence, psychological phenomena) like thoughts or ideas (like the idea, for example, that my father could possibly love me) that can be entertained and, given the right conditions, experienced, heart and soul. When I experience such and such my experience is alive because it exists in a passage of time. A linguistic analogy may make this clearer. If one thinks of experience as a verb and the thought experienced by the verb a noun, then once the noun is repressed the verb simply ceases to exist. The noun may subsequently be resurrected and, hence, its movement in time can begin anew. But a passage of time cannot, *in toto,* be repressed or forgotten. It simply dies by ceasing to exist at the moment the unwelcome idea or affect associated with it is rejected. The catalyst for erasing such experiences by repressing one's knowledge of them is the unsupportable pain or anxiety that suffering such experiences occasions. Later in analysis, the experience of my relationship with my analyst may remind me of a similar occurrence with my father, and the memory of this incident may, in turn, be recalled, but *without the attendant experience it originally elicited.* Subsequently, I may have to work over such revelations once they are manifested before I am capable of acknowledging the significance of the forgotten memory, not by understanding it better but by finally *suffering,* and hence, succumbing to an experience of it. The irony in this thesis is that so-called traumatic experiences are never actually *experienced* as such, but are deferred until a later date when, with the help of analysis, the repressed memory may be elicited and finally experienced, often for the first time.

These considerations may help to explain why the act of interpreting the patient's disclosures with the aim of aligning them with 'past' experience is a slippery slope upon which every analyst has tripped. The likelihood of transgressing the boundaries that designate the respective roles assigned to analyst and patient alike is built into the fabric of the analytic relationship because its outcome depends on the manner in which such interpretations are offered. Interpretation is an undeniably invaluable and no doubt indispensable resource, but only when employed for the purpose of helping patients gain access to a dimension of their experience that has become dormant, by seizing on the opportunity of coming to terms with a lost, unincorporated dimension of their existence, however painful such experiences may be.

It should be remembered that Laing's treatment of experience was offered some 40 years ago, long before the subsequent development of hermeneutic, relational, constructivist, and intersubjective schools of psy-choanalysis, that have in turn noted some of the same problems that Laing presaged but for which he rarely receives credit. One possible explanation for this oversight is that Laing's commentary is still, 40 years hence, rad-ical in comparison with contemporary treatments of this theme; indeed, virtually all the schools listed above continue to flirt with the notion of 'unconscious experience'!

The interpersonal tradition

Of all the psychoanalytic schools in America, the interpersonal school of Sullivan is the closest in temperament and spirit to Laing's phenomeno-logical perspective.[8] Sullivan was not himself a phenomenologist and apparently had no knowledge of its literature, but he was profoundly influenced by social theory and took considerable pains to reframe Freud's psychoanalytic vocabulary into one that was informed by a social, or 'interpersonal,' perspective, much of it indebted to Kurt Lewin and the American pragmatist, John Dewey. Sullivan's conception of the uncon-scious is a case in point. Perhaps because of Dewey, experience played an important role in Sullivan's thinking and led him to question the basis of Freud's drive theory and the idea that the unconscious is nothing more than a reservoir of repressed experiences. Sullivan situated Freud's con-ception of the unconscious in a social lens that relied less on the act of repressing fully formed (and hence 'experienced') knowledge than on the thesis that the experiences in question are not unconscious but 'unfor-mulated'. In other words, in keeping with what I have been saying, much of what is unconscious has never been *experienced*, as such, but is pre-experiential and, hence, not yet formulated (or in modern parlance, 'constructed'), so it couldn't have been repressed in the first place. According to Sullivan (1940):

> One has information about one's experience only to the extent that one has tended to communicate it to another or thought about it in the manner of communicative speech. Much of that which is ordinarily said to be repressed is merely unformulated. (p. 185)

Stern (1997), however, observes that Sullivan was not entirely successful in making a decisive distinction between his conception of unconscious experience and Freud's: 'Because the approach was a new one at the time, and not clearly differentiated from the classical theory of the defens-es, it is not always obvious when Sullivan means repression (expulsion or exclusion from consciousness of a fully formulated psychic element) and when he means lack of formulation' (p. 55). Stern's clarification of

Sullivan's murky treatment of this distinction is a considerable advancement over Sullivan's while remaining faithful to it in spirit. Perhaps Sullivan's clearest statement on what he meant by experience is contained in a footnote of his seminal work, *Schizophrenia as a Human Process* (1962, p. 106):

> Experience as here used refers to anything lived, undergone, or the like: to that which occurs in the organism, rather than directly to events in which the organism is involved. Experience is mental; i.e., it is reflected to a greater or lesser extent in behavior and thinking. At the same time, *experience often occurs without conscious awareness.* [emphasis added]

This ambiguous statement as to whether experience is, strictly speaking, unconscious (a fully formulated thought that has suffered repression) or may occur 'without conscious awareness' would appear to support the thesis that Sullivan rejected the notion that experiences reside 'in' the unconscious, as such. Compared to Laing, however, Sullivan does seem to entertain experiences that are not strictly 'conscious,' a notion that Laing rejected in principle. In an effort to correct some of Sullivan's oversights, contemporary interpersonalists such as Edgar Levenson, Donnel Stern, Philip Bromberg, and Robert Langan have been instrumental in situating many of Sullivan's insights into the contemporary relational, hermeneutic, constructivist, and intersubjective perspectives. Stern, in particular, has brilliantly rendered Sullivan's often incomprehensible conception of experience more accessible to contemporary psychoanalytic practitioners. Indeed, Stern (1997) has emphasized the crucial role of interpretation in the psychoanalytic experience and is in many ways more consistent with Laing's position (noted above) than was Sullivan's.

In an imaginative application of Gadamer's hermeneutic method to psychoanalytic interpretation, Stern has also drawn attention to the manner in which human beings are essentially interpretative creatures, and how the interpretive act is one in which we are *already* engaged at the moment we experience something. In fact, according to Stern (1997, pp. 181–4), what we experience is our interpretation of reality, not reality as such. This is very close to Laing's thesis (drawing from Heidegger) that in order to change one's experience of reality one much first change one's interpretation of it. This should not be surprising because the principal inspiration for Stern's adoption of the hermeneutic method is Gadamer, a former student of Heidegger. Although Gadamer adopts Heidegger's thesis that interpretation is a precondition to experience, he departs from Heidegger's ontological schema and replaces it with a hermeneutic one, emphasizing the manner in which individuals 'construct' their reality by virtue of the interpretation they give it, in the act of conversing with others. This appears to suggest, however, that the act of interpretation (or 'construction') is a conscious one, whereas Heidegger argues that the spontaneous act of interpretation that gives rise to experience is not conscious, as such, but one that is 'given' to consciousness, from the recesses of one's being. Hence, for Gadamer (and Stern) experience is constructed, whereas for Heidegger (and Laing) it is given to consciousness, after the fact. Thus it is only when we *bring into question* the interpretations we have already given that we engage in the interpretive act consciously or, as Gadamer would say, 'constructively.' Moreover, this is the role analysts assume when questioning the interpretations their patients give to experience, by inviting them to consider alternate interpretations, as well.

I believe both Sullivan's and especially Stern's respective conceptions of unformulated experience are advances over the problematic notion of unconscious experience and a step in the right direction, but they still do not quite reach the radical level of Heidegger's ontological critique of experience, for two reasons: 1) Heidegger's model is not constructivist but revelatory, not a revelation of 'knowledge,' *per se*, but of being; and 2) experiences that are not yet formulated (or conscious) are not actually *experienced* as such, whether one depicts them as formulated or unformulated.

The points of convergence between the two perspectives (between Laing's and Stern's), however, far outweigh their divergence. For example, whereas Freud would say that anxiety prompts the individual to repress painful experiences that are already fully formed, Stern characterizes the act of repression/dissociation that rejects unwanted experiences (which have or have not yet achieved formulation) as one where the individual does not want to *have to think* about it, a point I have made elsewhere (Thompson, 2001, pp. 418–24; see also above). Hence, according to Stern (1983, pp. 74–5):

> The self-system rejects all experiences and modes of relating which are associated with anxiety ... New experiences come to be mistrusted simply because they are new ... When this happens, the new disappears without ever having been noticed – or without being formulated ... That is, one keeps certain material unformulated in order not to 'know' it.

I concur with Stern (and Sullivan) that simply not thinking about something is the principal means available to the neurotic for not knowing what his or her experience is. My only argument with Stern – and this may be a semantic one – is that I would not characterize unformulated experiences as 'experiences', *per se*, but rather thoughts or perceptions that have not yet *been* experienced. Hence one is perfectly capable of 'apprehending' a thought or discovery without giving such apprehensions sufficient thought to experience them.

Moreover, Stern suggests that this intricate dance the individual employs in order not to know (or experience) what is staring him in the face is more aptly characterized by dissociation than repression because the conventional (or at any rate, classical) view of repression is that the repressed is a 'fully formed experience', whereas Stern's point is that dissociation takes hold before such experiences have had the opportunity to be formulated and, hence, experienced, properly speaking. Stern (1997, pp. 113–47; 2001) has examined the relationship between dissociation and unformulated experience in painstaking detail and depicts two types of dissociation. The first type is a more structured form of dissociation that more or less corresponds to repression, but differs from it in that the experience being defended against does not exist 'in' some psychic underground grotto 'from' which it can later emerge; rather it serves to impede efforts to construct a specific kind of experience that the individual is predisposed against experiencing. The second, less structured kind of dissociation is not typical of repression because the only reason the individual is dissociated from a given experience is because he is preoccupied with another, more acceptable experience. It is easy to see how either hysterics or obsessional patients typically suffer from both types, the one that they mount powerful defences against and the other that is readily available to them once they have been given an opportunity to entertain it.

The turn from utilizing repression as the fundamental defence mechanism (among classical analysts) to a more sophisticated conceptualization of dissociation (among contemporary analysts) has been spearheaded by interpersonal psychoanalysts such as Stern and more recently Bromberg (1998), who has discussed the role of dissociative states in severe forms of psychopathology. Bromberg rejects the 'receptacle' metaphor for the unconscious and agrees that the study of experience is fundamental for a proper understanding of so-called unconscious processes; moreover, he has also given a great deal of thought to the role dissociaton plays in defences against experience.[9] Similarly, Langan (1993) has invoked the perspectives of Laing, Binswanger, Heidegger, and Sartre in his relational take on the unconscious. Many of these authors owe a considerable debt, not only to Sullivan, but to Levenson (1972; 1983; 1991), who has played a decisive role in translating Sullivan's now outmoded terminology into the language of the consensus, while brilliantly demonstrating Sullivan's lasting relevance to, and continuing influence on, the most cutting-edge ideas in contemporary psychoanalysis. My only problem with these exciting and accessible thinkers is the tendency to position Freud as the straw man for everything that is corrupt and wrong-headed about classical analysis. Indeed, were Freud alive today he would feel at home among the interpersonalists and the existentialists, not the so-called classical analysts!

Freud's and Heidegger's respective conceptions of experience

Returning to Freud, I shall now review those aspects of Freud's conception of the unconscious that are compatible with Heidegger's philosophy,
and the respective importance that each assigns to the role of experience
in our lives. Over the past two centuries the German language has offered
perhaps the richest and most subtle variations on the kinds of experience
that English subsumes under the one term. It should not be surprising,
therefore, that German philosophers have dominated the nineteenth- and
twentieth-century investigations into the nature of experience that subsequently spilled over to other European countries, including France, Great
Britain, and Spain. I am thinking of Hegel, Schopenhauer, Dilthey,
Nietzsche, Husserl, and Heidegger specifically, each of whom elaborated
on the notion of experience in their respective philosophies, granting the
concept a central role in both phenomenology and existential philosophy.
Before exploring their impact on phenomenology, however, I shall say a
few words about the German conception of experience and the etymology from which the terms they employ are derived.

The first is the German *Erfahrung,* which contains the word *Fahrt,*
meaning 'journey'. Hence, *Erfahrung* suggests the notion of temporal
duration, such as, for example, when one accumulates experience over
time, including the accruing of wisdom that comes with old age. The
other German term for experience is *Erlebnis,* which derives from the
word *Leben,* meaning 'life.' Hence, the use of the word *Erlebnis* connotes
a vital immediacy in contrast to the more historical perspective of
Erfahrung. When invoking *Erlebnis,* the speaker is emphasizing a primitive unity that *precedes* intellectual reflection.[10] In the scientific
community the notion of experience suggests the accumulation of empirical knowledge through the use of experimentation, a supposedly
objective endeavour. On the other hand, experience may also suggest
something that happens to us when in a passive state and vulnerable to
stimuli, such as what occurs in a movie theatre. It may also suggest the
process whereby we submit to education, entailing the accumulation and
memorization of knowledge over a period of time. Finally, the term may
be used to connote a journey I have taken while travelling to a foreign
country, perhaps in wartime when I am faced with obstacles and danger,
the experience of which has expedited my journey into manhood.

You can see from these distinctions between the two types of experience we are capable of having that, even while offering tantalizing hints
as to what the term means, there remains something ineffable about the
concept itself. This presents us with a paradox because the word is often
employed, according to Martin Jay (1988) 'to gesture towards precisely

that which exceeds concepts and even language itself'. In fact, the word 'experience' has frequently been used as a marker for what is ineffable and so private or personal that it cannot be rendered in words. One's experience of love, for example, is an experience that many insist is impossible to express or grasp in words alone, precisely because it is experienced long before it is understood, if then. As Laing observed earlier, even when I try to communicate what I experience to others, only I can know what my experience is. Hence, our efforts to convey experience are imperfect because it cannot be reduced to words. This observation has enormous consequences for the experience of psychoanalysis for both patient and analyst, who rely almost entirely on the passage of words between them.

So what does the essential nature of experience entail? Is experience antithetical to our capacity to reason, as some have claimed, or is our ability to reason dependent on our capacity to experience the very thoughts that our words endeavour to convey? As we know, many of the last century's philosophers and academics sought to reduce human activity to language, suggesting that one's capacity to experience is mediated through words and, hence, is secondary to the power that words possess. This view implies that pre-verbal experience is inconceivable, so that even the experience of pain relies on one's 'knowledge' of what pain entails. Many of the features of structuralism, deconstructionism, poststructuralism, and the postmodernist perspective argue that the very notion of a conscious, sentient, self that is capable of determining its own truth is an antiquated idea that should be replaced with a schema that views the subject, not in terms of an experiencing agent, but as an effect, or 'construct,' of hidden forces.

In order to appreciate the contribution of phenomenology to our conception of experience it is important to note that, historically, empiricist philosophers such as Hume separated experience from rationality by consigning to experience sensual data alone. Hence, modern scientific methodology, which endeavours to combine the experience we derive from our senses with our capacity to think about and reflect upon the nature of such experiences, is unable to account for the experience of ideas, thoughts, and imagination. In other words, philosophers have traditionally 'split' human beings in half, assigning one portion of the human project to rationality, the mind, and the other portion to sense experience, the body.

The singular contribution of Husserl at the turn of the century was to reconcile the split between sense experience and rationality by suggesting that experience is already inherently thoughtful, because the nature of consciousness, according to Husserl, is intentional, so that the act of consciousness and its object are given at one stroke. One isn't 'related' (as per object relations theory) to the other because each is irrevocably dependent on the other, so that neither is capable of standing alone. As some Buddhists have argued, the presumed split to which Western thought has been devoted is illusory, because the two are actually one. Heidegger concluded that there are levels of experience – just as there are levels of awareness or consciousness – depending on my capacity to interpret to the depths what my experience discloses to me.

This thesis is especially relevant to the psychoanalyst who endeavours to direct patients' attention to their experiences by interpreting their ostensible meaning. Viewed from this angle, a good interpretation is not intended to explain one's experience, but to *deepen* it, in the phenomenological sense. Alternatively, *what the patient experiences and how it reveals to the analyst the person the patient happens to be.* Thus, as Laing noted earlier, patient and analyst alike are interested not only in their own experience of the situation they share together but in what each takes the other's experience to be, however imperfect one's ability to understand other's experience may be.

This helps to explain why Heidegger conceives experience as the 'revealing' of Being. Because experience discloses both who I am and the world I inhabit simultaneously, the two are inextricably connected. I am neither strictly constituted by the world, nor is the world I inhabit my invention: the two are interdependent because each serves to constitute the other. Thus the distinctive feature of experience from a Heideggerian perspective is its capacity to shock the slumber of my world at the roots, because experience not only reveals things that are hidden, it is also capable of changing *who* I am. In Heidegger's (1971, p. 57) own words:

> When we talk of 'undergoing' an experience, we mean specifically that the experience is not of our own making, [so that *in order* to undergo an experience] we [must] endure it, suffer it, [and] receive it as it strikes us, and [finally] submit to it.

By anticipating my experiences with a specific purpose in view I can use them in order to gain insight into the person I am. Moreover, there are degrees to experience; it isn't all or nothing. This is why I am also capable of resisting experience, avoiding it, and even forgetting experiences that are too painful to bear. In turn, the degree to which I am able to experience anything – a piece of music, the chapter you are now reading, even a psychoanalysis – is determined by how willing I am to submit to the experience in question.

So what does the ontological structure of experience have to do with the unconscious? Some would argue nothing. After all, psychoanalysis is concerned with exploring the unconscious whereas Heidegger's conception of phenomenology is devoted to the revelation of Being by critiquing one's experience. Despite what Freud says about the ego 'no longer being the master of its own house', experience plays a vital role in Freud's conception of analysis and the conflicts that patients typically suffer. Basically, Freud believed that our capacity to bear painful experience (*Erlebnis*) as children more or less determines whether we shall develop neurotic symptoms, or worse, when we grow up. This is actually a Heideggerian conception of experience, although Freud never knew this. According to Freud, if a child is faced with an experience that is too painful to bear, the child simply represses it from consciousness, making the child's experience of frustration disappear. As Freud himself noted, it is not the actual experience of frustration that is repressed but the *knowledge* or idea (or from a hermeneutic perspective, the 'interpretation' of what one takes the case to be) of the incident that elicited the experience in the first place. Hence, after this piece of knowledge (or idea) is repressed, the individual continues to experience moments of sadness or anxiety, for example, but doesn't know why. The only problem with this solution is that the repressed memory finds an alternate means of expression that transforms it into a symptom, which the adult subsequently suffers and complains about, though he hasn't a clue what caused the symptom or what purpose it serves.

For Freud, the purpose of pathogenic symptoms is to shield the individual from experiencing a disappointment of traumatic proportions that the person who suffers the symptom wants desperately to deny. Since the disappointment in question was repressed (or disavowed, projected, dissociated, and so forth) but not entirely eradicated, the individual instinctively *avoids experiencing similar disappointments and anything that may serve to remind him of it in the future*. Analytic patients are reluctant to risk disappointment because to really be disappointed is not only transformative but necessarily painful. But such disappointments are transformative only and to the degree to which they are finally experienced at the heart of one's being, in the give-and-take of the analytic encounter.

Just because one has a fleeting thought, idea, or intuition, for example, doesn't necessarily guarantee that one will have a full-throttle experience of it. The phenomenologist accounts for this phenomenon by suggesting that Freud's unconscious is nothing more than a *mode of thinking* (consciousness) that the patient is unaware of thinking. In other words, the patient has no experience of thinking the thoughts attributed to him because he failed to hear himself thinking the thoughts in question. At the moment such thoughts occurred to him, his mind was 'somewhere else'. The psychoanalyst says he was unconscious of what he was thinking, but the phenomenologist would say he simply failed to listen to, and hence experience, the thoughts in question, when they occurred to him.

Based on this hypothesis, psychoanalytic treatment is nothing more than an investigation into the patient's experience, suffered over the entirety of one's life. Hence, analysts seek to learn about the experiences (*Erfahrung*) that patients remember over the course of their history, just as they seek to understand the patient's experience of the analytic situation (*Erlebnis*) – the patient's *experience of his relationship with the analyst,* the so-called transference phenomenon. But analysts are also interested in eliciting what may be characterized as 'lost' experience (what Heidegger would call potential experience) through the patient's free associations. Change comes about through the patient's ability to speak of his experience instead of concealing it, as he has in the past. In other words, giving voice to experience deepens it, but only if the experience elicited plunges the patient to the depths of his suffering.

Concluding unscientific postscript

What does Heidegger's emphasis on the ontological dimension of experience tell us about the psychoanalytic conception of the unconscious? Does it do away with it entirely or does it offer another way of conceiving it? How, in turn, does it relate to Sartre's distinction between reflective and pre-reflective consciousness? Are Heidegger's and Sartre's respective views compatible or are they hopelessly irreconcilable? And finally, is it possible to be 'conscious' of something that one has no experience of, or is it necessary to experience something in order to know it, even 'pre-reflectively'? Or, on the other hand, is there a dimension to experience that one is not *aware* of experiencing, or is it essential to be conscious of experience in order to construe it as experience, as such, whether one is invoking *Erlebnis* or *Erfahrung*?

Recall that Sartre makes a distinction between *pre*-reflective consciousness and reflective consciousness (that which we ordinarily term 'conscious awareness'). Even while Sartre is indecisive on this point, for Heidegger Sartre's notion of pre-reflective consciousness makes sense only if it is conceived as a form of nascent awareness that is not immediately available to experience, properly speaking. Only when I *reflect on* my pre-reflective acts of consciousness am I capable of experiencing them and, hence, being with them. Thus, from a Heideggerian perspective, there is no such thing as 'unconscious experience', despite the views of most classical and conventional psychoanalysts. If Sartre's conception of pre-reflective consciousness is simply another term for what Freud calls primary process thinking, then *the unconscious may be conceived as a form of consciousness that is not yet available to experience.*

As noted earlier, Heidegger lost interest in exploring the distinctions between consciousness, awareness, and intentionality because he felt they were inadequate concepts for describing the nature of thought and why it is available to experience in some situations but not others. Thus the capacity to experience is the final arbiter for what it means to inhabit the world and to be-in-the-world authentically, as the person I genuinely am, because experience, whatever form it assumes, is irrevocably my own. Heidegger finally rejected the primacy of consciousness because he was concerned with how one comes to be who one is and the weight of anxiety that being oneself inevitably entails.

If Freud's conception of the unconscious is, for all intents and purposes, a scientific one, it is nevertheless imbued with ontological overtones that are evident, for example, when he characterizes the way we stumble upon it in our dreams, parapraxes, and symptoms. From this perspective, the unconscious is nothing more than an algebraic 'x' that serves to explain that which is not immediately given to experience. Moreover, one can discern parallels between Freud's and Sartre's (as well as Heidegger's) respective depictions of 'two types of thinking' that, when treated phenomenologically, betray ontological connotations to Freud's intuitions, if not his theoretical conceptualizations. Thus what Freud depicts as primary thought processes may be conceived as a version of Sartre's notion of pre-reflective consciousness, and what Freud depicts as secondary thought processes are editions of what Sartre terms 'reflective consciousness'. Seen from this angle the primary thought processes are a form of consciousness, but lack the reflective capacities that the ego is capable of obtaining only after the acquisition of language. Another way of understanding the distinction between *Erlebnis* and *Erhfarung* is to conceive the former as a form of pre-verbal experience (the experience of the infant) whereas the latter pertains to the child's (and later, the adult's) capacity to reflect on his or her experience after having acquired the capacity for language. The child's ability to learn from experience will evolve and develop, just as the *capacity to experience* will also evolve, from the most primitive aspects of *Erlebnis* to the more sophisticated editions of *Erfahrung*. Thus, Freud's topographical and structural models are indeed scientific, but only to the degree that psychoanalysis is a theoretical science that presumes to explain that which is inaccessible to experience. As a theoretical construct it may be accurate or not. We do not know, nor can we, whether and to what degree it is accurate, which no doubt explains why the history of psychoanalysis is littered with a seemingly endless array of alternative formulations to Freud's, each of which is just as credible (or not) as the next. Whichever theory one opts for – whether Klein's, Sullivan's, or Lacan's, for example – however compelling or attractive or elegant it may be – it is still just as theoretical, abstract, and impossible to prove (or disprove) as Freud's.

From Heidegger's ontological perspective, the unconscious is not a theoretical construct, nor is it 'in' my head, but 'out' *there*, in the world, an inescapable dimension of Being. It is my abode, my past, and my destiny converged, so that 'I', the one for whom the unconscious comes into Being, am simply the experience of this tripartite intersection. We apprehend it as an enigma, a dimension of our existence that lies hidden one moment, then slips into view the next, only to disappear again, in perpetuity. If our only access to it is through the vehicle of interpretation, it is not the interpretation ('translation') of this or that psychoanalytic theory into a language of the consensus but the kind of interpretation we render each moment of our lives, by the act of giving things a name and a significance. This is because everything we are capable of experiencing conveys meaning, and the only way to understand what something means is to determine what it means for *me*, at the moment it becomes available to experience, and how. Consequently, the unconscious is never unconscious for me, but a living presence in my world. This is why the purpose of analysis is not finally to 'know' the unconscious but to return the analytic patient to the ground of an experience from which he has lost his way, in order to claim it as his own.

Notes

1. An earlier version of this chapter was presented as the Presidential Address at the Eleventh Annual Interdisciplinary Conference of the International Federation for Psychoanalytic Education, Chicago, Illinois, 4 November 2000.
2 For a more thorough treatment of Freud's conception of psychic reality see Thompson (1994, pp. 1–50).
3 See Thompson (2000b), for a discussion on the sceptical dimension to Heidegger's and Freud's respective conceptions of the human condition.
4 See Thompson (1998 and 2000b), for a more detailed exploration of how Freud developed the principles of free association and neutrality.
5 See Medard Boss's account of Heidegger's take on Freud in Boss (1988, pp. 9–10).
6 See Thompson (1996a, 1996b, and 2000b) for a more detailed exploration of Freud's conception of free association and neutrality in light of the sceptic and phenomenological traditions.
7 The theme of experience preoccupied Laing throughout his lifetime. Two of his other books, The Politics of Experience (1967) and The Voice of Experience (1982), even contain the word 'experience' in their titles. (See more on the history of experience in Western culture in Thompson, 2000a.)
8 Indeed, after Laing visited the Alanson White Institute (founded by Sullivan and others) in the 1960s, he was made an Honorary Member of its society, and remained so throughout his life.
9 I am particularly indebted to both Bromberg and Stern for alerting me to some of the similarities between Sullivan's views on experience and my own.
10 As noted earlier, whereas Sartre holds that pre-reflective consciousness is a

form of experience (*Erlebnis*), Heidegger argues that in order for knowledge to become available to experience it must be thought. Hence, for Heidegger pre-flective consciousness may be intuited, but not experienced, per se. For this reason Heidegger rejected Dilthey's (and Sartre's) notion of *Erlebnis* as a feature of experience, properly speaking, though he would have probably found the term more acceptable if it were to connote an act that is reflectively conscious at the moment it is experienced. It is this, later, understanding of *Erlebnis* that I employ this article. (For more on Heidegger's perspective on experience see Heidegger, 1970.)

References

Agamben G (1993) Stanzas: Words and Phantasm in Western Culture. Minneapolis: University of Minnesota Press.

Agamben G (1999) Potentialities: Collected Essays in Philosophy. Stanford: Stanford University Press.

Appignanesi L, Forrester J (1993) Freud's Women. London: Virago.

Armstrong J (2001) The Intimate Philosophy of Art. London: Penguin.

Austin JL (1971) How To Do Things With Words. Oxford: Oxford University Press.

Bachelard G (1958) The Poetics of Space. Trans. Jolas M. Boston: Beacon Press.

Bacon R (2000) Theory and therapeutics: stress in the analytic identity. Free Associations 8(2): 1–20.

Barham P (1992) Closing the Asylum. London: Penguin.

Barham P (1993) Schizophrenia and Human Value. London: Free Association Books.

Barthes R (1972) Mythologies. Trans. Lavers A. London: Jonathan Cape.

Baudelaire C (1981) Selected Writings on Art and Artists. Trans. Charvet PE. Cambridge: Cambridge University Press.

Bauman Z (1989) Modernity and the Holocaust. Cambridge: Polity Press.

Beattie T (1999) God's Mother, Eve's Advocate: A Gynocentric Refiguration of Marian Symbolism in Engagement with Luce Irigaray. Bristol: Centre for Comparative Studies in Religion and Gender.

Berger J (2001) The Shape of the Pocket. London: Bloomsbury.

Bohm D (1980) Wholeness and the Implicate Order. London: Routledge & Kegan Paul.

Bolla P de (2001) Art Matters. Boston and London: Harvard University Press.

Boss M. (1988) Martin Heidegger's Zollikon Seminars. In Hoeller K (ed.) Heidegger and Psychology, a special issue of the Review of Existential Psychology and Psychiatry.

Breger L (2000) Freud. New York: John Wiley.

Bromberg P (1998) Standing in the Spaces: Essays on Clinical Process, Trauma, and Dissociation. Hillsdale NJ and London: The Analytic Press.

Brunner J (2001) Freud and the Politics of Psychoanalysis. New Brunswick/London: Transaction.

Budge W (Trans.) (1900) The Miracles of the Blessed Virgin Mary and the Life of Hanna (Saint Anne) and the Magical Prayers of Aheta Mikael. London: W Griggs.

Burston D (2000) The Crucible of Experience. Cambridge Mass: Harvard University Press.

Cavell S (1976) Must We Mean What We Say? Cambridge: Cambridge University Press.

Clark E (1983) Women in the Early Church. London: Michael Glazier.

Clark E (1986) Acts of Paul and Thecla. In Ascetic Piety and Women's Faith. Lewiston: Edward Mellon.

Cooper D (1978) The Language of Madness. Harmondsworth: Penguin Books.

Cooper R et al. (ed.) (1989) Thresholds between Philosophy and Psychoanalysis: Papers from the Philadelphia Association. London: Free Association Books.

Damasio A (2000) The Feeling of What Happens. London: Heinemann.

DeLillo D (1998) Underworld. London: Picador.

Derrida J (1995) The Gift of Death. Chicago: Chicago University Press.

Dhomhnaill Nuala Ni (1990) Pharaoh's Daughter. In Jouve NW (ed) (1998) Female Genesis: Creativity, Self and Gender. Cambridge: Polity Press.

Dineen T (1999) Manufacturing Victims: What the Psychology Industry is Doing to People. London: Constable.

Dunmore H (1998) Your Blue Eyed Boy. London: Penguin.

Dupre J (1993) The Disorder of Things. Cambridge Mass: Harvard University Press.

Eliot TS (1944) Four Quartets. London: Faber & Faber.

Evans R (1976) RD Laing: The Man and His Ideas. New York: Dutton.

Ewin S (1996) A Social History of Spin. New York: Basic Books.

Fanon F (1968) Black Skin, White Masks. Trans. Markmann CL. London: MacGibbon and Kee.

Fitzgerald R (trans) (1961) The Odyssey. London: Collins Harvill.

Foucault M (1979) Discipline and Punish. Harmondsworth: Penguin.

Freud S (1892) Case of a Successful Treatment by Hypnosis. Standard Edition. London: The Hogarth Press. Vol. I.

Freud S (1900) The Interpretation of Dreams. Standard Edition. London: The Hogarth Press. Vol. IV.

Freud S (1901) The Psychopathology of Everyday Life. Standard Edition. London: The Hogarth Press. Vol. VI.

Freud S (1911) Formulations on the Two Principles of Mental Functioning. Standard Edition. London: The Hogarth Press. Vol. XII.

Freud S (1912) On the Universal Tendency to Debasement in the Sphere of Love. Standard Edition. London, The Hogarth Press. Vol. XII.

Freud S (1913) Totem and Taboo. Standard Edition. London: The Hogarth Press. Vol. XIII.

Freud S (1914) The Moses of Michelangelo. Standard Edition. London: The Hogarth Press. Vol. XIII.

Freud S (1914–16) On Metapsychology. Standard Edition. London, The Hogarth Press. Vol. XIV.

Freud S (1916–17) Introductory Lectures on Psychoanalysis. Standard Edition. London: The Hogarth Press. Vol. XV.

Freud S (1923) A Seventeenth Century Demonological Neurosis. London: The Hogarth Press. Vol. XIX.

Freud S (1933) New Introductory Lectures on Psychoanalysis. Standard Edition. London: The Hogarth Press. Vol. XXII.

Freud S (1939) Moses and Monotheism: Three essays. London: The Hogarth Press. Vol. XXIII.

Friedman J. (1989) Therapeia, play and the therapeutic household. In Cooper R (ed.) Thresholds between Philosophy and Psychoanalysis: Papers from the Philadelphia Association. London: Free Association Books.

Frisch, M (1954) I am not Stiller. New York: Harvest.

Gaudin, C (1987) On Poetic Imagination and Reverie: Selections from Gaston Bachelard. Dallas: Spring Publications.

Gay P (1998) Freud: A Life for Our Time, New York, WW Norton.

Gergen K (1994) Realities and Relationships: Soundings in Social Construction. Cambridge Mass: Harvard University Press.

Goffen R (1993) Giovanni Bellini. New Haven/London: Yale University Press.

Goffen R (2002) Renaissance Rivals. Michelangelo, Leonardo, Raphael,Titian. New Haven/London: Yale University Press.

Gordon P (1999) Face to Face: Therapy as Ethics. London: Constable.

Gordon P (2003) Do you always listen to what your patients say? The ethics of therapy. In King L and Randall R (eds) The Future of Psychoanalytic Psychotherapy. London: Whurr.

Gordon RSC (2002) Primo Levi's Ordinary Virtues: From Testimony to Ethics. Oxford: Oxford University Press.

Gray JG (1968) Introduction to Heidegger. San Francisco: Harper & Row.

Griffin J (1980) Homer on Life and Death. Oxford: Clarendon Press.

Grossman D (2002) Be My Knife. London: Bloomsbury.

Grotstein J (1999) Who Is The Dreamer That Dreams The Dream? London: Karnac Books.

Heaton JM (1993) The sceptical tradition in psychotherapy. In Spurling L (ed.) From the Words of My Mouth: Tradition in Psychotherapy. London: Routledge.

Heaton JM (2000) Wittgenstein and Psychoanalysis. Cambridge: Icon Books.

Heaton JM (2003) Pyrronhian scepticisim and psychotherapy. Existential Analysis 14(1): 32–47.

Heidegger M (1962) Being and Time. Trans Macquarrie J. Oxford: Blackwell.

Heidegger M (1968) What is Called Thinking? Trans. Gray JG. San Francisco: Harper & Row.

Heidegger M (1970) Hegel's Concept of Experience. New York and London: Harper & Row.

Heidegger M (1971) On the Way to Language. Trans. Hertz PD. San Francisco: Harper & Row.

Heidegger M (1977) On the Essence of Truth. In Basic Writings (Krell DF ed.) New York and London: Harper & Row.

House R (2003) Therapy Beyond Modernity, London: Karnac.

Husserl E (1989) Philosophy as Rigorous Science. London: Routledge.

Illich I (1975) Tools for Conviviality. London: Fontana.

Irigaray L (1993) The Sex Which is Not One ... Trans. Porter C. Cambridge: Cambridge University Press.
Irigaray L (1997) Women-Mothers. The Silent Substratum of the Social Order. In Whitford M (ed.) The Irigaray Reader. Oxford: Blackwell.
Irigaray L (2002) To Speak is Never Neutral. London: Continuum.
Janik A (2001) Wittgenstein's Vienna Revisited. New Brunswick: Transaction Publishers.
Jay M (1998) The Crisis of Experience in a Post-Subjective Age. Public Lecture, University of California. Berkeley Calif, November 14.
Kant I (1998) Critique of Pure Reason. Trans. Guyer P and Wood AW. Cambridge: Cambridge University Press.
Kelman J (1998) Oh my darling. In The Good Times. London: Vintage.
Kierkegaard S (1938) The Journals of Soren Kierkegaard. Selected and trans. Dru A. Oxford: Oxford University Press.
Klee P (1961) The Thinking Eye. Trans. Mannheim R, Weidler C, Wittenborn J. London: Lund Humphries.
Kovachevski C (1991) The Madonna in Western Paintings. Trans. Georgiev N. London: Cromwell.
Kovel J (1981) The Age of Desire: Case Histories of a Radical Psychoanalyst. New York: Pantheon.
Kristeva J (1980) Powers of Horror: An Essay in Abjection. Trans Roudiez L. New York: Columbia University Press.
Lacan J (1988) The Seminar of Jacques Lacan. Book 1: Freud's Papers on Technique 1953–54. Trans. Forrester J. Cambridge: Cambridge University Press.
Laing RD (1960) The Divided Self. Harmondsworth: Penguin.
Laing RD (1967) The Politics of Experience. Harmondsworth: Penguin.
Laing RD (1969 [1961]) Self and Others (2nd revised edition). Harmondsworth: Penguin.
Laing RD (1982) The Voice of Experience. Harmondsworth: Penguin.
Laing RD and Esterson A (1964) Sanity, Madness and the Family. Harmondsworth: Penguin.
Laing RD, Phillipson H, Lee AR (1966) Interpersonal Perception: A Theory and a Method of Research. London: Tavistock Publications.
Langan R (1993) The depth of the field. Contemporary Psychoanalysis 29(4): 628–44.
Langer S (1967–1982) Mind: An Essay on Human Feeling. Vols I–III. Baltimore and London: Johns Hopkins University Press.
Laplanche J and Pontalis J-P (1973) The Language of Psycho-Analysis. London: Hogarth Press.
Lasch C (1977) Haven in a Heartless World: The Family under Siege. New York: Norton.
Lattimore R (trans) (1965) The Odyssey of Homer. New York: Harper & Row.
Leavy S (1970) John Keats' psychology of creative imagination. The Psychoanalytic Quarterly 39(2): 173–7.
Leavy S (1980) The Psychoanalytic Dialogue. New Haven: Yale University Press.

Leavy S (1988) In The Image of God: A Psychoanalyst's View. New Haven: Yale University Press.

Levenson E (1972) The Fallacy of Understanding: An Inquiry into the Changing Structure of Psychoanalysis. New York and London: Basic Books.

Levenson E (1983) The Ambiguity of Change: An Inquiry into the Nature of Psychoanalytic Reality. New York: Basic Books.

Levenson E (1991) The Purloined Self: Interpersonal Perspectives in Psychoanalysis. New York: Contemporary Psychoanalysis Books.

Loewald HW (1980) Papers on Psychoanalysis. New Haven: Yale University Press.

Lomas P (1966) Ritualistic elements in the management of childbirth. British Journal of Medical Psychology 39: 207–13.

Lomas P (1999) Doing Good? Psychotherapy Out of Its Depth. Oxford: Oxford University Press.

McDowell J (1998) Mind, Value and Reality. Cambridge Mass: Harvard University Press.

Macquarrie J (1994) Heidegger and Christianity. New York: Continuum Publishing Company.

Main T (1977) The Ailment and Other Psychoanalytic Essays. London: Free Association Books.

Main T (1980) Some basic concepts in therapeutic community work. In Jansen, E (ed.) The Therapeutic Community. London: Croom Helm.

Meltzer F (1999) Re-embodying: virginity secularised. In Caputo JD, Scanlon MJ (eds) God, The Gift and Postmodernism. Bloomington: Indiana University Press.

Merleau-Ponty M (1962) The Phenomenology of Perception. London: Routledge & Kegan Paul.

Midgely M (1989) Wisdom, Information and Wonder. London: Routledge.

Miles M (1989) Carnal Knowing: Female Nakedness and Religious Meaning in the Christian West. London: Burns & Oates.

Mills CW (1956) The Power Elite. London/New York: Oxford University Press.

Mitchell J (1974) Psychoanalysis and Feminism. New York: Pantheon Books.

Montaigne M (1958) Essays. Trans. Cohen JM. Harmondsworth: Penguin.

Montaigne M (1965) Complete Essays. Trans. Frame D. Stanford: Stanford University Press.

Moran R (2001) Authority and Estrangement: An Essay on Self-Knowledge. Princeton: Princeton University Press.

Morris J (2001) Trieste and the Meaning of Nowhere. London: Faber & Faber.

Mortley R (1991) French Philosophers in Conversation. London: Routledge.

Nichols G (1983) In my name. In Jouve NW (ed.) (1993) Female Genesis: Creativity, Self and Gender. Cambridge: Polity Press.

O'Connor N, Ryan J (1993) Wild Desires and Mistaken Identities: Lesbianism and Psychoanalysis. London: Virago.

Oliver K (ed.) (1997) The Portable Kristeva. New York: Columbia University Press.

Parker I (ed.) (1999) Deconstructing Psychotherapy. London: Sage Publications.

Paz O (1990) The Labyrinth of Solitude. London: Penguin.

Phillips A (1994) On Flirtation. London: Faber & Faber.

Polanyi M. (1958) Personal Knowledge. London: Routledge & Kegan Paul.

Rieff P (1979) Freud: The Mind of the Moralist. Chicago: University of Chicago Press.

Rivas M (2002) The Carpenter's Pencil. Trans. Dunne J. London: Harvill Press.

Roustang F (1986) Dire Mastery: Discipleship from Freud to Lacan. Trans. Lukacher N. Washington: American Psychiatric Press.

Rycroft C (1968) Imagination and Reality. New York: International Universities Press.

Sagan E (1988) Freud, Women and Morality: The Psychology of Good and Evil. New York: Basic Books.

Samuels A (1989) The Plural Psyche: Personality, Morality and the Father. London: Routledge.

Sartre J-P (1957a) Being and Nothingness. Trans. Barnes H. London: Methuen.

Sartre J-P (1957b) The Transcendence of the Ego. Trans. Williams G, Kirkpatrick R. New York: Noonday Press.

Sartre J-P (1962) Sketch for a Theory of the Emotions. Trans. Mairet P. London: Methuen.

Sartre J-P (1981) Existential Psychoanalysis. Trans. Barnes H. Washington DC: Regnary Gateway.

Sassoon S (1937) The Complete Memoirs of George Sherston. London: Faber & Faber.

Scherner KA (1861) Das Leben des Traumes. Berlin.

Schneiderman S (1983) Death of an Intellectual Hero. Cambridge Mass: Harvard University Press.

Seabrook J (2002) The soul of man under globalism. Race and Class 43(4): 1–25.

Simic C (2002) Review of Without End: New and selected poems by Adam Zagajewski. New York Review of Books, 9 May.

Sluga H, Stern DG (eds) (1996) The Cambridge Companion to Wittgenstein. Cambridge: Cambridge University Press.

Smail D (2001) The Nature of Unhappiness. London: Robinson.

Spence DP (1964) The Rhetorical Voice of Psychoanalysis. Cambridge Mass: Harvard University Press.

Steiner G (1989) Real Presences. London: Faber & Faber.

Stern DB (1983) Unformulated experience. Contemporary Psychoanalysis 19(1): 24–7.

Stern, DB (1997) Unformulated Experience: From Dissociation to Imagination in Psychoanalysis. Hillsdale NJ and London: The Analytic Press.

Sullivan HS (1940) Conceptions of Modern Psychiatry. New York: WW Norton & Co.

Sullivan HS (1962) Schizophrenia as a Human Process. New York: WW Norton & Co.

Thompson MG (1994) The Truth About Freud's Technique: The Encounter with the Real. New York and London: New York University Press.

Thompson MG (1996a) The rule of neutrality. Psychoanalysis and Contemporary Thought. 19(1): 57–84.

Thompson MG (1996b) Freud's conception of neutrality. Contemporary Psychoanalysis. 32(1): 25–42.

Thompson MG (1998) Manifestations of transference: love, friendship, rapport. Contemporary Psychoanalysis 34(1): 543–61.

Thompson MG (2000a) The crisis of experience in contemporary psychoanalysis. Contemporary Psychoanalysis 36(1): 29–56.

Thompson MG (2000b) The sceptic dimension to psychoanalysis: toward an ethic of experience. Contemporary Psychoanalysis 36(3): 457–81.

Thompson MG (2001) The enigma of honesty: the fundamental rule of psychoanalysis. Free Associations 8(3): 390–434.

Tracy D (1999) Fragments: The Spiritual Situation of our Times. In Caputo JD, Scanlon MJ (eds) (1999) God, The Gift and Postmodernism. Bloomington: Indiana University Press.

Vivante P (1985) Homer. New Haven & London: Yale University Press.

Weber M (1968) The Sociology of Max Weber. Harmondsworth: Penguin.

Wittgenstein L (1958) Philosophical Investigations. Trans. Anscombe GEM. Oxford: Blackwell.

Wittgenstein L (1969) On Certainty. Trans. Paul D, Anscombe GEM. Oxford: Blackwell.

Wittgenstein L (1975) Philosophical Remarks. Trans. Hargreaves R, White R. Oxford: Blackwell.

Wittgenstein L (1980) Culture and Value. Trans. Winch P. Oxford: Blackwell.

Index